"No one more than Christians
well-written words. Yet, with so much ... ...
have forgotten—or perhaps never really learned—how to read with care and
skill the words that have shaped human history for thousands of years. Whether
you are a student, teacher, parent, or pastor, *Recovering the Lost Art of Reading*
will instruct and delight you in God's wonderful gift of language and literature."

> **Karen Swallow Prior,** Research Professor of English and Christianity
> and Culture, Southeastern Baptist Theological Seminary; author, *On
> Reading Well*

"In this literate but accessible book, Leland Ryken and Glenda Faye Mathes
first rescue true literature from the trash heap of 'text' to which it has been
confined for the last half century and then provide their readers with tools for
engaging fully with the goodness, truth, and beauty of the imaginative poetry
and prose of the past and present."

> **Louis Markos,** Professor of English and Scholar in Residence, Houston
> Baptist University; author, *From Achilles to Christ* and *Literature: A
> Student's Guide*

"Both practical and inspirational, *Recovering the Lost Art of Reading* deserves a
wide audience. May it spur us, as 'people of the book,' to slow down and savor
the riches of literature and the great gift of literacy."

> **Janie Cheaney,** Senior Writer, *WORLD* magazine

"Thoughtful, challenging, and even harrowing, *Recovering the Lost Art of
Reading* persuasively exhorts us to recover the serenity, joy, and wonder of
serious reading. Those who seriously engage this book will find themselves
blessedly refreshed, educated, and motivated to pursue the good, the true,
and the beautiful."

> **David V. Urban,** Professor of English, Calvin University; author,
> *Milton and the Parables of Jesus*

Recovering the Lost Art of Reading

Recovering the
Lost Art of Reading

A Quest for the True, the Good, and the Beautiful

Leland Ryken and Glenda Faye Mathes

WHEATON, ILLINOIS

Recovering the Lost Art of Reading: A Quest for the True, the Good, and the Beautiful

Copyright © 2021 by Leland Ryken and Glenda Faye Mathes

Published by Crossway
    1300 Crescent Street
    Wheaton, Illinois 60187

Cover design: Amanda Hudson, Faceout Studios

Cover image: Getty Images

First printing 2021

Printed in the United States of America

Trade paperback ISBN: 978-1-4335-6427-7
ePub ISBN: 978-1-4335-6430-7
PDF ISBN: 978-1-4335-6428-4
Mobipocket ISBN: 978-1-4335-6429-1

Library of Congress Cataloging-in-Publication Data

Names: Ryken, Leland, author. | Mathes, Glenda Faye, author.
Title: Recovering the lost art of reading : a quest for the true, the good, and the beautiful / Leland Ryken and Glenda Faye Mathes.
Description: Wheaton, Illinois : Crossway, [2020] | Includes bibliographical references and index.
Identifiers: LCCN 2020025538 (print) | LCCN 2020025539 (ebook) | ISBN 9781433564277 (trade paperback) | ISBN 9781433564284 (pdf) | ISBN 9781433564291 (mobi) | ISBN 9781433564307 (epub)
Subjects: LCSH: Books and reading. | Bible as literature.
Classification: LCC Z1003 .R98 2020 (print) | LCC Z1003 (ebook) | DDC 028/.9—dc23
LC record available at https://lccn.loc.gov/2020025538
LC ebook record available at https://lccn.loc.gov/2020025539

Crossway is a publishing ministry of Good News Publishers.

VP		30	29	28	27	26	25	24	23	22	21
15	14	13	12	11	10	9	8	7	6	5	4	3	2	1

To our respective spouses, Mary Ryken and David Mathes,
whose partnership in the gospel enlivens our earthly pilgrimages.

Contents

Introduction

Welcome to the Conversation

PERHAPS YOU'RE WONDERING about this book's title. Does reading need to be recovered? What makes it an art? And is it really lost? After all, here you are—reading a book.

These are fair questions, which *Recovering the Lost Art of Reading* seeks to answer. Its three progressive parts address first the concept of reading as a lost art, then distinctive features of various types of literature and tips for reading them, and finally, ideas for ways to recover reading.

While this book shares aspects of literary theory, it is far from an academic tome. Although it teems with practical suggestions, it isn't a how-to book with numbered steps to reading success. It's a guidebook by two seasoned and enthusiastic reading travelers, who show all readers—from those who rarely pick up a book to English majors and everyone between—how to discover more delight in the reading journey.

Perhaps you're reading more than ever, on Facebook or Twitter or blog posts or websites, primarily on your smartphone. But the plethora of cyber information is not generating genuine joy in your soul. Kitten videos may be endearing but not enduring.

Society does little to help shape timeless values. Manufactured and manipulated news reports convey inaccuracies. Politicians and celebrities promote immorality. Bleak architecture and tawdry images surround us.

In today's technology-driven and value-bereft culture, reading has become a lost art. But it's an art that can be recovered and enjoyed by anyone, no matter what the individual's educational level or literary experience. Join us on a journey that will open your eyes and hearts to reading that delights your soul with the true, the good, and the beautiful.

PART 1

———————

READING IS A LOST ART

1

Is Reading Lost?

"READ ANY GOOD BOOKS LATELY?"

This question once functioned as a common conversation-starter, but now we're more likely to hear, "What are your plans for the weekend?" or "Did you catch the game last night?" There's nothing wrong with spending time with family and friends on weekends or cheering on favorite sports teams. But could the prevalence of such questions indicate that these activities are eclipsing thoughtful conversations about reading?

The question about reading good books may seem blasé or even a cliché. But it's still used to launch literary discussions, and it effectively reflects this chapter's focus.

The negative connotations surrounding this question could be rooted in the phrase's history. It began initiating conversations almost a century ago, during the Roaring Twenties. BBC radio personality Richard Murdoch popularized it with a humorous twist in the 1940s, when he interjected it into dialogue as a comic attempt to change an unwelcome subject. Amusing variations came into play during ensuing years, and the catch phrase lost validity as a serious conversation starter.[1] Despite existing negative perceptions, it continues to enjoy a measure of popularity. Bloggers sometimes ask the question to head posts about books they recommend. Prominent Christians Stephen Nichols and Sinclair Ferguson have employed it respectively for a church history podcast and as a book title.[2]

Maybe "Read any good books lately?" is making a serious comeback. It could be a legitimate way of jumpstarting more conversations. We're using it here because it encompasses much of this chapter's scope. Each word packs a specific punch.

Read = This chapter reflects this book's focus on reading.

Any = Research shows that many people don't read any books or can't name a single author.

Good = This chapter's discussion touches on the concepts of literary quality and reading competency.

Books = Reading on screens differs from reading physical books.

Lately = We're addressing the current situation by providing recent information and statistics.

You may recognize these elements as we explore this chapter's primary question: Is reading lost?

THE CURRENT STATE OF READING

Most adults have 24-hour access to a constant stream of information. You may peruse a physical newspaper while sipping your morning cup of coffee, but you're more likely to respond to emails, scroll your Facebook feed, or skim top news stories on your phone. The screen-reader could be scanning more words than the person reading the paper. With the incredible volume and easy accessibility of information today, aren't people reading more than ever?

Yes and no. Many people are reading a great deal of material, especially online. But they are not necessarily reading quality material or reading well.

Surveys consistently show that most people believe reading is a worthwhile use of time and they should do more of it. But some people don't read any books. Gene Edward Veith Jr. writes: "A growing problem is illiteracy—many people do not know how to read. A more severe problem, though, is 'aliteracy'—a vast number of people know how to read but never do it."[3] Most of us could (and suspect we should) read more and read better.

Our worm of suspicion may even evolve into a dragon of guilt. Or we may think of reading as a duty we're neglecting, while feeling overwhelmed at the very idea of crowding one more thing into our busy lives. In this book, we aim to alleviate any reading guilt or anxiety. We want you, whether you read a little or a lot, to experience more joy in reading (and therefore in life). We want to dispel the notion of reading as duty and instill the concept of reading as delight.

Perhaps reading had declined in recent decades, but isn't it increasing now? The 2009 report by the National Endowment for the Arts, *Reading on the Rise*, celebrated (according to its subtitle) "a new chapter in American literacy." The NEA might well rejoice in any increase over the statistics reflected in its pessimistic 2004 report, *Reading at Risk*, which bemoaned previous decades of decline.[4] While Americans can join in the NEA's joy, we should pause for further consideration before patting ourselves on the back.

The Pew Charitable Foundation reported in 2018 that nearly a quarter of American adults had not read a book in any form within the past year.[5] This figure painted a slightly brighter picture than the high of 27 percent non-book readers in 2015. Still, it's a sobering statistic. Think of the people walking our city streets. Out of every four adults, one has not cracked open a physical book, downloaded a digital copy onto a device, or even listened to an audiobook.

British research expands our understanding of current reading culture. A recent statistic from the Royal Society of Literature sounds similar to the Pew report's finding. The 2017 RSL report showed that one out of five people could not name an author—any author.

On the positive side, the report showed people have a keen desire to read more literature. Nearly all respondents believed everyone should read literature, which they viewed as *not* limited to classics or academics. Over a third of those who already read want to read more in the future, while over half of those who currently do not read literature expressed a desire to do so. But many of those surveyed find literature—even material not considered classic or academic—difficult to read.[6]

The amount of time Americans spend reading each day increases with age, with retirees reading the most. But even those in the seventy-five and above age bracket read only 50 minutes per day. Not a single age group averages as much as an hour of daily reading.[7]

Compare that with the time people spend on digital media, which according to one study averages a whopping 5.9 hours per day. This nearly six hours per day may not be so surprising when you consider it includes smartphones, computers, game consoles, and other devices for streaming information.[8] Pew Research indicates about three-fourths of Americans go online daily. More than a quarter of US residents admit to being online "almost constantly."[9] No wonder many people express concern about society's burgeoning information technology and its possible relation to recent reading trends.

FINDING PEACE IN A READING WAR

Research on reading reveals a fascinating recurrence of references to Leo Tolstoy's *War and Peace*. Why are so many people writing about a Russian novel published more than a hundred and fifty years ago? Probably because *War and Peace* is often regarded as a litmus test for reading ability and perseverance.

Professor Margaret Anne Doody explains: "*War and Peace* is one of those few texts . . . too often read as some kind of endurance test or rite of passage, only to be either abandoned halfway or displayed as a shelf-bound trophy, never to be touched again. It is indeed very long, but it is a novel that abundantly repays close attention and re-reading."[10]

Careful attention appears to be a vanishing reading skill in our busy, technology-glutted lives. Writer Nicholas Carr famously asked, "Is Google Making Us Stupid?" While he noted the benefits of online research and accessible information, Carr found that he and many others struggle to read as well as they formerly did. One of his friends can no longer read *War and Peace* because scanning short online texts has given him a "staccato" thinking quality.[11]

In response to Carr's article, writer and speaker Clay Shirky celebrated the demise of literary reading and its culture. He wrote, "But here's the thing: it's not just Carr's friend, and it's not just because of the web—no one reads *War and Peace*. It's too long, and not so interesting."[12] Quite the blanket statement, but is it valid?

Professor Alan Jacobs sarcastically assessed Shirky's statement by noting how the "reading public has chosen to pronounce this devastating verdict against Tolstoy's masterpiece by purchasing over one hundred thousand copies" of *War and Peace* in the past four years, which he observes is "an odd way of making its disparagement known."[13] Any modern writer with that many copies sold in four years would be making the talk show rounds and juggling offers from major publishers.

At 560,000 words, there's no denying *War and Peace* is a hefty read. But several other novels—including Proust's *Remembrance of Things Past* with 1.5 million words—are significantly longer.[14] Penguin's Vintage Classic edition of *War and Peace* runs 1296 pages and still sells well enough for Amazon to flag it as a "#1 Best Seller" in Russian literature.

Literary critic James Wood recommends this translation for its accuracy in reflecting Tolstoy's style as well as the original language. Wood finds it feels "alive, and very much so" (quoting from Tolstoy's diary) "to be caught up in the bright sweep" of War and Peace. "It is to succumb to the contagion of vitality. As his characters infect each other with the high temperature of their existence, so they infect us."[15] Stirring words, which almost make one want to be numbered among the one hundred thousand purchasers.

Author and critic Philip Hensher calls War and Peace "the best novel ever written," although he admits it has "the worst opening sentence of any major novel, ever" and the "very worst closing sentence by a country mile." Between the two is a novel he views not only as the best ever written but also "the warmest, the roundest, the best story and the most interesting."[16]

These facts fail to support Shirky's claim. A great many people still read War and Peace, some find it neither too long nor uninteresting. But it can certainly be intimidating, especially keeping track of characters with multiple Russian names.

After author Michael Harris had read the first fifty pages five times, he returned to War and Peace, determined to finish it. As he withdrew from external influences and the pull of connectivity, he was able to focus on the story. He became immersed in the characters and their lives. His reading improved and he did more than finally complete the novel; he enjoyed it.[17]

Although War and Peace seems an accepted measure of reading competency, we don't endorse any particular novel as a standard. We want everyone to discover the delight of reading literature in any genre or format.

When considering other formats, one has to admire the rare feat of Clive Thompson, who read *War and Peace* on his iPhone. Thompson is someone who views "Tolstoy's phone-book-sized epic" as a reading test. "Make it to the end, and you get your Deep Literary Concentration Prize! You're a cultured individual!" Although distractions initially threatened to derail his phone-reading effort, he became captivated. "The phone's extreme portability allowed me to fit Tolstoy's book into my life, and thus to get swept up in it," he writes. "And it was *being* swept up that, ironically, made the phone's distractions melt away."[18]

Thompson makes positive observations about reading on a screen, and Alan Jacobs credits his Kindle as the device that rescued his reading habits.[19] But many others view screen reading and online activity as less than helpful, even harmful.

BRAIN CHANGES

In *The Shallows: What the Internet Is Doing to Our Brains*, Nicholas Carr provides numerous anecdotes and statistics to support his belief that the Internet is changing our brains in profound and negative ways. He writes, "Dozens of studies by psychologists, neurobiologists, educators, and Web designers point to the same conclusion: when we go online, we enter an environment that promotes cursory reading, hurried and distracted thinking, and superficial learning." He sees the internet itself as harmful.

> One thing is very clear: if, knowing what we know today about the brain's plasticity, you were to set out to invent a medium that would rewire our mental circuits as quickly and thoroughly as possible, you would probably end up designing something that looks and works a lot like the Internet.[20]

Particularly disturbing is how technology intentionally targets young people at their most vulnerable moments. Psychologist Richard Freed warns about "The Tech Industry's War on Kids":

> Persuasive technology's use of digital media to target children, deploying the weapon of psychological manipulation at just the right moment, is what makes it so powerful. These design techniques provide tech corporations a window into kids' hearts and minds to measure their particular vulnerabilities, which can then be used to control their behavior as consumers.[21]

Freed's article is packed with alarming facts and concerning quotations, some from tech professionals. It seems a few people within the industry are beginning to realize the harmful ways technology changes young brains.

In *Proust and the Squid: The Story and Science of the Reading Brain*, Maryanne Wolf wonders, "What would be lost to us if we replaced the skills honed by the reading brain with those now being formed in our new generation of 'digital natives,' who sit and read transfixed before a screen?" She believes they

> are not illiterate, but they may never become true expert readers. During the phase in their reading development when critical skills are guided, modeled, practiced, and honed, they may have not been challenged to exploit the acme of the fully developed, reading brain: time to think for themselves.[22]

Most online reading does not allow time for analytical thought. Hyperlinks are designed to lead readers to other sites, further fracturing their focus. Author Sven Birkerts suggests the problem may be twofold. "More and more we hear the complaint, even from practiced readers, that it is hard to maintain attentive focus. The works have presumably not changed. What has changed are either the conditions of reading or something in the cognitive reflexes of the reader. Or both."[23]

THE DEATH OF ARTFUL READING

These brain changes may be more important than most people realize. While reading a book and reading a screen both require the same eye movement and decoding of symbols, there is a huge difference in how people process and internalize the words. Screen reading is primarily scanning through short articles designed for distraction. Reading a book immerses oneself into an extensive work. When this is done receptively and thoughtfully, it becomes artful reading. Some people call it "deep reading" and believe it is in deep trouble.

Writer Annie Murphy Paul views such reading as "an endangered practice" that we should "take steps to preserve as we would a historic building or a significant work of art." She believes, "its disappearance would imperil the intellectual and emotional development of generations growing up online, as well as the perpetuation of a critical part of our culture: the novels, poems and other kinds of literature that can be appreciated only by readers whose brains, quite literally, have been trained to apprehend them."[24]

Nicholas Carr grieves the loss of his own ability to read. "The deep reading that used to come naturally has become a struggle," he writes. "My mind now expects to take in information the way the Net distributes it: in a swiftly moving stream of particles. Once I was a scuba diver in the sea of words. Now I zip along the surface like a guy on a Jet Ski."[25]

Author Michael Harris goes even farther to confess, "I have forgotten how to read." He found many friends shared his problem. "This doesn't mean we're reading less" in our "text-gorged society," he writes. "What's at stake is not whether we read. It's how we read." He makes this thought-provoking statement: "In a very real way, to lose old styles of reading is to lose a part of ourselves."[26]

What we've lost goes far beyond a simple behavior. Birkerts sees a loss of depth and wisdom, which he defines as "the knowing not of facts but of truths about human nature and the processes of life." He believes "we no longer think in these larger and necessarily more imprecise terms" because we are "swamped by data, and in thrall to the technologies that manipulate it." He adds, "In our lateral age, living in the bureaucracies of information, we don't venture a claim to that kind of understanding. Indeed, we tend to act embarrassed around those once-freighted terms—*truth, meaning, soul, destiny.*"[27]

Such concepts are important for everyone but particularly Christians. Who should care more about reading timeless truths than children of the Book? If we—like Michael Harris—have forgotten how to read, we've lost more than delight in literary treasures. We've lost the ability to read the Bible consistently and attentively. What then happens to our relationship with God? We have, indeed, lost part of ourselves in ways infinitely worse than Harris imagines.

Author Philip Yancey conveys the extent of this risk in the title of his article, "The Death of Reading Is Threatening the Soul." He concludes that a commitment to reading is a continuing battle similar to the struggle against the "seduction of Internet pornography." What does he recommend? "We have to build a fortress with walls strong enough to withstand the temptations of that powerful dopamine rush while also providing shelter for an environment that allows deep reading to flourish. Christians especially need that sheltering space, for quiet meditation is one of the most important spiritual disciplines."[28]

Some Christians tend to dismiss the concept of meditation as being too mystic, but God commands us: "Be still, and know that I am God" (Ps. 46:10). Elijah didn't hear God speak in the wind, the earthquake, or the fire. He heard God in the still small voice (1 Kings 19:12). We are called to quiet our souls and commune with God through an open Bible. If digital media continually fractures our focus, can we meditate on God and his word, receptively and thoughtfully? Artfully reading the Good Book and other good books is a treasure we dare not lose.

2

What Have We Lost?

A WELL-KNOWN INSURANCE company showcased a series of TV ads around the punch line, "We know a thing or two because we've seen a thing or two." Having been a college English professor for over half a century, I (Leland) have also seen a thing or two.

One memorable occasion relates directly to this chapter's question. A student seated in my office announced he could not justify reading Charles Dickens's *Great Expectations* during his last semester in college, preferring instead to spend time with his friends. I've often pondered and lamented what he lost by refusing to read a work of literature that may have had far-reaching and positive influence on his life.

The incident brings to my mind two statements by famous authors that guide our discussion of specific reading losses. In the penultimate paragraph of *An Experiment in Criticism*, C. S. Lewis writes,

> Those of us who have been true readers all our life seldom fully realize the enormous extension of our being which we owe to authors. We realize it best when we talk with an unliterary friend. He may be full of goodness and good sense but he inhabits a tiny world.[1]

Lewis makes the bold claim that a lack of reading limits a person's vision and experience.

Three centuries earlier, Francis Bacon stated the same truth in a positive way. In his essay "Of Studies," Bacon said that reading makes a full person, conference (or conversation) a ready person, and writing an exact person.[2] Lewis and Bacon help us to sense the richness we miss by not reading or not reading well.

LOSS OF MEANINGFUL LEISURE

Reading is by its very nature a leisure time activity. Although some people speak of reading as a compulsion and something they cannot live without, reading is usually something we do after we've handled life's routine physical and social demands.

Through the centuries, certain words dignified the sphere known as leisure. With the decline of reading and parallel activities, words that once elevated leisure have become debased. *Recreation*, for example, once denoted re-creation—the renewal of the human spirit. This lofty ideal has now shrunk to the point where the word may convey a "rec room" with a ping-pong table and large-screen TV, or a community recreation commission that provides sports programs for children of all ages, or a Recreational Vehicle (RV) for camping with all the comforts of home. While there's nothing wrong with games or sports or traveling, these newer uses of the term *recreation* all fall short of the former ideal of re-creation.

The term *entertainment* has suffered a similar diminishment. It once meant a pleasurable activity that people pursued in their free time. The Latin word for *hold* was part of the word's origin, implying that the activity involved had the power to rivet one's attention. To our surprise, we discovered that the word *amusement* was a synonym for *entertainment*, so that as late as 1920, T. S. Eliot defended the reading of literature as being "superior amusement."[3] Today, *entertainment* suggests a Hollywood celebrity world, and *amusement* is associated with a comedy show or a park with rides.

Leisure has lost its dignity. The word's etymology implies its higher reaches. Roots of the word *leisure* denote time free from necessary occupation with connotations of expanding potential and enrichment. A Christian leisure theorist aptly summarizes these concepts: "Leisure is the growing time for the human spirit. Leisure provides the occasion for learning and freedom, for growth and expression, for rest and restoration, for rediscovering life in its entirety."[4]

In contrast to this original and lofty standard, our culture (including the Christian segment of it) has drifted toward reducing leisure to mere diversion and distraction. Of course leisure cannot be exclusively mental and sedentary; we also need physical and relational activities. But discarding contemplative reading, once the staple of leisure in the English-speaking world, has diminished personal and cultural enrichment.

Most leisure pursuits today do not grow the human spirit. They often fail to engage the mind and imagination (the re-creating element). Staring at a smartphone for hours does not even meet the minimum requirement for leisure, a break from obligations. A Christian publisher releasing a book titled *Still Bored in a Culture of Entertainment* shows that believers struggle with boredom alongside unbelievers.[5] Artfully reading a wide range of good books is an antidote to boredom and fosters spiritual growth. Literature refreshes at deeper levels than many other leisure activities. God wants us to be all that we can be, in our leisure as well as in our work.

LOSS OF SELF-TRANSCENDENCE

As we immerse ourselves in the reading experience, we forget self-centered concerns and thoughts. We rise above ourselves to focus on other people or large themes or even God. This experience is best labeled as self-transcendence, despite the term's occasionally spiritualistic uses.

Getting beyond ourselves involves not only self-forgetfulness but also leaving behind our daily preoccupations: worries, work, relationships, and the myriad of regular concerns. Our human constitution requires breaks from burdensome reality. Constant immersion in obligation can make us feel joyless, irritable, and oppressed.

Biblical wisdom promotes the concept of rest. Christians generally are aware of work as a calling from God but often are ignorant that leisure is also a calling. After six days of creation, God "rested from all his work that he had done" (Gen. 2:3) and "was refreshed" by that rest (Ex. 31:17). As image-bearers, our calling is clear: our lives are incomplete if we do not follow God's lead in balancing work with leisure. Rest from labor becomes a direct command in the Decalogue: "Six days you shall labor, and do all your work, but the seventh day is a Sabbath to the LORD your God. On it you shall not do any work" (Ex. 20:9–10). God ordained rest as an opportunity to rise above the self by focusing on fellowship with others and God.

One of the best ways of resting from routine can be found in reading. While physical exercise temporarily removes us from the workaday world, it does not take us "out of ourselves." On the flip side, watching television diverts our minds from daily obligations, but most television and other forms of screen time can hardly be dignified with the lofty ideal of self-transcendence. Much of the time that people formerly used for reading is now spent staring at screens, primarily the ubiquitous smartphone.

Little of this screen time represents the health-giving act of forgetting self and identifying with something beyond normal experience. Literary scholar Helen Gardner praises the reading of literature for the way in which it "wonderfully distracts us from our self-concern [and] takes us out of ourselves, restoring . . . us."[6] Our failures to read and read well have deprived us of an essential way to transcend our confining world of private preoccupations and worries.

LOSS OF BEAUTY

One source of beauty is nature. Another is the arts, including literature. If we do not read, we have lost a primary avenue for fostering our sense of beauty. Is this important?

As with leisure, the Bible clearly shows that God wants us to have beauty in our lives. God created a world that is beautiful as well as useful. The garden he planted for our first parents was not only "good for food" but also "pleasant to the sight" (Gen. 2:9). In the New Testament, Jesus's discourse against anxiety and greed (Matt. 6:25–34) includes the command to "consider the lilies of the field," which is a call to contemplate beauty. At the literary level, the writer of Ecclesiastes informs his readers that he "sought to find words of delight" (Eccles. 12:10).

God intends human life to be abundant, and this includes fulfilling our God-implanted desire for the beautiful. Abraham Kuyper wrote that "as image-bearer of God, man possesses the possibility both to create something beautiful, and to delight in it."[7] Unfortunately, the long-time cultural trend has been to cauterize people's capacity for beauty through neglect of it. We see this trend in the bland, prosaic language of our church music and colloquializing translations of the Bible. One way we can reclaim a biblical view of beauty is by reading great literature and connecting with visual art and masterpieces of music.

Too often, the Internet and modern advertising fill our minds and imaginations with images of the cheap and tawdry. Literature and the arts can enlarge our spirits with images of greatness and beauty.

LOSS OF CONTACT WITH THE PAST

Although modern and contemporary eras have produced great literature, the bulk of it comes to us from the past. A weighty consideration for Christians is that their sacred book and salvation's redemptive acts are rooted in the past. But there is more to the picture than this principial one.

Matthew Arnold, a Victorian-era apologist for culture, bequeathed a marvelous formula when he said that to live a full life we need to be acquainted with "the best that is known and thought in the world."[8] A majority of the best that has been thought and said and produced in the arts comes from the past. We are more likely to find the true, the good, and the beautiful in classics of history than in contemporary and modern art. We need to be clear here that it is not the "pastness" of literature that makes it worthy. It is the presence of the true, the good, and the beautiful.

Additionally, acquaintance with the past liberates us from bondage to the contemporary. C. S. Lewis has written on this with his usual good sense. In an essay titled "Learning in War-time," Lewis asserts that "we need intimate knowledge of the past," not because "the past has any magic about it, but because we . . . need something to set against the present." Then he shares the following analogy: "A man who has lived in many places is not likely to be deceived by the local errors of his native village; the [person who knows the past] has lived in many times and is therefore in some degree immune from the great cataract of nonsense that pours from the press and the microphone of his own age."[9]

Other literary scholars have sounded the same note. Northrop Frye claimed that when we read literature from the past "we are led into a different kind of culture, with unfamiliar assumptions, beliefs, and values," and that contact with this unfamiliar world "is what expands our own view of human possibilities."[10] Wendell Berry writes about the past as something we need to "commune with, to speak with," and that if "we remove this sense of continuity, we are left with the thoughtless present tense."[11]

The decline of reading has led to the loss of the stabilizing influence and enriching treasures from the past. They speak with an outside voice into the repressive tyranny of the secular and politically-correct present.

LOSS OF CONTACT WITH ESSENTIAL HUMAN EXPERIENCE

A leading theme throughout this book is that literature testifies to the human experience. The loss of reading leads to a disconnection with biblical and bedrock aspects of humanity.

The first benefit of connecting with the portrayal and analysis of human experience in literature is an increased understanding of life. We erroneously assume daily living automatically leads to an understanding of essential human experience. The situation is nearly the reverse: we are too harried by life's demands to fully understand the first principles of living and of human nature. As literature projects human experience, we see our own lives more clearly and accurately. In this way, the literary enterprise shapes and forms us. The very nature of reading is contemplation of the human experience and the world in which it exists.

Self-understanding and a sense of self-identity also accompany such reading. At a commemorative ceremony at the tomb of Flemish painter Pieter Brueghel in 1924, Felix Timmermans said something that is true of literature as well as of painting: "In your work are reflected . . . our joys and our sorrows, our strengths and our weaknesses. . . . You are our mirror; in order to know . . . what we are, we have only to thumb through the book of your art, and we can know ourselves."[12] To live well, we need to know who we are.

Another dimension is the human urge for expression. We want our longings and fears to be given a voice. We desire our experiences to be registered. This explains why authors and painters and musicians ply their trade, and why the public seeks out their offerings.

Ralph Waldo Emerson, in his essay, "The Poet," observed that "all [people] live by truth and stand in need of expression."[13] The problem is that "adequate expression is rare." Literary authors become our representatives, "sent into the world to the end of expression," articulating our deepest feelings better than we can.

Literature can also serve a corrective function in its portrayal of human experience. The universality and broad expanse of literature, past and present, gradually builds up within readers an awareness of enduring values and norms for living. Literature keeps calling us back to the basics, which are discernible under the details of a literary work. William Faulkner, in his 1950 Nobel Prize acceptance speech, said that the literary author's task is to call humanity back to "the old verities and truths of the heart . . . love and honor and pity and pride and compassion and sacrifice." Without that foundation, "any story is ephemeral and doomed."[14] Life itself is ephemeral if we do not connect with permanent principles of existence.

Another way literature serves as corrective is in its archetypes. These are literature's recurrent master images and motifs. It is no exaggeration to call archetypes the building blocks of the literary imagination. Authors cannot avoid them if they try. But the reason archetypes are everywhere in literature is that they are everywhere in life. Psychologist Carl Jung, who helped establish the modern understanding of archetypes, championed the view that the human race shares common psychic responses to certain universal images and patterns. These images "make up the groundwork of the human psyche. It is only possible to live the fullest life when we are in harmony with these symbols; wisdom is a return to them."[15] Reading literature is a primary activity in our return.

The portrayal of human experience in literature also reflects a celebratory aspect. Recognizing our experiences creates a sense of personal identity. We feel "this is who we are." That identity is not all good, but it is authentic. Christians are familiar with the act of confession, both confessing what we've done wrong and professing what we believe. Literature is a confession of the human race. We have a stake in it.

Entering the world of literature can accurately be labeled as "welcome to the human race." All it takes to accept the invitation is to read a book or poem. To reject the invitation is to live in a diminished world, not fully participating in literature's understanding and affirmation of human experience.

LOSS OF EDIFICATION

While we have many sources of edification in our lives, we lose an important source by not reading literature. Christian readers naturally gravitate to literature that affirms a biblical viewpoint and portrays Christian experience, but such writings should not constitute our entire reading diet. On the other hand, something is wrong when Christians immerse themselves in material that assaults rather than supports their biblical values. The songs of Zion are better than the songs of Babylon. Following the promptings of the Holy Spirit, when Christian readers take stock of what reading means to them personally, most will identify reading as a major source of spiritual input. Christian writers become spokespersons for the faith, and readers celebrate the truth these authors express. After his conversion, one-time British atheist Malcolm Muggeridge wrote that "books like *Resurrection* and *The Brothers Karamazov* give me an almost overpowering sense of how uniquely marvelous a Christian way of looking at life is, and a passionate desire to share it."[16]

In addition to *the literature of Christian affirmation*, literature that affirms a biblical viewpoint, there is an even larger body of literature that we can call *the literature of common experience*. It does not espouse a specifically Christian view of life, but it is entirely congruent with Christianity. In fact, much of this literature is written by Christians.

This literature embodies general truth, not distinctively Christian truth. It is the communal wisdom of the human race, made possible by God's common grace bestowed on all humanity. What is edifying about immersing ourselves in literature of common experience? General truth is genuine truth, and Christians "rejoice with the truth" (1 Cor. 13:6) wherever they find it.

At the far end of the literary continuum, we find *the literature of unbelief*—literature that contradicts what the Christian faith asserts. We would not say that such literature is edifying, but *our encounter with it* can be. As we resist what is being commended to us, we celebrate what we have in Christ. Reading modern literature of despair can make us even more aware of our joy in the Lord. Literature categories edify in different ways, but most reading experiences can be edifying if we read self-consciously as Christians. Not reading prevents these new avenues of edification from developing in our lives.

LOSS OF AN ENLARGED VISION

Our concluding item in this inventory of losses occasioned by the decline of reading brings us back to where we started, the idea that a non-reader "inhabits a tiny world," while reading produces a full person.[17] C. S. Lewis advocated a theory of literature that became widely accepted. In brief, Lewis believes that "we seek an enlargement of our being. We want to be more than ourselves. . . . We want to see with other eyes, to imagine with other imaginations, to feel with other hearts, as well as with our own."[18]

Reading is not the only way to enlarge our fund of experiences. Traveling or conversation or television viewing can do so as well. But reading has some built-in advantages. One is the transport by which we can access a world of experiences and viewpoints different from our own and those of our contemporary world. All it requires is opening a book. Compared to the vast sweep of viewpoints and experiences represented by literature through the ages, our community and contemporary books comprise a very tiny circle.

We need to consider not only the *quantity* of experiences in literature but also their *quality*. Literature is a realm of the imagination. Anything is possible. Imagination instantly takes us farther than any travel in the real world. It frees us from time and place and ushers us into an expansive world. Few events in life give us anything close to literature's beauty and range of style. Most activities, like a visit to the local coffee shop, confine us to the mundane and prosaic. The human spirit craves the emancipation of excursions into the imaginative realm created by eloquent wordsmiths.

Literature not only imitates the world around us, as classical art theory promoted but adds to our world's materials. Literary authors are sub-creators under God. For avid readers, many of the places and events and characters of an invented world are more real, more inspiring, and more interesting than the local grocery store and the people in it. Individuals who know only the actual things live in a shrunken world.

WHAT HAVE WE LOST?

The decline of reading has impoverished our culture and individual lives. We have lost mental sharpness, verbal skills, and ability to think and imagine. Our leisure has little meaning, and we're consumed with self. We fail to recognize beauty or the value of either the past or essential human experience. We suffer from a lack of edification and a shrunken vision.

Too many people drift aimlessly in a rowboat without oars when they could be sailing on a fully-equipped cruise ship, feasting on delicious food, visiting fascinating ports of call, lounging on white beaches, and diving into an amazing underwater world. Sadly, they may not even realize what they're missing.

3

Why Consider Reading an Art?

DURING THE YEAR BEFORE I (Glenda) began attending Pella Christian Grade School, I cried every morning my older brother and sister boarded the big, yellow school bus. I'd sit on the basement steps, watching my mother manually feed wet laundry through the washing machine wringer. As water poured from squeezed blue jeans, tears streamed down my cheeks. I repeatedly begged, "When will I learn how to read?" Mom calmly answered, "When you go to school."

The following year, my first stop each morning in the Kindergarten room was the teacher's desk. I'd ask, "When will we learn to read?" Mrs. Vander Wiel invariably replied, "As soon as we finish our *Think and Do* books."

We eventually completed those wretched workbooks and took them home at Christmas break. When returning after the new year, my excitement ran high. *Today*, I thought. *Today I'm finally going to learn how to read!*

My anticipation was justified. I didn't even bother to question my teacher because a stack of Dick and Jane readers sat on her desk. After our classroom's usual beginning formalities, she turned to the blackboard and picked up a piece of chalk. "Today, class, we're going to learn how to read." I squirmed in my seat at the half-moon table I shared with another girl.

Mrs. Vander Wiel formed white letters on the chalkboard. "Today, we're going to learn how to read 'Oh' and 'Look.'"

Oh? Look? That's it? My spirit plummeted into my black and white saddle shoes. *I already know how to read those two words!*

Perched on the arm of an upholstered chair in our living room, following along as my mother read aloud or as siblings rehearsed catechism answers, I'd learned how to read without realizing it.

Once this realization set in, I read everything from cereal boxes to newspaper headlines. If I didn't recognize a word, I sounded it out. But I didn't unleash the power of reading until I discovered chapter books, like the one about the Bobbsey Twins I brought to school in second grade. While my classmates took turns reading aloud from a textbook, one excruciatingly-slow paragraph at a time, I lifted the lid of my desk enough to retrieve my Bobbsey Twins book. Then I held it inside my propped-up textbook and surreptitiously read it. When Miss Ella called on me, I had no idea which paragraph we were ready for in the textbook. Rather than paying attention to my classroom in Pella, I'd been participating in the camaraderie of the Bobbsey household in Lakeport.

While the Bobbsey Twins may not have been great literary art, this personal anecdote demonstrates the power of not only transport but also participation. Participation elevates reading skill to an art. This chapter's purpose is to encourage our consideration of reading as an art and to introduce a biblical view of the arts.

SKILL OR ART?

We learn to read in various ways. Children may learn best by recognizing sight words in a whole language approach or through the sounds of phonics or a combination of both. Some students quickly catch on to reading, while others struggle for years. Why can learning to read be so challenging?

Author Maryanne Wolf believes it is because our brains are not wired for it. But as the neural connections for reading form, our brains surpass basic decoding functions to encompass analytical thought. "Developmental differences in the circuit systems between a beginning, decoding brain and a fully automatic, comprehending brain span the length and breadth of the brain's two hemispheres," she writes. "A system that can become streamlined through specialization and automaticity has more time to think. This is the miraculous gift of the reading brain."[1]

The ability to go beyond simple decoding to complex thinking is certainly a gift. Anyone who has struggled with learning to read or teaching someone how to read will appreciate this miraculous aspect. Still, we tend to think of reading as a skill rather than as an art. What makes the difference?

Both what we read and how we read affect our consideration of reading as an art. Informational reading and online skimming require only basic skill. Imaginative literature goes beyond simple skill to artful reading.

When we read a recipe or an instruction manual or an encyclopedia entry, we gather information. We can read quickly, without thinking deeply or weighing our response. If we're making a cake, we mix the listed ingredients. If we're putting together an entertainment center, we follow the steps and diagrams. If a curious child asks about that different-colored country below the United States on the globe, we search for "Mexico" online or may even pull the encyclopedia's M volume from the bookcase and flip through pages describing details about Mexico.

Although the Internet brings worlds of words to our screens and speeds along tedious research, too much online reading consists of clicking social media posts that lead down a rabbit warren of mind-numbing hyperlinks. This type of reading requires little thought.

The way we read imaginative literature differs significantly. Receptively and thoughtfully reading a novel or a memoir or a poem allows us to become an active participant in its art. What the author conveys may either appall or enthrall us. Good literature both enlightens and delights.

In his "The Art of Reading" course, Professor Timothy Spurgin calls these two types of reading "everyday reading" and "artful reading." Thinking of reading as an art, he explains, helps you do three things: (1) take reading more seriously, (2) see a difference between reading and reading well ("getting through a book and getting something out of it"), and (3) consider this type reading as its own reward.[2]

We agree with Professor Spurgin. We believe reading can be considered an art when the reader participates in imaginative literature's artistic experience, discovering the power of creativity from a biblical perspective.

PARTICIPATION

When we talk about participation, we're not advocating an approach limiting meaning to mere reader response. It's important to make this clarification because literary theory has changed over the years. Early theories focused on the author, with little consideration to what the reader brought to the reading experience. Modern theories shifted attention to the text and reader. Deconstructionism placed so much emphasis on the response of individual readers that the writer was almost completely ignored, resulting in what some have called "the death of the author." Peter J. Leithart writes, "In the early part of the twentieth century, modernism shifted attention from the author and his biography to the text as a literary object, and postmodernism has finished the job by wresting the text completely from its author's grasp."[3] We, in writing this book, want to promote a balanced approach that encompasses the author, text, and reader within the context of a biblical perspective.

Other people have experienced revelations similar to Glenda's opening anecdote. Damon Young shares how reading Sherlock Holmes stories first generated an awareness of himself as "something powerful: a reader." He realized that "without a reader, the magic stops."[4]

This magic is the art of reading. An imaginative current flows between the written words and the mind's eye. An author creates a work of literature. A reader receives and responds to it, which empowers participation in its art. How does this happen?

Initially, we simply receive it. C. S. Lewis writes: "The first demand any work of art makes upon us is surrender. Look. Listen. Receive. Get yourself out of the way. . . . The distinction can hardly be better expressed than by saying that the many *use* art and the few *receive* it."[5] Whether we view a masterpiece in the National Gallery of Art or read a novel on the plane to Washington, D.C., we best receive it by being open to its artistry.

In *Art Needs No Justification*, Hans Rookmaaker acknowledges art's "manifold" uses. But he writes, "Art has its own meaning. A work of art can stand in the art gallery and be cherished for its own sake."[6] Instead of viewing art as something we can use or as a means to an end, we value it for itself.

But our reception of literature is not static. Damon Young calls it an "active passivity." He describes artful reading as a "dance" that is a "fragile poise between proclivities: thought and feeling, spontaneity and habit, deference and critique, haste and slowness, boldness and caution, commitment and detachment."[7] His dance imagery beautifully expresses the reader's balance between these juxtapositions of human response.

Christians gain additional insight from Lewis, as he clarifies his advice to receive: "I do not mean by this that the right spectator is passive. His also is an imaginative activity; but an obedient one. He seems passive at first because he is making sure of his orders. . . ."[8] Those orders for the Christian, of course, come from our commander, Jesus Christ.

PONDERING PERSPECTIVES

The imagery of the poised reader, making sure of orders, describes someone pondering perspectives. People have differing views about the world and what should be valued. Readers better engage in the reading experience when they are aware of their own worldview and that of the author.

James Sire, greatly influenced by Francis Shaeffer, describes the importance of worldviews in reading:

> When writers write they do so from the perspective of their own world view. What they presuppose about themselves, God, the good life and the validity of human knowledge governs both what they say and how they say it. That is why reading with world views in mind (your own and that of the author) will help you understand not only what is written in the lines but what is written between the lines—that is, what is presumed before a pen ever reaches the page.[9]

Authors often express worldviews in subtle ways. Thoughtful readers recognize nuances or assumptions that either resonate with their own beliefs or fail to do so. This doesn't mean Christians should read only literature falling inline with their faith. It does mean, however, that their faith informs their reading. With our commander Jesus's orders in mind, we are free to explore a variety of vistas and recognize ways that even harsh terrains reveal truth or goodness or beauty.

C. S. Lewis recognized the individuality of worldview. "Each of us by nature sees the whole world from one point of view with a perspective and a selectiveness peculiar to himself." He goes on to describe the desire to explore experiences beyond our own with his famous quotation: "We demand windows. Literature as Logos is a series of windows, even of doors."[10] The concept of literature as Logos applies directly to reading as an art.

LOGOS AND POWER

The Greek word *logos* has various meanings and connotations, but it can be defined as a literary device relating to logic. This definition grew from Aristotle's concept of *logos* as the method of persuasion that appealed to logic (his other two were *pathos*, an appeal to emotions, and *ethos*, an appeal to ethics). Greek philosophy considered logos the fundamental aspect regulating the universe, and some literary theories view it as the writer's foundation.

All these definitions of the word seem to reflect (albeit palely) the biblical meaning of *Logos*: the Word and Wisdom, who is Christ. The apostle John beautifully describes Christ's creative power: "In the beginning was the Word, and the Word was with God, and the Word was God. He was in the beginning with God. All things were made through him, and without him was not any thing made that was made" (John 1:1–3). Paul calls Christ "the power of God and the wisdom of God" (1 Cor. 1:24). The second person of the Trinity, Jesus Christ, embodies both creative power and continuing wisdom.

Within the context of reading as an art, the reader participates in the power of the author's imagination and creativity. The reading experience itself is a threefold process that reflects the trinitarian character of God.

In *The Mind of the Maker*, Dorothy Sayers explores how the three-fold nature of human creativity reflects the triune character of the Creator God. She then extends this analogy to the reader:

> For the reader . . . the book itself is presented as a threefold being. First: The Book as Thought—the Idea of the book existing in the writer's mind. . . . Secondly: the Book as Written—the Energy or Word incarnate, the express image of the Idea. . . . Thirdly: the Book as Read—the Power of its effect upon and in the responsive mind.[11]

Her expression "Word incarnate" and its connection with the second person of the Trinity help us understand the idea Lewis expressed of literature as Logos. Because people are image-bearers of God, it makes biblical sense that human creativity reflects divine creativity. And we can see how that applies to the three aspects of a book as thought, written, and read. We participate in literature's artistic experience by pondering the author's idea, receiving the energy in the words, and responding to the work's power.

Sayers sees power in both an author's creativity and a reader's participation: "When the writer's Idea is revealed or incarnate by his Energy, then, and only then, can his Power work on the world. More briefly and obviously, a book has no influence till somebody can read it." Power is latent in the words themselves and becomes active when they are read. She writes, "The habit, very prevalent today, of dismissing words as 'just words' takes no account of their power."[12] Literature as logos and the power of the written word propel reading into the realm of art.

BIBLICAL AESTHETIC

Our word choices in the term "biblical aesthetic" are intentional. We're using the adjective biblical rather than Christian because, sadly, much of what is called "Christian art" today is not artistic. This is particularly true when it comes to books. The popular genre of Christian fiction contains too few literary gems. We're using aesthetic as a noun rather than its more common use as an adjective to reflect the word's definition as "a particular theory or conception of beauty or art: a particular taste for or approach to what is pleasing to the senses and especially sight."[13] When we write about a biblical aesthetic, we mean a perspective on the arts that is steeped in scriptural knowledge and informed by artistic awareness.

We have mentioned the true, the good, and the beautiful, which is a threefold paradigm often used to guide a perspective on art. Later chapters will expand on this triad and explore each aspect individually. For now, we simply want to establish that looking for the true, the good, and the beautiful is a foundational concept in developing a biblical aesthetic.

Christians live in God's world as people of his word, conscious of their worth and responsibilities as his image-bearers. For those reasons, believers—more than any other people—ought to appreciate imaginative literature and embrace a biblical view of all art. Awareness of the Creator elevates the Christian's view of nature over that of the unbeliever.

Clyde S. Kilby (who excels at articulating and encouraging a biblical aesthetic) writes,

> Does it not confer a far greater dynamism and potential upon nature to view God as its cause? . . . Thus artistic experience may become for the Christian believer a more thrilling experience than for the unbeliever. The beauty of a Turner landscape or a Rembrandt still life contains for him a double beauty—the hand of the artist and also the hand of a personal and loving God.[14]

The Christian knows God as both the Almighty Creator and as a tender Father. This dual knowledge of God exponentially increases the Christian's pleasure in art.

We're not advocating separate categories of Christian art as opposed to secular art. Because all artists are made in God's image and live in a world that reveals him (whether they realize it or not), both Christians and unbelievers are capable of producing artistic works. As Kilby writes, "To suppose a secular and Christian art is to denigrate the unity of the universe, the *imago Dei* in man, and the very nature of God."[15] God's act of creation brought unity out of chaos. He created man in his own image and a cosmos reflecting aspects of his character.

In lovely language, the *Belgic Confession* speaks of the universe, "which is before our eyes as a most elegant book." It adds that "all creatures, great and small, are as so many characters leading us to *see clearly the invisible things of God, even his everlasting power and divinity.*"[16] The *Belgic Confession* supports this with Romans 1:20, "For his invisible attributes, namely, his eternal power and divine nature, have been clearly perceived, ever since the creation of the world, in the things that have been made." The verse confirms the concept's biblical truth, while the terms "elegant book" and "characters" resonate with writers and readers.

God's two methods of revelation, his word and his world, help us understand him and humanity better. Great art reaffirms or expands this understanding. As Calvin famously writes, "Our wisdom, in so far as it ought to be deemed true and solid wisdom, consists almost entirely of two parts: the knowledge of God and of ourselves." While the twofold knowledge is intertwined, a priority should be kept in mind. Calvin later adds, "But though the knowledge of God and the knowledge of ourselves are bound together by a mutual tie, due arrangement requires that we treat the former in the first place, and then descend to the latter."[17] The primary consideration in a biblical aesthetic is how art reflects God, but the second factor is how art increases our understanding of ourselves.

Kilby summarizes the human aspect well: "Great art reveals the human condition—past, present, and future—helping man to understand himself, the universe, and life itself."[18] When we read imaginative literature artfully, we better understand ourselves and the meaning of life. We identify with universal truths and emotions, while becoming more aware of ourselves as unique individuals. Such discoveries strum our heartstrings, reverberating humanity's common chords.

Our individuality is a gift from the God who not only named day, night, heaven, earth, sea, and stars but also has every Christian's name engraved on his hand and will give each one a new name at the end of time (Gen. 1; Isa. 40:26; 49:16; Eph. 3:15; Rev. 2:17). God created all things for a purpose, creating sentient humans as the crown of his creation.

Kilby sees this God-given individuality as what sets the Christian view of art apart from other perspectives:

> The uniqueness characteristic of true art is ascribed by the Christian to the selfhood given all things by God. The universals with which art deals he ascribes to a moral and unified creation with a single great Maker. He holds that the best art is that which sees man, not as mere mechanism or accident, but as purposive in a theistic order. He believes that art is a supreme expression of man, enabling him to look contemplatively at himself and the meaning of his life and permitting him through the works of others to test, comprehend, and enlarge his own experience.[19]

Learning to read is a gift that keeps giving. Careful reading of imaginative literature elevates reading skill into an art. We participate in the artistic experience by receiving and responding to the work's power. A truly Christian perspective is steeped in Scripture and informed by aesthetic standards of the true, good, and beautiful.

We hope this first part has encouraged you to think of reading as an art that is being lost at great cost to both the individual and society as a whole. The next part will explore reasons *why* to read literature and offer suggestions on *how* to read specific genres.

PART 2

READING LITERATURE

4

What Is Literature?

WHILE DOING RESEARCH in the early eighties for a book on literature in Christian perspective, I (Leland) was exhilarated to find a new
anthology titled *What Is Literature?* Leading literary scholars of the
time explored the subject in essays, published by a university press. My
excitement turned to shock when I discovered that all the contributors
claimed we cannot answer the question posed in the book's title. It is
impossible to define literature!

We do not agree with those authors. But before we explore a definition, we want to explain the historical context for our discussion.

The disappearance of a definition for literature could never have
been predicted until it happened. Through the centuries, beginning
with Aristotle and the ancient Greeks, the concept of defining literature was a given. Even though literary experts disagreed on some fine
points regarding what literature is, there was never any doubt that it
could be defined. Why would there be? All we need to do is look at a
specimen of literature and describe what we observe. Half a century
ago, however, this suddenly ceased to be self-evident in the discipline
of literary studies. Academia rejected the idea of defining literature.

The fallout was predictable: if it is impossible to define the differentiating properties of literature as a form of writing, then all writing

and even non-writing becomes fair game to be considered literature. This is precisely what happened. When literary scholars in the 1980s substituted the word "texts" for the traditional term "*works* of literature," the change of nomenclature signaled a seismic shift in literary studies. The generic term *text* opened the door to teach any written document—in fact, the term quickly expanded to encompass nonverbal artifacts. Here is a representative list of courses currently offered in literature departments at prestigious universities: "The Politics of Hip-Hop"; "Digital Game Studies"; "The Art of Insult." (That last one was allowed as a substitute for a course in Shakespeare.) A student I (Leland) know reported taking a literature course that had no texts at all. Instead of scrutinizing great works of literature, the class did activities such as visiting a toy store to see what packaging was gender-biased and spending an evening in a gay bar.

Readers should be aware of the cultural and academic context within which we now proceed to define what literature is. Contrary to trends in college literature departments, it is not impossible to define literature, and the best thinking on the subject for twenty centuries will guide our journey to this definition.

EXAMINING A SPECIMEN

While we wish to encourage all types of good reading, our passion and expertise focus on imaginative literature. This is also the sphere in which we can most decisively speak of having lost the art of reading. We will begin by looking at a literary specimen and drawing some preliminary conclusions about the nature of literature.

Most obviously, literature consists of words. So do newspapers, textbooks, and other informational reading materials. This type of reading, as distinguished from literary reading, continues to happen in our society. Most jobs and regular duties require some reading, as do our spiritual routines. We conduct the daily business of life in expository discourse. It is customary to contrast literary writing with this other main style, known as expository writing.

The following piece of expository writing expresses how a botanist formulates the scientific facts about a landscape:

> Environment is highly complex and integrated. . . . The problem of measuring those physical conditions that really govern plant behavior is much more difficult than is commonly conceived. . . . The intensity of most factors varies with the hour, day, and season, and the rates of change, the durations of particular intensities. . . . The common practice of integrating measurements taken over a period of time as mean values may obscure very important time aspects of factor variation.[1]

The most obvious feature of the passage is its analytic approach, with the emphasis on things such as measuring the features of plants and determining mean values. The language is abstract, and its account of the landscape conveys nothing sensory about observing a sunrise in a natural environment.

Here is a literary rendition of the same phenomenon:

> The dawn creeps in stealthily; the solid walls of black forest soften to gray, and vast stretches of the river open up and reveal themselves; the water is glass-smooth, gives off spectral wreaths of white mist; there is not the faintest breath of wind, nor stir of leaf; the tranquility is profound and infinitely satisfying. . . . Well, that is all beautiful; soft and rich and beautiful; and when the sun gets well up, and distributes a pink flush here and a powder of gold yonder and a purple haze where it will yield the best effect, you grant that you have seen something that is worth remembering.[2]

Mark Twain's description of daybreak from his *Life on the Mississippi* epitomizes the literary use of language. It captures and conveys the rich experience of seeing a river landscape gradually revealed in the growing light. Rather than provide information, it awakens imagination. We share in what the author felt and saw.

The botanist's account is objective and analytical, while the literary account is highly personal and affective (suffused with feeling). The literary passage appeals to our imagination (our image-making and image-perceiving capacity). An obvious feature of the literary language is its concreteness (as opposed to abstractness). To the botanist, environment is "highly complex and integrated"; to the literary writer, it is "beautiful." This preliminary foray into our subject is designed to guide our thinking in a certain way.

A biblical signpost confirms we're heading in the correct direction. Consider the parable Jesus told about the good Samaritan. The rich young ruler's question, "Who is my neighbor?" presents a perfect opportunity for Jesus to give a dictionary definition of the word *neighbor*. He could have responded with something like, "Our neighbor is anyone in need with whom we come into contact," which would be expository writing in its pure form. But Jesus instead told a story about an attacked man, heartless religious leaders, and a compassionate foreigner. The story teems with concrete details. Teachers of literary writing belabor the theme that the author's task is to "show, don't tell." Rather than explain in abstract terms, literary writers embody through concrete images.

Equipped with some historical background and an understanding of the differences between expository and literary writing, we are now ready to explore five foundational principles that underlie literature. Literature is: experiential, concrete, universal, interpretive, and artistic.

LITERATURE IS EXPERIENTIAL

To say that literature is experiential means first that its subject is human experience. Authors do not seek to convey information *about* human experience but to recreate experiences that readers vicariously live in their imaginations and emotions. A literary scholar put it this way: "Literature provides a *living-through*, not simply *knowledge about*: not the fact that lovers have died young and fair, but a living-through of *Romeo and Juliet*; not theories about Rome, but a living-through of the conflicts in *Julius Caesar*."[3]

C. S. Lewis was on the same page in his essay on the nature of literary language. He begins (as we did above) by contrasting expository and literary writing, with the latter represented by John Keats's description of a cold winter night. The discussion winds its way to the conclusion, "This is the most remarkable of the powers of [literary] language: to convey to us the quality of experiences."[4] This concurs with the whole history of thinking about the nature of literature.

For twenty centuries, the classical tradition agreed that literature is an imitation of reality, acknowledging how literature resembles human experience as lived in the world. Shakespeare popularized a formula for this concept in his play *Hamlet*: the writer "holds the mirror up to nature [life]."

When the romantic movement arrived in the nineteenth century, it became evident that the concept of imitation does not do justice either to the creative element in composition or to literature's unlifelike details. Accordingly, imagination replaced imitation as the key concept. But this new theory did not abandon the truth of literature's subject as human experience. Dorothy Sayers expressed the more recent theory: "Suppose, having rejected the words *copy, imitation,* and *representation* as inadequate we substitute the word *image* and say that what the artist is doing is *to image forth* something or the other."[5] What the writer "images forth" is life.

The subject of literature is human experience. When we read a story or poem, we vicariously live a segment of life. We both studied under an English teacher at the Christian high school in our hometown of Pella, Iowa, whose mantra encapsulated this point: "Literature is life." Literary works specialize in *truthfulness to life*.

LITERATURE IS CONCRETE

Our look at the contrasting descriptions of dawn showed how literature uses concrete images rather than abstract descriptions. Concreteness is necessary to express human experience effectively. The theological concept of incarnation provides a helpful analogy for understanding this. The second person of the Trinity, Jesus Christ, took the form of a body and walked on earth as a visible man. C. S. Lewis once wrote that literature "is a little incarnation, giving body" to its subject.[6] The word *embodies* is a good synonym for *incarnates* in this context.

A couple of biblical examples demonstrate how concreteness embodies truth. The sixth commandment commands propositionally, "You shall not murder" (Ex. 20:13). The story of Cain (Gen. 4:1–16) embodies the same truth in a narrative form of plot, setting, and character. A theology book defines *providence* as God's provision for his creatures and his direction of events in people's lives. Psalm 23 concretely embodies that truth in the description of a shepherd's provision for his sheep during the course of a typical day.

LITERATURE IS UNIVERSAL

If literature is inherently concrete and filled with particulars, its uncanny ability to express what is universal in human experience is surprising. Literature embodies experiences familiar to all people in all places at all times. This view of literature can be traced back to Aristotle, who claimed that the writer imitates the universal (whereas history imitates the particular). This does not negate the obvious way a poem is filled with images and a story with actions, settings, and characters. But these details, said C. S. Lewis in his classic essay "On Stories," are only a net whereby to capture the universal.[7] Literary scholars speak of literature as a concrete universal: it is filled with particulars that express universal human experience.

A good way to remember this dimension of literature is that a history book and newspaper tell us what *happened*, while literature tells us what *happens*. In the words of literary scholar Northrop Frye, the author's role "is not to tell you what happened, but what happens; not what did take place, but the kind of thing that always does take place."[8]

To see literature's universal element sometimes requires analysis. This is easy if we begin with a conviction that we can see life as we know and experience it behind literature's surface details. Literature is a window to our world. A work of literature is bifocal: we look *at* the details of a story or poem but also *through* them to life. Comprehending this aspect of literature as life helps us grasp the relevance of what we read.

LITERATURE IS INTERPRETIVE

As noted, poets and storytellers present human experience as concretely as possible. They appeal to imagination over intellect. But they do more than *present* human experience; they also *interpret* it. Works of literature embody ideas, which can be extracted from the text. Novelist Joyce Cary expressed it this way:

> All great artists have a theme, an idea of life profoundly felt and founded in some personal and compelling experience. . . . All writers have, and must have, to compose any kind of story, some picture of the world, and of what is right and wrong in that world.[9]

Having a "picture of the world" builds on our earlier point about literature's concreteness and touches on the previous chapter's discussion of worldviews. Authors have their own conceptions about what is right and wrong, ideas which are embodied in literature.

Literature acquaints us with the great ideas by which the human race has ordered life. These ideas are important, but not every view is true. Christian readers should compare what is conveyed in works of literature to biblical truth. In other words, we read through the lens of our Christian worldview. Even though literature does not always tell us the truth at an ideational level, contemplating such ideas can be a catalyst to our realization of what is true.

LITERATURE IS ARTISTIC

So far, our discussion has centered on literature's content. But an additional, equally important, dimension to literature is its form—the "how" of a literary work rather than the "what."

The initial thing to establish about literary form is that content does not exist apart from form. There is no "what" without the "how." This concept should be self-evident but is often overlooked. We mention it first because the utilitarian function is the vehicle through which meaning exists. The meaning we discover in a literary work springs from the form in which it is embodied. We can express this very broadly: anything having to do with *how* writers express themselves is "form."

The second function of literary form is artistic. Literary writers affirm the importance of form and beauty as part of their task. Victorian poet Gerard Manley Hopkins, author of some of the most treasured devotional poems ever written, claimed that the form of a poem exists "for its own sake and interest even over and above its interest of meaning."[10] Modern Welsh poet Dylan Thomas claimed, "I like to treat words as a craftsman does his wood or stone . . . to hew, carve, mold, coil, polish, and plane them into patterns, sequences, sculptures of sound."[11] Writers incessantly revise their works in progress, not as an attempt to express their ideas better but in order to perfect their form. Ernest Hemingway rewrote the ending of *A Farewell to Arms* over thirty times "to get it right."[12]

Knowing how seriously writers take literary form is important to our understanding of what literature is. Literary artistry and the beauty it represents are important aspects of literature that should not be ignored but regarded as self-rewarding. Refuting a popular view that only literature's ideas matter, C. S. Lewis writes that to regard a work of literature "as primarily a vehicle for . . . philosophy is an outrage to the thing the poet has made for us. . . . [A literary work] is not merely *logos* (something said) but *poeima* (something made). . . . One of the prime achievements in every good fiction has nothing to do with truth or philosophy."[13]

Our take-away point as it relates to our definition of literature is that beauty of form is an essential ingredient. Because authors work hard to craft beauty into their compositions, readers should pay attention to their intentional artistry.

FINAL THOUGHTS

What is literature? It can be briefly defined as a concrete, interpretive presentation of human experience in an artistic form. Why is it important to define the attributes of literature as this chapter has done?

The goal of definition is to see something more precisely in order to understand and enjoy it. Knowing what to look for in literature helps us experience it more fully. C. S. Lewis said that "the first qualification for judging any piece of workmanship from a corkscrew to a cathedral is to know *what* it is—what it was intended to do and how it is meant to be used."[14] The principle applies to all of literature as a whole. To master literature, we need to know its specific traits.

Now that we understand what literature is, we can explore its value. Why is literature important in our lives? The subsequent chapter takes the logical next step to discovering its rewards.

5

Why Does Literature Matter?

BY THE END OF the book of Ecclesiastes, its writer has exhausted his search for meaning in life and come to a conclusion: "Fear God and keep his commandments" (Eccles.12:13). He has shown how existence in this world makes no sense apart from faith in God. In other words, life under the sun is meaningless until life above the sun gives it meaning. From this wise perspective, he shares his philosophy of composition. He "taught the people knowledge" and "sought to find words of delight" (Eccles. 12:9–10). We view his wisdom as foundational in articulating a defense of literature. Reading literature matters because it conveys knowledge and confers delight.

Writing in Rome twenty years before the birth of Jesus, Horace bequeathed a similar literary formula that has been a touchstone ever since: *utile et dulci*—useful and pleasant. Through the years, his twofold formula has been expressed in various words to convey instruction and enjoyment. We can think of literature as edifying as well as entertaining.

Another way to organize a defense of literature is to tie it to the writer's threefold task, reflected in the previous chapter's definition of literature. The writer's task is to present human experience as concretely as possible, to interpret the presented experiences, and to create artistic beauty. Each of these identifying traits of literature performs its own function, and these functions can be shown to be valuable in corporate society and individual lives.

HOW WE KNOW THAT LITERATURE IS IMPORTANT

While this chapter focuses on *why* literature matters, we want to make a preliminary point *that* it matters. Christians can begin their defense of literature armed with a conviction of success. We know God wants us to have literature in our lives because he has revealed himself to the human race in a book that is primarily literary in nature. If we apply the criteria for literature explored in the preceding chapter, at least 80 percent of the Bible meets the definition of being literature, and with a generous application of the criteria, the percentage is even higher. It is therefore accurate and helpful to think of the overall genre of the Bible as a literary anthology—a collection of predominantly literary works composed by numerous authors over a span of many years.

A noted literary scholar of an earlier era wrote that "Christianity is the most literary religion in the world: it is crammed with characters and stories, much of its doctrine was enshrined in poetry. . . . It is a religion in which the word has a special sanctity."[1] Although this scholar did not apply his insight specifically to Scripture, his statement fits the Bible perfectly. Because we'll discuss the Bible's literary nature in chapter 13, we'll simply note now that the very *example* of the Bible establishes the necessity of literature in a Christian's life. Scripture does more than *sanction* literature; it shows us that literature is *indispensable* in knowing and communicating our most important truth.

SEEING LIFE STEADILY AND WHOLE

Literature helps us see life. When a friend of the French poet Mallarmé complained that he was finding it impossible to write sonnets despite all the ideas in his head, Mallarmé responded, "You can't make a poem with ideas."[2] Human experience constitutes the content of literature. English novelist Joseph Conrad claimed that his task was "by the power of the written word to make you hear, to make you feel—it is, before all, to make you *see*."[3] In a similar vein, American Southern fiction writer Flannery O'Connor asserted that "fiction is an art that calls for the strictest attention to the real," adding that writers "should never be ashamed of staring."[4]

Literary authors observe life and then place it before us in the form of a poem or story or drama. When we read their work, we follow their lead in staring at life. A literary scholar has correctly said that the writer's task "is to *stare*, to *look* at the created world, and to lure the rest of us into a similar act of contemplation."[5] The more closely we look at anything, the better we understand it.

We can speak of this as knowledge in right seeing. Robert Frost offered the word *wisdom* as a synonym for what we have called knowledge, defining *wisdom* as "a clarification of life."[6] Literature clarifies life by leading us to observe it closely.

Seeing things accurately is a necessary—and powerful—foundation for living well. We become acquainted with various matters of life and are able to make sense of its confusing aspects. Matthew Arnold praised an author "who saw life steadily, and saw it whole." Arnold expanded on the value of reading such literature: "the grand power" of literature is its ability to put us "in contact with the essential nature of objects [i.e., life], to be no longer bewildered and oppressed by them, but to have their secret, and to be in harmony with them."[7]

Why does literature matter? It matters because seeing human experience and the world accurately matters. If we regularly read literature, we will see life not only steadily but also in its whole scope.

ENCOUNTERING THE GREAT IDEAS

While defenses of literature often place too much or an incorrect emphasis on ideas, we shouldn't discount the presence and value of ideas embedded in literature. But we want to think clearly about how those ideas operate. In the twentieth century, a familiar mantra among literary authors and critics was "no ideas but in things" to convey how literature "shows" rather than "tells." But poet Denise Levertov offered the corrective that "'no ideas but in things' . . . does not mean 'no ideas.'"[8] The ideas reflected by things remain ideas.

Let's start with the common assumption that literature and the arts are a leading means by which the human race grapples with reality and seeks to understand it. Wrestling with reality involves extracting and formulating truth about life in the form of ideas—in other words, making intellectual and spiritual sense of the world.

When we consider the entire body of literature the world has produced, viewpoints obviously contradict each other. We cannot assert that literature as a whole embodies right ideas about God, people, and nature. A more realistic assessment is that literature embodies the great ideas by which the human race has ordered its affairs. On one level, this is simply interesting to know. But there is a practical usefulness as well. The ideas conveyed in literature serve as a stimulus to our own thinking. Encountering these ideas forces us to codify what we, as readers, believe to be the truth. This process sometimes expands our understanding and more often leads us to repudiate error and confirm our commitment to truth. The Bible calls us to understand, embrace, and walk in the truth.

Literature's intellectual dimension is not only useful but also one of its pleasures. If we speak of literature's imaginative and emotional enjoyment, we should also speak of its intellectual delights. Ralph Waldo Emerson said that the poet (and by extension the storyteller) has the power of "rejoicing the intellect."[9] Someone else has claimed that the joy experienced by writers and readers of literature is "the joy that arises from discerning the truth."[10] Discovering truth on an intellectual level produces emotional pleasure.

We should not set literature's ideas in opposition to its accurate portrayal of human experience. Lifelong readers often relate how they first or most memorably encountered powerful ideas in literature. Matthew Arnold championed the importance of holding fast to this: "that the greatness of a poet lies in his powerful and beautiful application of ideas to life."[11] Disembodied ideas do not constitute power in literature. It is their *application to life*.

Why does literature matter? It matters because it can help shape us into thinking people, armed with God's answers to life's questions.

BEAUTY AND REFRESHMENT

Recall our definition of literature as a concrete, interpretive presentation of human experience in an artistic form. Arnold touches on all three concepts when he mentions *ideas* (interpretive), *applied to life* (human experience), in a *beautiful* form (artistic). Defenses of literature have too often slighted the important aesthetic component.

A work of literature features form as well as content. Form should be construed very broadly as covering all aspects of *how* an author has packaged content. Verbal beauty, genre, and structure reflect a work's form. Characterization falls under the rubric of form, as do poetic metaphors and figures of speech. Whatever strikes us as skillfully created in a literary work is part of its form. What Robert Frost said about poetry applies equally to other literary genres: it is "a performance in words," like a musical exhibition or athletic feat in which we admire the performer's skill.[12]

Form and content are both important in composing and reading literature. Literary authors are in no danger of minimizing the centrality of form in their craft, but readers run this risk. C. S. Lewis spoke metaphorically of literature as having two parents, with its mother being the mass of experiences and ideas writers have at their disposal, and the father being the form into which the content is cast. "By studying only the mother," writes Lewis, "criticism becomes one-sided." In an oft-quoted aphorism, Lewis added, "It is easy to forget that the man who writes a good love sonnet needs not only to be enamoured of a woman, but also to be enamoured of the Sonnet."[13]

Once we acknowledge the importance of literary form, the further question is what function this artistic aspect serves. Throughout history the customary term for artistic form is *beauty*. In fact, beauty is virtually synonymous with the idea of art or aesthetics. Someone has expressed it this way: "Our primal aesthetic experience is . . . a response of enchantment to beauty."[14] While nearly everyone sees beauty in music and painting, people are less able to see it in literature.

If the function of literary form is partly to express beauty, we immediately need to add the word *pleasure* to the mix. Beauty exists to give us a certain type of pleasure. One of the most famous definitions of beauty was bequeathed by the medieval Catholic theologian Thomas Aquinas, who defined beauty as "that which, being seen, pleases."[15] English poet Samuel Taylor Coleridge similarly claimed that the "immediate purpose" of poetry is "pleasure through the medium of beauty."[16]

Why does beauty matter? It matters for two reasons. The first is that the human spirit craves beauty and withers without it. Our own practices of seeking out beauty confirm this. Matthew Arnold uses the constitution of human nature to explain why we have an urge for beauty. He finds four "powers" that make up human life: (1) conduct,

(2) intellect and knowledge, (3) beauty, and (4) social life and manners. Arnold then rightly claims that "human nature is built up by these powers; we have the need for them all. . . . Such is human nature."[17]

We can appeal to more than human nature's constitution in asserting beauty's value. The Bible declares the importance of beauty from the first page (the story of God's creation of a beautiful world) to the last (the description of the new Jerusalem). God is the source of beauty and gives it as a gift to the human race.

Why does literature matter? It matters because we need artistic beauty in order to live happily and fully. Without the pleasures of beauty in our life, we are less than God intends us to be.

WHY LITERATURE IS GOOD FOR YOU

Our defense of literature has explored the three most important aspects of the topic (portraying human experience, seeing ideas rightly, and enjoying beauty), but it also leaves much unsaid. Modern writer Annie Dillard responds to our chapter's primary question with her own eloquent series of questions:

> Why are we reading, if not in hope of beauty laid bare, life heightened and its deepest mystery probed? Can the writer isolate and vivify all in experience that most deeply engages our intellects and our hearts? Can the writer renew our hope for literary forms? Why are we reading if not in hope that the writer will magnify and dramatize our days, will illuminate and inspire us with wisdom, courage, and the possibility of meaningfulness, and will press upon our minds the deepest mysteries, so we may feel again their majesty and power?[18]

We suggest you read what she has written again, slowly. Few people can express more beautifully the essence of why we read literature.

The previous chapter's discussion of literature's nature and traits contained a latent defense of it, which we have now made explicit. Defining what literature *is* had to be augmented by what it *does*. A necessary next step is to explore the *values* these functions fulfill in people's lives, which we will do in the next chapter.

6

What Does Literature Offer?

IN JULY OF 1976, my husband, David, and I (Glenda), celebrated the U.S.'s bicentennial by traveling to visit friends in Michigan via motorcycle. When I asked about the unusual pictures on the calendar in their apartment, my friend explained they depicted scenes from the books of J. R. R. Tolkien. Although I had been a voracious reader from childhood, this was the first I'd heard about this author and his books. The revelation of missed literature swept over me like a rogue wave. Before many more years passed, I read for the first time, "In a hole in the ground there lived a hobbit."[1]

As I read those words, something extraordinary happened. My tiny trailer home in Pella, IA, faded away as my consciousness magically transported to Bag End in Middle Earth. The journey so enchanted me, I flew "there and back again" every winter for nearly thirty years. This is the enduring power of transport, one of literature's chief delights.

Having defined literature and discussed its functions in the previous two chapters, this chapter completes our defense for reading literature by exploring the values and pleasures it offers.

As we describe these joys, we believe something will resonate with every reader. Committed readers will recognize these pleasures as old friends. Other readers will find some joys familiar, while still other readers will be newly introduced to these delights. We encourage all readers to join in literature's party. We invite those who feel as if they're on the outside, looking in, to enter the warmth and fun. No reader—no matter how reluctant or unconfident—is barred from literature's pleasures.

TRANSPORT

Reading a work of literature begins with a magical moment of transport. This transport includes both a leave-taking from our ordinary world and an arrival in an imaginary one, but we'll focus first on the departure. As soon as we become engaged in a story or poem or drama, our everyday concerns and physical surroundings recede from our consciousness. This initial wonder is therapeutic to the human spirit. There are many joys in reading literature, but transport alone makes it worthwhile for even the most reluctant reader.

Do other types of reading also transport us in this way? Screen reading rarely does. When we read on a digital device or computer monitor, we do not leave concerns behind but remain very much connected to them. Writer Joseph Epstein believes "there is a mysterious but quite real difference between words on pixel and words in print." He summarizes: "Pixels for information and convenience . . . print for knowledge and pleasure is my sense of the difference between the two."[2] Physical books are the primary vehicle for providing reading's delight. But not all books are created equal. Reading a history or biography or travel narrative may remove us from our world of ordinary concerns, but reading literature provides a more unique and complete transport.

Several authors and scholars have communicated this concept in helpful ways. Emily Dickinson's short poem encapsulates the power of transport:

There is no Frigate like a Book
To take us Lands away,
Nor any Coursers like a Page
Of prancing Poetry.
This Traverse may the poorest take
Without oppress of Toll—
How frugal is the Chariot
That bears a Human soul.[3]

This poem expresses three ideas about literature's transport: (1) its power surpasses all rivals, (2) it is free for the taking to anyone who wants it, and (3) the transaction involves nothing less than the human soul.

Elizabeth Goudge offers another helpful slant. As a fiction writer and editor of numerous literary anthologies, Goudge knows about reading inside and out. In one anthology preface, she briefly notes how reading is characterized by "stillness, quietness and forgetfulness of self."[4] Self-forgetfulness is one benefit accompanying transport. People need regular times when we move beyond preoccupation with ourselves and our concerns. Reading's leave-taking provides such release.

C. S. Lewis wrote about transport that "one of the things we feel after reading a great work is 'I have got out,'"[5] that is, out of the enclosing world around and inside us. The very act of reading admits us to a particular state, which in itself is pleasurable and beneficial, quite apart from the content of what we are reading.

Sven Birkerts has written on this with great clarity. He describes reading as "a state or condition" and then asks whether specific reading experiences share certain universal qualities that make up the reading state. He believes a shared quality exists. When working in bookstores, he sees browsers who display "a need to keep getting back to" the reading state, which "they know . . . and . . . seek." What they want, concludes Birkerts, "is a vehicle that will bear them off to the reading state." He adds, "The elsewhere state of being while reading was once—in childhood—a momentous discovery." Regular readers would agree with him that as years have unfolded, "I value the state a book puts me in more than I value the specific contents."[6]

What does literature offer? It offers the power of transport, a holiday of the imagination and spirit.

ENTERING AN IMAGINED WORLD

As we leave our physical and mental surroundings, we simultaneously arrive in an alternate world that is merely imagined. We cannot touch it with our hands or see it with our eyes. Its specific qualities depend on the genre and literary work we are reading. The broad genre most obviously creating this world is narrative or story, which includes sub-genres such as fiction and creative nonfiction. But other genres conjure imaginative worlds as well. When we read a devotional poem by George Herbert or a nature poem by William Wordsworth, we inhabit a world the poem itself creates. Even when reading an informal essay, we follow the author's reflections and the scenes or events generating them.

The twofold action of transport cannot happen without the existence of an alternate world. Being aware of the transaction allows us to more willingly give ourselves to the journey. Some people who do not see the point of literature assume it's just like everyday life. While literature is life at a certain level, it is not *just like real life*. Literature achieves its effects by temporarily removing us from life and placing us in another world.

Discovering the nature of the world the author has created is an obvious pleasure. C. S. Lewis describes how surrender enables us to "cross the frontier into that new region which [a work of art] has added to the world."[7] In the sentence directly following his quotation about getting out, Lewis writes, "From another point of view, [we feel] I have got in . . . and discovered what it is like inside."[8] Encountering something new is one of the things literature offers us, accomplished by activating our imagination to dwell in an alternate world.

As we situate ourselves in a different world, we find both the familiar and the unfamiliar. No literary work can exist without reflecting life in the real world. A landscape in a fantasy may be something we'd never find in our world, but it is still a landscape. Conversely, we might think a short story's detailed description of an inner-city street scene is like a photograph of the setting, but it is not. A scene in a piece of realistic fiction is more heightened, more simplified, and more distilled than we would experience when walking through it.

Literature offers a concentrated version of a chosen subject. It defamiliarizes a subject in a way that helps us see it more clearly than we do in real life. To cite an example from the sister art of painting, a still life of fruit in a bowl makes us notice the fruit's properties in a new and heightened way. As we fix our gaze on the painting, we are captivated by three things: the artist's skill in producing what we are looking at, the luminous clarity with which an aspect of our experience is held before us, and the novelty of seeing real life from an unfamiliar perspective. Those same three things engage us when reading a work of literature. They are what literature offers us: the creative skill of the author in making a recognizable picture of human experience and presenting it in an unfamiliar pose.

Life as we live it is often chaotic. Literature offers an imaginary world in which the features of life stand silhouetted with clarity.

THE RETURN JOURNEY

We've discussed what literature offers by looking at reading as a metaphoric journey. John Keats wondrously referred to this as traveling in the "realms of gold."[9] Our journey begins with a leave-taking from everyday life. While we are reading, we reside in an imagined world. Eventually we put the book down and return to the life we are living. What does literature offer when we make the return journey?

If we have been reading something good and satisfying, we experience a feeling of disappointment as we close the book. Such disappointment is revealing. It tells us that the leave-taking and temporary residence in an imaginary world have been meaningful and desirable, in itself a tribute to the value of reading.

It is useful to recall how reading literature is a bifocal activity. We not only look *at* the work of literature but also *through* it to real life. T. S. Eliot encapsulated this duality in his statement that "it is a function of all art to give us some perception of an order in life, by imposing an order upon it."[10] The order authors impose on life is the story or poem or essay itself, including its world of the imagination. This imaginative world is not only a beneficial holiday from life, but it is also a roadmap that may help us chart our course in daily life.

We can understand this better by considering a formula literary scholar Kenneth Burke bequeathed in his landmark essay, "Literature as Equipment for Living."[11] What kind of equipment do we bring back from our excursions into the golden realms of literature? In answer, we will describe the ideal reading experience—a potential experience to which we need to contribute, not something that happens automatically.

The first thing we possess after an optimal reading experience is clarity of vision. As the author says "look" and points, we as readers stare at that aspect of life. If a writer has "gotten it right" (and literary writers almost always do in terms of observing and recording life accurately), we feel that we see our lives and world more clearly than we did before. Seeing life accurately gives us a confidence for negotiating life that we would otherwise lack. Dorothy Sayers claimed that when we read a work of literature, "it is as though a light were turned on us. We say, 'Ah! I recognise that!' . . . I can possess and take hold of it and make it my own, and turn it into a source of knowledge and strength."[12]

Our excursions into literature can also make us thinking people, depending on our ability to extract embedded ideas and our willingness to consider them. At the very least, a work of literature asks—and prompts us to ask—the right questions about life experiences. Great works of literature also provide answers to the questions they raise. As Christian readers, we have an obligation to weigh the answers and decide whether they conform to biblical thinking or deviate from it. In all instances, analyzing the ideas of literature can feed our intellectual life. This is equipment for living.

Socrates famously said that the unexamined life is not worth living. If we reflect on the experiences and ideas presented in the literature we read, our reading can lead to an examined life. The word *edification* is appropriate here. From many of our reading experiences, we resume our lives feeling edified by what we have read.

REFRESHMENT

Literature's refreshment value extends like an umbrella over all that we have discussed so far in this chapter. The break from our immediate physical world and its weight upon us, the temporary residence in an imagined world, the return to life with new equipment for living—all combine to refresh the human spirit. Other activities also refresh us. But literature's multiple levels of pleasure and refreshment elevate reading over most leisure activities.

What are the levels at which reading literature pleases and refreshes us? Reading intensifies our involvement with life and our understanding of it. Having vicariously experienced life under an author's expert guidance, we carry away clarity of vision. Many leisure activities offer something only during the time we spend on them. Along with increased understanding from seeing life portrayed accurately, we derive intellectual pleasure from pondering and interacting with the embedded ideas of literature. To be a thinking person is useful as well as pleasurable and something God expects of us.

Imagination is at the very heart of the literary enterprise. An author exercises creative imagination, but the creation exists initially as a potential. It comes into being only as we create in our own imagination what the author places before us as a prompt. Eighteenth-century essayist Joseph Addison did a good thing in writing several papers addressing the pleasures of the imagination.[13] Literature is a triumph of the imagination.

Additionally, literature is an art form. An essential part of the author's task is creating beauty, which is a product of creativity and craft. Beauty can be as large as a novel's unifying structure or as small as lovely phrases and precise words. Artistic beauty manifests itself in forms, so whatever we enjoy about the *how* of a story or poem can be regarded as art and beauty. We can enjoy beauty even if we do not consider exactly how the effects are achieved, although such analysis also provides pleasure.

Finally, literature can be a source of spiritual refreshment. Some literary works express and commend a Christian attitude. We most naturally think of devotional poetry as providing spiritual refreshment, but all literature of Christian affirmation can be read devotionally. In fact, nearly any reading experience can become an encounter with God and his truth. We simply need to activate a devotional stance.

What does reading literature offer us? It offers us meaningful leisure at contemplative, intellectual, imaginative, and spiritual levels. As a total package, reading literature is impossible to surpass as a recreational activity.

The joy is before you. Open a book and enter.

7

Reading Stories

Tell Me a Story

WHO DOESN'T LOVE A STORY? Almost any adult easily visualizes a wide-eyed child, gazing into your face and imploring, "Tell me a story!" Those four words sum up the universal human impulse of storytelling. Isak Dineson said, "To be a person is to have a story to tell."[1]

People have told stories from the beginning of time. Secular scholars cite the *Epic of Gilgamesh* and other ancient myths, in which Christians hear biblical echoes. God reveals himself through the Bible, a unified story filled with individual stories and punctuated with parables. Because God loves to tell stories, it is no wonder that people created in his image do also.

Family members tell each other stories about their day. Friends enjoy a meal and exchange stories about recent events. Author John Shea has written that "humankind is addicted to stories. No matter our mood, in reverie or expectation, panic or peace, we can be found stringing together incidents, and unfolding episodes."[2] We live in a story-shaped world.

Life itself has a narrative quality. Because this is true, a real link exists between the fictional stories we read and the lives we live. Stories form a central core for most readers.

While stressing the centrality of story in reading, we needn't succumb to the current trend of privileging story over other literary genres. The genre pie can be divided in different ways. Some people might consider its primary categories as poetry and prose or fiction and nonfiction. In academic communities, the standard division is poetry and narrative. As we proceed, we can understand the terms *story* and *narrative* as interchangeable.

The previous three chapters helped us understand *why* we should read literature. This is the first of several chapters exploring *how* to read specific types of literature, logically beginning with the overarching concept of story. We'll first describe the three key elements forming a story. Then we will speak about the functions and entertainment value of stories before concluding with some tips for getting the most from reading stories.

WHAT IS A STORY?

To fully enjoy reading any story, we need a foundational grasp of its three basic ingredients: setting, plot, and characters. Chapter 9 on novels contains examples of these and other elements from literature, but these three things are essential for all stories, nonfictional as well as fictional.

Setting

Simply put, setting is the story's place or location. Fiction writer Elizabeth Bowen made this classic comment on the importance of setting, "Nothing can happen nowhere."[3] A setting functions on multiple levels, and discovering them can be delightful.

In the first place, settings *enable* the action that occurs within them. An author who has produced some of the best writing on this subject describes *scene* as a fit container for the actions and agents within it. Because this is true, we can speak of a scene-act ratio and scene-agent ratio, with the word *ratio* meaning correspondence.[4] Secondly, settings make a story vivid in our imaginations, placing us on the scene of the action. They also create atmosphere (fear, safety, oppression, etc.) and can be part of a storyteller's strategy of foreshadowing. Additionally, settings tend almost inevitably to take on symbolic meanings, conveying positive or negative associations.

Setting is present everywhere in stories, but many readers fail to recognize how various scenes contribute to it. You can become more aware of setting by learning to identify specific scenes. This is easily done by combining the word *scene* and a blank in one of two formulas: [blank] scene (i.e., street scene, murder scene, encounter scene) or a scene of [blank] (i.e., scene of violence, scene of wandering, scene of defeat). Getting the word *scene* into the mix works wonders in opening up your understanding of setting.

We also need to consider setting's bigger picture. When we read a story, we enter a comprehensive imaginative world. This world goes beyond the physical location and atmosphere to encompass the people with their characteristic customs and values as well as events and actions. An assumed premise of literary narrative is that the world of the story is being offered by the author as an accurate view of reality and as the correct worldview.

Fiction writer Flannery O'Connor went so far as to state that "it is from the kind of world the writer creates, from the kind of character and details he invests it with, that a reader can find the intellectual meaning of a book."[5] This is a huge claim: the imagined world of a story embodies the ideas ("the intellectual meaning") an author intends to assert about existence. A grasp of setting is crucial for understanding any story.

Plot

The second key ingredient of stories is plot. Stories generally follow a linear sequence consisting of beginning, middle, and end. This shapely structure is built around unifying story patterns, such as quest or courtship or battle or coming of age. Plots always deal with one or more conflicts and often describe a cause-effect chain of related events. Recognizing these elements helps us more fully experience a story and its meaning.

We can also familiarize ourselves with the repertoire of conventional plot devices that have been part of storytelling from time immemorial—dramatic irony, suspense, foreshadowing, poetic justice (virtue rewarded and vice punished), surprise, reversal, and epiphany (when the reader shares in a moment of revelation and insight achieved by one or more characters late in the story).

Characters

Characters are the third ingredient of story. Readers can begin by identifying the cast of characters and what may be most important about each one for the story's purposes. The *protagonist* (based on the Greek for "first struggler") is the primary character the reader accompanies through the conflicts and events in the story. Forces (human or otherwise) arrayed against the protagonist are *antagonists*. The rule for interpreting characters is simple: get to know the characters as fully as the information allows. We can assume the storyteller has told as much as we need to know in our consideration of the story's purposes.

The characters in a story are *examples* of human conduct and values—positive examples to emulate or negative examples to repudiate. Narrative characters represent people generally (including ourselves) and embody universal experiences (even though characters in a story are also highly particularized). Partly because literary characters are simplified and heightened, they often seem more real than actual people. The most memorable ones take on a life of their own that we carry with us beyond our reading of the story in which they appear.

THE FUNCTIONS OF STORIES

Stories serve important functions in the lives of individuals and societies. The most obvious one is entertainment. What makes stories entertaining? One answer lies in their power of transport. The genius of narrative is its ability to remove us from the physical world around us and plant us in an imaginary world replete with its own places, characters, and events. This occurs easily because stories unfold as a sequence, creating their own momentum, drawing us in and placing us under their enchantment. The phenomenon expressed by the familiar phrase "lost in a book" is preeminently true of stories.

While we intuitively enjoy a book without necessarily thinking about what produces the pleasure, we can also notice delightful techniques. A story's aesthetic pleasure lies in seeing and relishing creative skill and its beauty. We admire a storyteller's inventiveness in crafting captivating scenes, characters, and episodes. The author's way with words and chosen prose style can generate pleasure.

A further function emerges when we consider why we tell stories. John Shea has written that "we turn our pain into narrative so we can bear it; we turn our ecstasy into narrative so we can prolong it."[6] People feel a strong compulsion to tell about their experiences. What characterizes the story we share when a friend or spouse asks how our day went? The story is selective and interpretive. We speak of having had a good or bad, boring or challenging day. Our story is more condensed than the day's experiences, and we highlight important aspects. These traits are equally true of the literary stories we read. They too are simplified and organized, silhouetting important material with heightened clarity.

Shea's observation about how naturally we turn our pains and joys into stories leads to the important aspect of psychology. What psychological needs do stories fill in our lives? A literary scholar named Simon Lesser explored this subject in depth in *Fiction and the Unconscious.*[7] We agree with many of his observations but will summarize only a few:

- Stories give shape and expression to our own experiences.

- We gravitate to stories that portray our fears and longings.

- Stories compensate for what is missing in our lives by being more exciting or by clarifying confusing issues. Other types of stories confirm negative features of life, reconciling us to life in a fallen world and providing comfort in knowing how human misery is shared.

- It is a universal impulse to want to see our experiences given a voice, and we derive satisfaction from knowing our own and other people's experiences (both good and bad) have been given a voice.

The clarifying power of the above points is possible because when we read, we relax and contemplate life's anxieties from a safe distance. If we think about ways this occurs in our own reading, we discover revelations. Our choice of stories and responses to them both shape and reveal ourselves. Daniel Taylor writes, "You are your stories. You are the product of all the stories you have heard and lived—and many that you have never heard. They have shaped how you see yourself, the world, and your place in it."[8]

The stories we read also show our identity as members of specific narrative communities. If we are St. Louis Cardinal fans, we know Cardinal stories, which are part of our identity. Our enthusiasm for the Chronicles of Narnia stories or *The Lord of the Rings* affirms our affinity with those groups of fantasy readers. Whenever we read *Great Expectations*, we confirm our identity as someone who enjoys humor, loves the land and people of England, delights in verbal beauty, and recognizes how true values are inner and moral rather than external and material. The stories we embrace define us. Narrative scholars commonly assert that the stories we choose to read define who we *are*, but we also *become* the products of the stories we read. Stories reflect individual identity and have the power to modify it.

This is also true for societies and nations. Stories form a chief means through which groups codify, preserve, and pass on their beliefs and values. Cultural values influence storytellers, who frequently become spokespersons for their society. But it also works the other way. Stories disseminated in a society influence the people living in it. The identity of groups depends on the presence of shared stories, and when the stories are lost, the identity of the group is lost. Conversely, when a group changes its identity, it discards the stories it once embraced. For proof, one need only compare current American perspectives with those that shaped the formation of the United States.

THE ENTERTAINMENT VALUE OF STORIES

Storytellers compose their works with a twofold purpose—to entertain and to make a statement. Both of these deserve separate scrutiny.

Writers and readers alike acknowledge that stories entertain. Some of our earliest pictures of storytelling appear in Homer's *Odyssey*, when epic stories were performed as after-banquet entertainment. Odysseus describes the event held in his honor as "just the perfection of gracious life: . . . rows of guests enjoying themselves heartily and listening to the [story accompanied by] music, plenty to eat on the table. . . . I think that is the best thing men can have."[9] In the sixteenth century, English poet Sir Philip Sidney famously paid tribute to the power of stories to "hold children from play, and old men from the chimney corner."[10] When a student asked Flannery O'Conner what enlightenment she expected the reader to derive from her stories, O'Conner responded by urging her "to forget about enlightenment and just try to enjoy them."[11]

People have always preferred specific types of content in stories. Readers love heroes and heroism, but they are equally enamored of villains and villainy. Romantic love is a winner, and so are journey and battle. The popular taste expects to see the threatening side of life, but it greatly prefers happy endings in which good defeats evil. Of course, action needs to be engaging, in keeping with Thomas Hardy's dictum that "a story must be striking enough to be worth telling."[12]

Readers and listeners through the ages have also enjoyed numerous narrative techniques, such as characters who represent our own hopes and fears undergoing some kind of testing; adventure, suspense, or mystery; surprise and reunion scenes (especially homecomings). This brief list reflects only a portion of narrative techniques storytellers employ. The more we recognize techniques, the more we can enjoy a story.

Our delight is enhanced when we notice how a story pleases us. We find pleasure on different levels: reading to find out what happens next and how it turns out (plot), entering an imagined world, discovering characters' unique personalities, recognizing great archetypes (universal patterns), and seeing skillful technique and beautiful style. It is also helpful to know that some stories turn upon the changing fortunes of people (stories of plot), others on the characters of people (stories of character), and others upon the storyteller's skill at description (stories of place).

MAKING A STATEMENT

Authors compose a story not only to entertain but also to make a statement—about life, about reality, about morality. "To tell a story," writes John Shea, "is to create a world, adopt an attitude, suggest a behavior."[13] These, in turn, are offered to a reader as a statement of truth and guide to living.

We can extract the themes of a story in multiple ways. We can regard characters as people who undertake an experiment leading to success or failure, and then identify the experiment in living. The outcome always reflects the author's interpretation or assessment of what has preceded in the story. A successful outcome represents a positive verdict on a character's experiment in living. Failure is an implied verdict to avoid emulating the experience in our own lives.

A complementary way to understand storytelling goes by the quaint name of "example theory." It is the nature of stories to put examples of character and conduct before us. What storytellers wish to say about life is embodied in these positive or negative examples. Storytellers embed devices of disclosure in their stories to guide our interpretation, with outcome being one of the most important.

Another useful paradigm is how stories comment on the three great issues of life—reality (what really exists), morality (what constitutes good and bad behavior), and values (what matters most, less, or not at all). As we contemplate these elements, a view of God, people, and the world emerges.

It is usually not difficult to determine what a story is saying about life. But the time for reflecting on intellectual meaning is *after* we have enjoyed it as a story.

GETTING THE MOST FROM THE STORIES WE READ

This chapter has painted a large picture. We can bring it into focus with the following tips for reading stories:

- Plot, setting, and character are the building blocks of a story. Paying conscious attention to all three increases our reading pleasure.

- While we can derive *some* pleasure and profit from stories without applying the analytic tools presented in this chapter, we will derive *more* if we consider content and technique. Thoughtful contemplation itself can provide enjoyment.

- Stories are constructed on a principle of back and forth rhythm—between the build-up and release of tension, for example, or between two story lines or two characters or two settings. We will have a much better grasp of what is happening if we note these back and forth swings.

- Individual episodes or chapters have an intended purpose in the flow of the overall story. It will pay enjoyment dividends to name each chapter or episode function(s) after the action has transpired.

Experts on narratology (the study of narrative) have been far too glib in making the claim that we read stories in order to find out who we are. But in one indisputable way this is true: considering why some stories satisfy us and others do not helps us discover important things about ourselves. Stories also open our eyes to revelations about our world, other people, and God. Writing and reading stories forms such a crucial part of life because we all love to tell and hear a good story.

8

Reading Poems

Songs of the Soul

OUR CHAPTER TITLE resonates with people who regularly read poetry. Those who prefer poetry to novels or other prose genres may anticipate that this will be the best chapter in this book. Most people, however, do not read poetry. Some may even consider skipping this chapter. We encourage you to stay here and read because we hope our delight in reading poetry will generate an appreciation for poems as songs of the soul.

Few poetic works reflect personal essence with as much emotional depth as the biblical book of Psalms. In John Calvin's introduction to his commentary on Psalms, he explained that he was accustomed to calling the book "An Anatomy of all the Parts of the Soul." He believed this was appropriate as "there is not an emotion of which any one can be conscious that is not here represented as in a mirror. . . . the Holy Spirit has here drawn . . . all the griefs, sorrows, fears, doubts, hopes, cares, perplexities, in short, all the distracting emotions with which the minds of men are wont to be agitated."[1] With the psalmists, we cry to God, and we shout with praise. We plunge to depths of sorrow and despair, and we climb to heights of joy and beauty. Great poetry sings the songs in our souls, even the ones we find difficult to hear or articulate.

This chapter will begin by showing why we need poetry. We then will define poetry by explaining how it is familiar and by examining its distinctive traits. We'll conclude with suggestions for how to read poetry.

WHY WE NEED POETRY IN OUR LIVES

Although our chapter's subtitle implies poetry's spiritual component, we will be so bold as to assert four reasons why Christians cannot live without poetry: (1) God expects us to appreciate poetry, (2) Jesus regularly employed poetic devices, (3) everyone unconsciously speaks poetically, and (4) poetry is a natural form of expression.

We know that God expects us to appreciate poetry because approximately a third of the Bible is poetic in form. Proof begins with entirely poetic books, such as Psalms and Song of Solomon. Vast portions of the prophetic books are expressed in the biblical verse form of parallelism. While the book of Revelation avoids parallelism in deference to prose, it conveys truth chiefly through the poetic means of images and symbols. Finally, imagery and metaphors saturate the epistles. If God did not expect us to understand and enjoy poetry, why would he give us such a heavily poetic Bible?

Additionally, Jesus is one of the world's most famous poets. This isn't the controversial claim it may initially seem. Of course, Jesus was a religious teacher, not a proclaimed poet. But his discourses rely heavily on poetic speech:

"You are the light of the world" (Matt. 5:14) → metaphor
The "first will be last" (Matt. 19:30) → paradox
"The kingdom of heaven is like a grain of mustard seed" (Matt. 13:31) → simile

"God so clothes the grass of the field" (Matt. 6:30) →
personification

The sayings of Jesus masterfully display poetry's verbal beauty and aphoristic splendor. If we begin with the obvious fact that Jesus's discourses and sayings are among the most famous in the world, and then add our awareness of his utterances as frequently poetic in form, it is no stretch whatever to think of Jesus as a famous poet.

We can continue to build a case for poetry's importance by observing that everyone unconsciously speaks poetry during the course of a typical day. We speak metaphorically of the "sun rising" even though we know that the sun does not literally rise. When someone makes a conciliatory offer, we refer to it as "holding out an olive branch" when in reality no olive branch is in hand and most people have never seen an olive branch. Why do we persist in speaking like poets? Because at a deep level we sense that poetic speech conveys truth effectively, often more effectively than literal prose. In these instances, we *could* express ourselves literally, and yet we intuitively choose to speak poetically.

But isn't poetry an unnatural form of discourse? It is not. Poetry isn't our *normal* way of speaking and writing, but it is not an *unnatural* form of expression. Poetry "predates literacy and precedes prose in all literatures," writes an authority on the subject.[2] That being the case, literary scholar Northrop Frye can legitimately ask, "How could this happen if prose were really the language of ordinary speech?"[3] Owen Barfield championed the idea that when we look at a word's etymology, most of our words began as concrete images, the language of poetry.[4]

Where does this leave us? It should leave us totally skeptical of the common assumption that ordinary people cannot comprehend and enjoy poetry. Positively, it proves that all people can claim poetry as their possession. Christians can embrace poetry's spiritual significance, but we can appreciate poetry more if we understand what it is and how to read it.

WHAT IS POETRY?

The first step in defining poetry is to show how it is actually something familiar, despite surface features that may make it seem strange. We begin to recognize this familiarity by placing poetry into its primary literary family, which is simply literature. Literature itself, en masse, is a genre with differentiating traits shared by more specific genres like story and poetry.

Literature's subject is human experience. No matter how remote poetry may seem from life in the neighborhood, it is filled with common human emotions and everyday sensory perceptions. In the opening pages of a poet's aptly-titled book, *Poetry and the Common Life*, the author writes: "Too often poetry is thought to be impossibly far apart from ordinary human existence. Everyone's mind is a teeming gallery of sensations and memories. Housewife, murderer, plumber, schoolboy, each has a mind full of blue or gray skies, the touch or absence of love. . . . We all know the taste of things sweet or bland or sour. . . . The poet reaches into" this reservoir of shared human experience and finds words to express it.[5] Like all literature, a poem holds some aspect of human experience before us to observe and vicariously live.

In addition to presenting an experience, every work of literature offers an embedded interpretation. As readers, we reflect on the author's viewpoint and either affirm or correct it. It is often easier to see what a poem is saying about life than what a story is saying about it. The form in which this experience-plus-interpretation comes to us is known as the poetic idiom.

Finally, the content of any literary work is embodied in an artistic form. The poetic idiom presents meaning concretely rather than abstractly and consists primarily of images and figurative language. The writer's skill in crafting techniques becomes an artistic experience in which we enjoy not only *what* is said but *how* it is said. Like all literature, poetry achieves its effect by showing rather than telling. But poets display their artistry even more than storytellers.

Having seen how poetry shares the same rock-bottom traits as other genres of literature, we now consider what makes it distinctive. The most obvious is the language poets use (not surprisingly, the title of a book on the subject).[6] Poetic language is concrete and employs comparisons. It conveys meaning indirectly, with an artistry surpassing other genres in its intentionality and scope. A primary characteristic of poetry is its compression.

Poets speak concretely, naming actions or things through images. They want us to see and feel and hear. C. S. Lewis has written, "From Homer, who never omits to tell us that the ships were black and the sea salt, or even wet . . . , poets are always telling us that grass is green, or thunder loud, or lips red."[7]

Poets compare things to each other in figures of speech. Most images in poetry are not singular but instead are the first half of a comparison or analogy. Figures of speech such as metaphors and similes use one area of human experience to shed light on another. When Emily Dickinson describes grief as "the hour of lead," she draws upon lead's literal properties to convey how grief feels heavy and seems gray.[8]

While many poems (especially nature poetry) straightforwardly describe a scene or experience, poetry primarily works through indirection. Robert Frost expressed this prevalence by saying that "poetry provides the one permissible way of saying one thing and meaning another."[9] When John Keats *says* he has often "traveled in the realms of gold," he *means* he has read a lot of literature.[10]

A helpful way to understand this indirection is to accept poetry as a branch of fantasy. Poets using such figures of speech as hyperbole and personification operate on the principle of make-believe, asserting things not literally true or possible. Realizing poetry belongs to the fantasy realm of imagination frees us from wrongly thinking we are reading something factual. Reflecting on life's fleetingness, Shakespeare compares life to a walking shadow, an obvious bit of fantasy. And consider that God is not literally a rock (i.e., Ps. 18:31; Isa. 26:4), though the metaphor points by analogy to certain facts about God: he is stable, mighty, dependable, and protective.

Poetry's indirection provides a pleasing complexity. Poetry is adept at giving us two for the price of one. Poets place concrete images before us on the understanding that the images (level A) are analogies for the actual subject of the poem (level B). But the image puts us in touch with the "level A" realm of experience too. For example, in contemplating his own advancing age, Shakespeare says that we can see in him

that time of year . . .
when yellow leaves or none or few do hang
upon those boughs which shake against the cold.[11]

The poem is about approaching death, not about autumn, but Shakespeare's magical lines run through our minds when we see a fall landscape in cold weather. Because poets speak a language of analogy and indirection in which A is compared to B, a single poem often puts us in touch with multiple layers of life. We can think of this as poetry's bonus, symbolizing its inherent richness and abundance.

While poetry shares artistic characteristics with other types of literature, poetic artistry surpasses other genres in its intentionality and scope. Poets define their enterprise as creating artistic beauty. Edgar Allan Poe described poetry as "the rhythmical creation of beauty."[12] A century earlier, in tribute to this careful construction, Ben Jonson said that a poem is the product of the poet's "skill or craft of making."[13]

Most poems demonstrate artistry in construction, most obviously the appearance of the lines on a page. A famous example is George Herbert's "Easter Wings," whose stylized lines form shapes that look like angel wings.[14] Lines frequently end in rhyming sounds, with formal stanza arrangements demonstrating further layers of skill. Specific forms can fold within themselves like the pleated effect of a sestina or villanelle.[15] Other artistic constructions require a closer look at content. One or more primary contrasts operate throughout many poems. And poems usually progress through thought or feeling in a carefully orchestrated sequence. For example, Psalm 1 contrasts the blessedness of the godly person to the misery of the wicked. It progresses from its initial portrait of the godly person (vv. 1–2), through the fruitfulness of a godly life in contrast to the worthlessness of a wicked life (vv. 3–4), and concludes with final blessing of the godly and destruction of the wicked (vv. 5–6).

Poets add to this abundance of organization and patterning with an extraordinary show of verbal skill. They pack beauty and eloquence into each line, choosing words for how they complement each other in both sound and meaning. C. S. Lewis spoke of this quality of poetry as "phrase by phrase deliciousness."[16] English Romantic poet Samuel Taylor Coleridge defined poetry as "the best words in the best order."[17]

Poetry's compression sets it apart from prose. Because poems are generally brief, they are concentrated, sharply focused, and well defined. Words are carefully chosen for their connotation and power. Often the experience presented in a poem is a momentary one—a moment of prayer or observing a sunrise. But even when a longer event is described, the poet uses vivid images and powerful verbs to portray it succinctly and beautifully.

Let's summarize what poetry is. It shares familiar characteristics of literature: presenting and interpreting an aspect of life in an artistic form. Poetry stands apart in its vivid language of images and comparisons, which convey meaning primarily through indirection. Poetry surpasses prose in its artistry and the power of its compression. If prose is like walking to the door of human experience, poetry is like dancing through it to the reader's soul.

HOW TO READ A POEM

Simply knowing what poetry is will not enable us to enjoy a poem. But translating poetry's traits into tips for reading and interpreting can greatly increase our delight in reading poetry.

The most important tip for reading a poem has nothing to do with its technical aspects but everything to do with reading speed. Poetry requires a slow read. Because poetry is concentrated and compressed, packed with a maximum of meaning and technique, our pace must slow to allow pondering and rereading. Most poems are so brief that even if we read them three times, we spend less time than with most other genres. Flannery O'Connor's famous advice that writers "should never be ashamed of staring" applies to poetry readers as well.[18]

Merely staring at a poem, however, will not unfold its glories to us. We need to know what to look *for*. As we list things calling for our attention, bear in mind that a complete grasp of them is not necessary to be on the right path. The longer we live with a poem, the clearer the focus becomes, and this process of clarification can be greatly aided by excursions into published explications of the poem (including readily available commentary online).

A plausible starting point is to identify in general terms what a poem is about (its *topic*). Usually this will be the human experiences presented for our contemplation. Examples might be nature, romantic love, spiritual devotion, or a contemplated idea. These universal experiences might be presented as specific events—a walk in the woods, a narrator speaking to a beloved, a person addressing God in prayer. A poem asks us to share an experience first of all. It does not advertise what it is about, so we should take time to consider the situation. As we continue to stare at the poem's content, we gradually become aware of the poet's perspective or interpretation (the *theme* of the poem), which is often simply either to commend the experience or cast it in a negative light.

Another thing to identify as early as possible is its type or *genre* (under the general umbrella of poem). Is it a nature poem, a meditative landscape poem, or a praise poem? As in other genre areas, the more experience we have with poetry (perhaps aided by commentators who serve as travel guides), the more adept we become at understanding it.

Additionally, it's helpful to determine the poem's *occasion*. Many poems hint at the influence of an external event in the poet's life or times. Milton wrote a famous sonnet after becoming totally blind at the age of forty-four. Usually there is an implied situation *within* a poem—a speaker addressing a beloved, a walk on the beach, or the shepherd's daily cycle of care for his sheep in Psalm 23.

The above four things (topic, theme, genre, and occasion) are general aspects that form a poem's content core. Identifying a poem's big picture helps us recognize its skill and beauty.

We step from big effects to more specific elements of a poem when we look at its structure or organization. That organization is sequential, first of all—the carefully constructed flow from one unit of the poem to the next. In mastering a poem, we should identify successive units and give each an accurate label. We do this with an awareness that individual units are variations on the poem's unifying theme. Most poems fall into one of two styles: reflective/meditative or affective/emotional. In a reflective poem, we learn more and more about the speaker's thoughts. In an affective poem, the speaker shares increasingly more feelings.

At a final stage of analysis, we reach the "fine print," consisting of the individual images and figures of speech. This is called *poetic texture* (as differentiated from structure). Poetry is the most concentrated form of writing, achieving that status through the details of a poetic idiom. Figures of speech invite pondering and unpacking their multiple meanings. If the poet tells us that a traitor's "speech was smooth as butter" and "his words . . . softer than oil" (Ps. 55:21), we can consider how the literal properties of butter and oil accurately portray the poem's real subject. Anyone who's ever been betrayed by a friend can identify with this description of deceitful words spoken with destructive intent.

For those impatient with poetry's close reading, recall how a third of the Bible is embodied in poetry and Jesus frequently spoke in poetic form. We invite you to compare Exodus 14's narrative account of Israel crossing the Red Sea to the song of victory recorded in Exodus 15:1–21. Both inspire awe as they describe the same remarkable event, but the song pulses with poetic beauty that touches the soul.

In a culture known increasingly for its frenzied pace of life, reading poetry offers a welcome respite. Poems stand as proof that good things can come in small packages, and for that very reason, they are a manageable form of reading even in a busy schedule. Poetry is not dull or boring. It conveys power through emotive language and vivid imagery that appeal to the very essence of the reader. A slow and thoughtful reader hears the soul's song.

9

Reading Novels

Come Away with Me

WHY EVEN TALK about how to read novels? Can't we simply pick one up, sink into an easy chair, and dive into the story?

There's nothing wrong with reading novels purely for enjoyment. A good story entertains. Everyone needs to escape at times from the cares and concerns of life into the realm of imagination. *Escaping* connotes a temporary reprieve from duties, while *escapism* reflects an effort to abdicate responsibility. Examining motives can help us distinguish the difference: Are we indulging sloth or cultivating rest? The Bible permits literary refreshment apart from the daily grind. Christians needn't hesitate to responsibly enjoy literature as they do all of God's gifts. We know that whether we eat or drink, or whatever we do, we should do all to the glory of God (1 Cor. 10:31). C. S. Lewis echoed that concept when he wrote: "the Christian . . . has no objection to comedies that merely amuse and tales that merely refresh. . . . We can play, as we can eat, to the glory of God."[1]

That phrase "to the glory of God" ought to guide our thinking about everything we do. Reading novels may seem a trivial subject or merely a matter of personal taste. But like anything else, it can

be done in a way that honors or dishonors God. And thoughtful reading of novels can enrich our lives in more ways than you
might imagine.

WHY WE SHOULD TALK ABOUT READING NOVELS

A discussion about reading imaginative fiction is necessary because
our perspectives may be warped by modern theories, popular culture,
or a lack of a biblical aesthetic.

Modern literary criticism frequently reduces literature's significance. Literary deconstructionist or postmodern approaches often
limit meaning to mere reader response. Relativism encourages individuals to determine their own truth. Without biblically-grounded
criteria, a novel becomes whatever the reader wants it to be. When
authors and readers do not believe in objective truth, literature loses
transcendent meaning.

While not all readers are familiar with modern literary theory,
most are heavily influenced by cultural perspectives and pursuits.
Without even realizing it, they absorb unbiblical perspectives that have
become part of society's fabric. They focus on personal advancement
and mindless entertainment. They read novels much like they watch
TV, passively absorbing images and action with little thought to the
quality of the content or the values it promotes.

Even Christians disagree about how to view literature and other
fine arts. Os Guinness writes that "most Christians lack a Christian
aesthetic, an agreed Christ-centered philosophy of the arts. Christians
therefore tend to swing between two extremes—puritanically dismissing the arts as irreligious or seeking to exploit them as a means of
promoting faith and morals."[2]

This is too often the case when it comes to novels. Some Christian
readers consider fiction a secular invention to be avoided. Novelists
who are Christians frequently wield their pens with evangelistic or

moralistic fervor. Both extremes stem from a failure to appreciate literary quality.

The aesthetic lack is especially apparent in today's Christian fiction market. Too many of these novels are bland romances with flat characters and pat endings. Although exceptions exist, Christian fiction written according to modern formulas tends to lack character complexity, imaginative language, and creative execution.

No wonder some believers view reading novels as a waste of time! But individuals who summarily dismiss all novels miss opportunities to experience an amazing array of benefits, ranging from traveling to places and times we can never visit in real life to becoming more aware of the feelings and circumstances of persons very different from ourselves. Reading literary fiction expands our horizons and enriches our lives. Shared emotions touch our hearts and help us understand how much we have in common with people from all ages and all walks in life.

WHAT IS A NOVEL?

While there is some disagreement about the novel's origin, the prevailing opinion is that the novel as a fiction genre is relatively new. Some people view imaginary fiction as rooted in unheroic Roman prose composed in the first and second centuries. A few look to the east and credit an eleventh century Japanese tale as the world's first novel. Others consider prose versions of medieval chivalric romances as initial novels, particularly Thomas Malory's tale about King Arthur and his knights of the round table, published in 1485. But the most common consensus seems to date the novel in Western literature from the seventeenth century, when *Don Quixote* was published (1605). On the great timeline of world history, the novel is a rather—well—novel invention.

In its most simplistic definition, a novel is a book-length story of fictional prose. Constructed with a recognizable plot, it portrays authentic characters who say and do believable things in an easily-envisioned setting. These elements are generally imaginary, but real persons and places sometimes appear in novels.

Historical or biblical fiction is often based on real people and actual events. Current Christian fiction also includes subsets such as mystery, thriller, and contemporary fiction, some of which is designated specifically for women. Romance is a separate category but frequently appears as a primary feature in the others.

Mainstream novels are published in similar and an expanding array of additional categories. Novels considered classics are well-known works of literature universally recognized as having lasting value. While the listings of classics vary according to personal taste, such groupings usually include many British novels from the Victorian era and American novels from more modern decades.

Definitions of literary fiction can be somewhat diverse, but it's used here to describe well-written novels with timeless qualities that transcend popular trends. What separates popular fiction from literary fiction?

Writer Bret Lott explains the differences this way to his college students:

> I tell them that literary fiction is fiction that examines the character of the people involved in the story, and that popular fiction is driven by plot. Whereas popular fiction, I tell them, is meant primarily as a means of escape, one way or another, from this present life, a kind of book equivalent of comfort food, literary fiction confronts us with who we are and makes us look deeply at the human condition.[3]

In addition to authoring novels and teaching writing, Lott has written short stories and edited collections of them. A short story shares many elements of a novel, but it is far more condensed. The titles for two volumes of Lott's short story collections reflect the Narnian description of Aslan: *Not Safe, But Good*. These titles convey the idea that Christians who write fiction needn't avoid harsh aspects of life, as long as those realities are balanced with the biblical truth of grace. Lott hopes such short stories fill the fiction gap between popular Christian writing and literary art. They are, he writes, "proof positive that 'Christian literary fiction' is not an oxymoron."[4]

Literary fiction goes beyond page-turning action and predictable plots to a skillfully-constructed narrative about complex characters. It engages the mind and emotions with excellent craftsmanship. The best literary fiction reflects God's beauty and creativity in an imaginative and biblically-realistic way.

WHAT'S NOVEL ABOUT THE NOVEL?

Literary novels vary widely but have several defining characteristics. The most obvious is length. In contrast to a short story, a novel is book-length: generally from 80,000 to 120,000 words, although many are longer.

Another easily-spotted feature is the novel's point of view. The author writes the story from an imaginary narrator's perspective. This may be first-person (I), rarely second-person (you), or third-person (he, she, they). In general, first person pulls the reader into the narrator's life more quickly and deeply, but third person can do this effectively as well. First person is more common in modern novels than in classical literature. Authors in earlier centuries often intruded with direct remarks to readers that today's editors wouldn't allow.

Because all novels tell a story, they contain the basic elements of story discussed earlier. A plot is the way the narrative is constructed.

It most often has a beginning, in which we meet the main character(s) and conflict is introduced; a middle, in which complications arise and character development may progress; and an end, which provides resolution to conflict and shows how characters have changed. Most plots follow a chronological organization, relating events as they happen but not all.

Author Charles Martin, for example, frequently juxtaposes current events with flashbacks or reflections to create intriguing plots that gradually reveal backstory. The reader is gripped by a desire to know what is going on and enjoys each subtle revelation.

To maintain reader interest and provide a satisfying conclusion, a plot must involve some type of conflict that is eventually resolved. Gene Edward Veith Jr. offers this delightful explanation of plot:

> A story, of course, needs a plot; something has to happen. A plot is not just random action. First of all, a plot will almost always involve some sort of conflict. Every story will hinge upon a struggle, a problem, or a battle of contending forces or ideas. I used to put off my children's requests for a bedtime story by saying, "Once upon a time, there was a little boy and little girl who lived in a castle in the deep woods. And they lived happily ever after." My children, astute literary critics at an early age, rightly complained, "That's not a *story!* Tell us a story." When I would bring a monster into the castle, or a wicked stepmother, or sibling rivalry, or some sort of difficulty that the characters would have to overcome, then we would have a story.[5]

A clear resolution of conflict provides the reader with satisfaction, but readers may enjoy drawing their own conclusions after an ambiguous ending. Some artfully-constructed plots tie the ending back to the beginning. No matter how the author portrays final resolution, readers may feel cheated if crucial loose ends are not tied up.

While plot is *what* happens, setting is *where* it happens. Setting can be almost invisible or play a large role. In some novels, it almost becomes a separate character. Authentic settings go beyond mere physical location to encompass an area's atmosphere and colloquialisms. Author Wendell Berry is considered a master at creating setting for his believable portrayals of the fictional town of Port William.

Berry's audience cares primarily about the people in Port William, not the town itself. Authentic characters draw us into a novel. They ought to reflect the depth and complexity of real people, rather than being predictable stereotypes as flat as paper dolls. Readers must want to find out what happens to the characters, whether they really like them or not.

Characters talk to each other. Effective dialogue conveys information and propels the plot. Jane Austen masterfully showed personalities and dynamics through dialogue. Consider how much the reader learns about Mr. and Mrs. Bennett as this early conversation in *Pride and Prejudice* concludes:

> "Mr. Bennett, how can you abuse your own children in such a way? You take delight in vexing me. You have no compassion on my poor nerves."
>
> "You mistake me, my dear. I have a high respect for your nerves. I have heard you mention them with consideration these twenty years at least."[6]

Dialogue is an important element in making a novel come alive. It helps show readers what is happening rather than telling them. Realistic dialogue is more than capturing particular dialects or idioms. It also reflects individual personality and effectively demonstrates conflict or progress.

No matter a novel's length or point of view, the plot's arc and setting details contribute to a reader's pleasure and satisfaction.

Becoming aware of those elements helps the reader enjoy the heart of the narrative: the interaction of the characters and their progression in the story.

SUGGESTIONS FOR READING NOVELS

Implementing some basic reading strategies helps us recognize literary quality in novels and increases our enjoyment of them. The following suggestions can be remembered easily as the "Four R's":

- Read thoughtfully
- Raise questions
- Rediscover classics
- Recognize skills

As we consider each of these recommendations, we'll look at examples from literary fiction to help illustrate them. The Puritan Thomas Brooks wrote, "[A]s many fish and catch nothing . . . so many read good books and get nothing, because they read them over cursorily, slightly, superficially."[7]

You may be amazed at what you can get from reading more thoughtfully. For instance, you could pick up *Gilead* by Marilynne Robinson and read only the first two sentences:

> I told you last night that I might be gone sometime, and you said, Where, and I said, To be with the Good Lord, and you said, Why, and I said, Because I'm old, and you said, I don't think you're old. And you put your hand in my hand and you said, You aren't very old, as if that settled it.[8]

The first thing you'll notice is how the dialogue is written with no quotation marks or paragraph breaks. It's recorded more as stream of consciousness than normal dialogue. An unknown author couldn't get away with this, but Marilynne Robinson had the strength of her very successful reputation behind her when she wrote *Gilead*.

The pronoun "I" indicates this story is written in the first person point of view. But we also see the pronoun "you." Since "I" is addressing "you," it's like a letter. A novel written in the form of a letter is called an *epistolary novel*.

What do these sentences tell us about "I"? "I" is old (or at least thinks so); in fact, "I" is dying. But "I" is a Christian who believes in "the Good Lord" and life after death. "You" appears to be a child, perhaps even the speaker's child. Certainly there is a bond between the two that allows the younger person to put what seems to be a smaller hand into the larger hand of the narrator. "You" seems sweet and serious; it's easy to imagine a little child speaking this way.

You can get quite a bit of information about this novel by considering only these first two sentences. Of course, no one wants to stop and analyze every two sentences of a novel, but most of us can benefit from reading more thoughtfully.

Reading thoughtfully raises questions. Open-ended ones requiring more than a simple "yes" or "no" are especially beneficial. Questions like:

- What is true about this novel?
- How are the characters authentic?
- In what ways do they change?
- How is the central conflict resolved?
- In what ways has the novel increased my understanding of others?

These kinds of questions enhance our enjoyment and help us connect with transcendent meaning. This is especially true when we read novels that have been universally recognized as classic literature.

Perhaps your eyes glazed in high school or college classes that explored *Moby Dick*'s interminable passages describing the processing of whale blubber. But R. C. Sproul rated Melville's classic as "the Great American Novel" and recommended it for every Christian to read.[9] Sproul described its theme as "The Unholy Pursuit of God in Moby Dick."[10] If one of America's most beloved theologians saw such high value in the book, it may be worth reading with a thoughtful and open mind. Perhaps you'll find yourself mulling about how the numerous biblical allusions contribute to meaning. You may even admit how those detailed descriptions evidence Melville's extensive research and knowledge.

Although classics sometimes employ archaic language or an unfamiliar style, reading such literature allows us to participate in civilization's ongoing conversation. Classics help us understand the human condition and ourselves, leading to increased comprehension of many modern works. Rediscovering classics can also help us recognize literary skills.

Two important literary techniques that novels showcase are description and style. Description enlivens a novel by helping readers envision scenes and ground themselves in the setting. Good descriptions can be works of art, but they shouldn't be written simply to show off. They should have a purpose of conveying information or creating atmosphere.

Marilynne Robinson writes some beautiful descriptions in *Gilead*, such as a scene in which the pastor narrator describes his son blowing bubbles: "I saw a bubble float past my window, fat and wobbly and ripening toward that dragonfly blue they turn just before they burst."[11] The entire paragraph vividly pictures the scene, while effectively conveying the narrator's feelings about his wife and child.

Style is the way in which a work is written. Some authors write in a lyrical, almost poetical manner, such as Michael O'Brien in *Island of the World*. The novel's heart-breaking content could hardly be absorbed unless presented in this style. The narrator referring to himself in the third person throughout the bulk of the book creates a measure of distance, which also helps cushion the harsh realities. The exception is the crucial prologue, when the narrator speaks in the first person as an old man reflecting on life:

> We are born, we eat, and learn, and die. We leave a tracery of messages in the lives of others, a little shifting of the soil, a stone moved from here to there, a word uttered, a song, a poem left behind. I was here, each of these declare. I was here.[12]

On the other end of the style spectrum, Ernest Hemingway is known for a minimalist style that is often sparse and simple. When he was reportedly challenged to write an entire story in only six words, he responded with, "For sale: baby shoes, never worn."[13]

Learning to recognize and appreciate vivid descriptions and different styles contributes to our delight in reading fiction. We can revel in the beautiful language and complex characters of well-written novels. As God's image-bearers, Christians can enjoy the many ways imaginative stories refresh weary minds and spirits.

10

Reading Fantasy

A Far Journey

WHAT IS THE POINT of reading fantastic tales about imaginary worlds? This is a question on which the human race seems almost evenly divided. Literature as a whole exists on a continuum between the poles of realism and fantasy. Realism creates a replica of the world in which we live. Fantasy whisks us on a far journey to an alternate world. Between these two poles, we find degrees of realism and fantasy.

Many readers through the ages have gravitated toward one or the other in its varying degrees. There is no necessary quarrel between them, and ideally we should value both. In this chapter, we will identify fantasy's distinguishing traits, delineate its particular excellencies, and defend fantasy against a common misconception.

THE ESSENCE OF FANTASY

The defining trait of fantasy is that it presents settings, characters, and actions that do not exist in the real world but belong solely to the world of the imagination. Of course, no work of literature consists *entirely* of unreal ingredients, but fantasy highlights the unreal element. Such details as a flying scroll that devours wood and stone houses (Zech. 5:1–4) and a great red dragon whose tail sweeps a third of the stars down to earth (Rev. 12:4) are classic illustrations of the unlifelike aspect of fantasy.

Fantasy is not simply fictional or made-up as opposed to being historically or empirically factual. In fantasy, the made-up details are literally nonexistent in our world and experience. With this bottom-line definition in place, we turn to a discussion of the pleasures and uses of fantasy.

THE PLEASURES OF FANTASY

The most apparent pleasure of fantasy is what we can call the sense of otherness or the lure of the remote. Fantasy's goal is to break from the world of waking reality as completely as possible. Fantasy lovers entering the fictional world of a realistic novel find only a halfway excursion, not the complete journey that their imagination craves.

This pleasure of the distant is the delight of the travelogue and the holiday. That is why fantasy writers take pains to create their own geography, characters, and customs. They construct plots requiring us to travel extensively to get to this imaginary realm and back again. It is the pleasure of foreignness, the same joy we receive when we visit another country. C. S. Lewis observed that realists do not understand the appeal of imaginary geography, "but everyone who has ever made an imaginary map responds at once."[1] Fantasy taps into the human love of the merely imagined as an alternative to everyday realism.

What commends a green knight or a one-eyed giant over a check-out clerk as a potential character for a work of fiction? For those who prefer the green knight and one-eyed giant, the answer is simply that they are more interesting and entertaining than the checkout clerk. J. R. R. Tolkien coined the phrase "arresting strangeness" to designate this quality of fantasy.[2]

Along with the pleasures of otherness and arresting strangeness is the pleasure of enchantment—the atmosphere of mystery, magic, and the marvelous that is a trademark quality of fantasy. For many fantasy lovers (including C. S. Lewis), this is closely linked with the kindling of longing and desire. To read a good fantasy work is to experience a renaissance of wonder, often awakening the child within. J. R. R. Tolkien famously recalled that in his childhood "I desired dragons with a profound desire."[3] The very language Tolkien uses here shows how fantasy involves more than delight in a certain type of story. It also awakens desire or longing.

THE USES OF FANTASY

The first use of fantasy has already been covered, namely, enjoyment. When we speak of the pleasure and use of literature, we tend to regard these as different categories and overlook how pleasure is itself a "use" of literature. If literature provides the material and occasion for enlightened leisure, it has served an important function in our lives. We all need beneficial escapes from burdensome and monotonous reality; traveling to fantasyland can provide such escape.

A second use of fantasy is its clarifying power. In a world stripped of the realistic details making up our daily routine, we take note of what is universal and enduring. The best source on fantasy is J. R. R. Tolkien's essay "On Fairy-Stories," and one trait the famous fantasy writer ascribes to this type of literature is the "regaining of a clear view."[4] In fantasy's simplified world, nearly everything stands out in heightened clarity.

What chiefly becomes clear is the nature of good and evil. The best fantasy portrays good as attractive and evil as repulsive. Tolkien contrasts the moral clarity of fantasy to the modern spirit, with its tendency to confuse the categories of good and evil, and not infrequently to approve and even valorize evil. Writers of fantasy through the ages overwhelmingly give us not only a picture of their imagined world but also of what is right and wrong in it.

We should explain that this chapter addresses traditional fantasy stories from Homer's *Odyssey* and *Beowulf* through those of C. S. Lewis and J. R. R. Tolkien. Some present-day works reflect traditional values, but the modern spirit has infiltrated the ranks of fantasy. Many tawdry books sailing under the fantasy banner represent a degeneration of the high ideals of the genre as it has existed through the ages. A host of these recent counterfeits glorify evil, and readers must be on guard against them. Even some book covers of reprints of high-quality fantasy stories are a distortion of the actual content.

The moral vision of fantasy literature through the ages is traditional and universal. In Tolkien's *The Two Towers*, Eomer asked how a person is to judge what to do in such times. "'As he has ever judged,' said Aragorn. 'Good and ill have not changed. . . .'"[5] Fantasy's moral vision does not belong to modernism and postmodernism but to what G. K. Chesterton called "the sunny country of common sense."[6] It is no wonder that Christians resonate with fantasy as a genre (though not with every work within it).

A further aspect of fantasy's clarifying power is its ability to defamiliarize what has become trite and cliché-ridden. Tolkien speaks of the ability of fantasy "to clean our windows; so that the things seen clearly may be freed from the drab blur of triteness and familiarity."[7] For example, the tired cliché about "the victimization of the individual" suddenly takes on life when we read in the opening line of Kafka's *Metamorphosis* that "Gregor Samsa awoke one morning from uneasy dreams" to find himself "transformed in his bed into a gigantic insect," after which he endures a terrifying journey into ostracism and isolation.[8]

DOES FANTASY TELL THE TRUTH?

In its surface details, fantasy makes no pretense to replicate the factual world of external reality. But there are more levels of truth than literal truthfulness to the physical and human worlds in which we live. A look at how the Bible uses fantasy provides an entry into this subject.

Although the Bible is a predominantly realistic and historically factual book, fantasy permeates it as well. Jesus was capable of touches of fantasy, as when he pictured a person swallowing a camel (Matt. 23:24) and a mustard plant that becomes as large as a tree, reaching into the sky and accommodating the nests of birds (Matt. 13:31–32). The prophets continually drew upon the resources of fantasy, with Isaiah, for example, picturing a deep river overflowing the entire land of Judah, "reaching even to the neck, and its outspread wings will fill the breadth of your land" (Isa. 8:8). No literal river inundated Judah like that, nor do rivers have wings. The apocalyptic sections of the Bible are as filled with fantasy as the prophetic writings, with their visions of a bright red horse (Rev. 6:4) and hundred-pound hailstones (Rev. 16:21).

The question whether fantasy can embody truth receives a preliminary affirmative answer. If the writers of the Bible use fantasy, we know it can express truth. But what kind of truth does fantasy reflect?

The fantasy in the Bible and elsewhere embodies the same types of truth that realism and historical writing do, only in a different mode. The fantastic river of Isaiah's vision portrayed the coming military invasion of the Assyrian army, and the imaginary hundred-pound hailstones of the Apocalypse picture the coming cataclysmic destruction of the earth under God's final judgment. The Narnia stories of C. S. Lewis portray the Christian life and courage as accurately as a missionary biography. The difference is that we must *translate* fantasy's details into known realities and experiences.

This requires a greater interpretive act than when we assimilate the straightforward presentations of realism and historical writing, but it is within anyone's ability. We simply need to become accustomed to looking for the realities being portrayed. A knight fighting a monster embodies the same reality as a soldier facing an enemy on the frontline of a modern war. A fire-breathing dragon ravaging a land embodies the same power of evil we see and fear in our own society.

Tolkien's way of expressing the situation is to declare that although fantasy is not *real*, it is *true*.[9] It is not real in many surface details, but it can be truthful to human experience and spiritual reality.

FANTASY AND THE SUPERNATURAL

While people of all ages (especially children) and all religious or non-religious persuasions can love fantasy, it holds a special place among Christians. In fact, a debunker of C. S. Lewis once declared that lovers of his fantasy stories are either children or Christians. There is logic at work here, as the author went on to say that these two groups "share one quality of imagination—a common willingness to extend reality beyond the visible."[10]

Madeleine L'Engle, a writer of children's fantasy stories, went so far as to say, "I'm never surprised when I discover that one of my favorite science fiction writers is Christian."[11] Why is this? It has partly to do with the connection between the way both fantasy and Christianity embrace a supernatural level of reality. L'Engle notes how the world of fantasy "is inimical to the secular world, and in total opposition to it," adding "in the Bible we are constantly being given glimpses of a reality quite different from that taught in school."[12]

We need to tread cautiously here, lest we baptize every manifestation of the fantastic imagination as being automatically Christian. Many false religions have believed in a supernatural world. To say the Christian faith shares an important premise with fantasy is not to presume that a given piece of fantasy gives us *the Christian* supernatural. If fantasy can be a road into Jerusalem (as mythology was for C. S. Lewis), in a day of aberrant versions of the supernatural, it can also be a ring road around Jerusalem.

With that qualification in place, we can still make *something* of the supernaturalism of fantasy. It is easy to see why Christian authors and readers have embraced fantasy as a genre. One of the things it does particularly well is to assert with clarity and conviction that a spiritual level of reality exists beyond the earthly sphere.

IS FANTASY ESCAPIST?

A common charge made against fantasy is that it is escapist. In this view, fantasy transports us to a merely imaginary realm, which has no connection with our own world. This issue requires unpacking, after which it will be clear that fantasy is not inherently escapist, any more than realistic fiction is.

The best starting point is C. S. Lewis's distinction between *escape* and *escapism* in reading. Lewis begins with the very important point that "all reading whatever is an escape. It involves a temporary transference of the mind from our surroundings to things merely imagined or conceived." A history or science book, a realistic novel or fantasy story, all remove us from our immediate world to a realm of the mind that engages our attention.

"Escape," writes Lewis, "is common to many good and bad kinds of reading." Escap*ism* is "a confirmed habit of escaping too often, or for too long, or into the wrong things, or using escape as a substitute for action where action is appropriate." The bottom line: "Escape is not necessarily joined to escapism."[13] We all need beneficial escapes, a principle that extends to all of the genres discussed in this book and to the literary enterprise itself.

The alleged dangers of escapism in fantasy literature have been greatly exaggerated. The test of whether a fantasy work is escapist is simple, and it applies equally to realistic fiction: Does reading this book unfit me for life in everyday reality, or does it send me back to life with renewed understanding and zest? C. S. Lewis made the following comment about the unlifelike details in Kenneth Grahame's children's story *The Wind in the Willows*:

> It might be expected that such a book would unfit us for the harshness of reality and send us back to our daily lives unsettled and discontented. I do not find that it does so. . . . The whole story, paradoxically enough, strengthens our relish for real life. This excursion into the preposterous sends us back with renewed pleasure to the actual.[14]

The key to understanding how the preposterous details of fantasy deal with the same realities as literary realism was well stated by science fiction writer Ursula LeGuin. Rejecting the charge that "we who hobnob with hobbits and tell tall tales about little green men" are mere entertainers or escapists, she claimed that the far-flung details of fantasy are "precise and profound metaphors of the human condition."[15] *Metaphors of the human condition*—this is the vital link between fantasy and everyday life. One of LeGuin's illustrations is "a scientist who creates a monster." Nothing could be more up to date as a picture of what is happening in our world today.

Medieval English author Geoffrey Chaucer composed a rollicking animal fable about a rooster named Chaunticleer and his wife (a hen, of course) named Pertelote. How can a story of talking animals possibly relate to everyday reality? Once we recognize this rooster and hen as the archetypal husband and wife with opposite temperaments striving for supremacy over each other, the story is as close to real life as any realistic novel about married life.

One of the paradoxes of fantasy is that it actually stays close to life's physical and emotional realities. As Tolkien's observed, "Fairy-stories deal . . . mainly with simple or fundamental things . . . made all the more luminous by their setting. . . . It was in fairy-stories that I first divined the potency of the words and the wonder of . . . things such as stone, and wood, and iron; tree and grass; house and fire; bread and wine."[16]

Fantasy illustrates particularly well a principle applying to all literature, art, and music. Pablo Picasso stated it this way: "We all know that art is not [factual] truth. Art is a lie [at the literal level] that makes us realize truth."[17]

TIPS FOR READING FANTASY

- Realize from the start that you are not reading a piece of realism. People who never see the point of fantasy are the ones who go to the text expecting to find realism and are baffled by what they encounter.
- Abandon yourself to the unlifelike qualities of fantasy. Fantasy represents the liberation of the imagination. Allow yourself to be transported to a strange world, realizing that sometimes you need to escape from the mundane.
- Do not relinquish your conviction that the subject of literature is human experience. Having allowed yourself to be transported to a strange world, ask what universal experiences and everyday realities are embodied in the fantastic details. Beneath the surface details, at a principial level, fantasy deals with the same range of human experience as realism.
- A helpful exercise for seeing how fantasy gives metaphors of reality is to complete the formula *images of . . .* : images of good, evil, fear, courage, love, redemption, devotion to God, and so on.
- Carry some of fantasy's adventure into real life. C. S. Lewis claimed that a person "does not despise real woods because he has read of enchanted woods: the reading makes all real woods a little enchanted."[18]

Some people have a taste for fantasy, while others prefer realism. With both, we stand a better chance of enjoying them if we understand what we are reading. This understanding has two sides—knowing what to expect and knowing what not to expect. When reading fantasy, we shouldn't expect a depiction of real life. But we can anticipate a delightful journey to a far country with echoes of home.

11

Reading Children's Books

Once Upon a Time

A HARRIED PARENT plops beside a reluctant sleeper's bed and begins, "Once upon a time," not knowing what will happen from there. But as soon as the ancient phrase is spoken, parent and child soar on the magic carpet of imagination.

People have always told children stories, but children's literature as a genre didn't exist until the mid-eighteenth century with the advent of books written for children's entertainment. The genre enjoyed a golden age from the mid-1800s to the early 1900s, and the industry boomed after the Second World War. Most of these children's books conveyed biblical values, often with positive references to prayer or God.

A huge shift occurred in the 1960s, when many authors started exploring previously-taboo topics from a secular perspective. Mature themes filtered down into material for younger readers. As children's book sales soar into the twenty-first century, increasingly dark subjects and unbiblical views are dished up to children on attractive reading platters.

How can we promote healthy reading alternatives to today's junk-food, literary fare for children? We can recognize the unique nature of children's literature and become aware of current concerns. Then we can choose good books and integrate reading into family life through strategies like reading aloud and controlling technology.

UNIQUE NATURE

Children's books share story elements of other genres as well as literature's twofold function of delight and edification. But they differ from literature for adults in one foundational aspect and some structural features.

The unique nature of children themselves is the primary factor that makes children's literature unique. Children in general experience emotions more keenly than adults. Their vivid imaginations and naïve spontaneity plunge them into a story's action and emotive experiences. Sometimes parents must reassure, "It's only a story." But it's real to children. They believe what they hear or read, developing their understanding of life from its portrayal in books. Children lack the emotional and intellectual maturity to temper the reading experience with an adult's reserve or analysis. Books affect them far more profoundly.

This is why the most crucial aspect of children's literature is its *incredible capacity to shape impressionable young minds*. This is also why it's so important for loving and godly adults to guide children in going beyond merely learning to read to reading with discernment and delight.

Entertainment was the initial characteristic defining children's literature. The few books for children prior to the mid-eighteenth century were moralistic or educational, but John Newbery's *A Pretty Little Pocket-Book* (1744) appealed to children's imaginations. His legacy lives on in the annual American award named after him, which distinguishes a children's book for literary quality but "not for didactic content or popularity."[1]

The genre's emphasis on entertainment does not preclude an educational aspect. Literature conveys meaning and values, which children absorb like little sponges.

Children's books are unique in structural features of length, language, and content that generally correspond to age-related categories. Board books and picture books are short, with illustrations matching simple concepts. As the categories progress for older children, book length increases, language becomes more complex, and content becomes more mature. Young Adult books often contain sexual or violent scenes, but concerns about mature content exist across the spectrum of children's literature.

CURRENT CONCERNS

Concerns about children's literature fall into two broad categories: quality and content. Although both lamentable quality and questionable content permeate many of today's books for young readers, poor literary quality has long been a concern.

This charge of poor quality is often leveled at large series characterized by formulaic and predictable plots. It arose in the early 1900s, when Edward Stratemeyer's syndicate introduced many series, including *The Hardy Boys* (1927) and *Nancy Drew* (1930). These and most of the syndicate's series contained the work of multiple authors under one pseudonym. For a fee of about $100 per book, writers followed Stratemeyer's formula and churned out manuscripts at astounding speed (sometimes in as little as three weeks). Small wonder librarians and educators dismissed the books as of poor literary quality. Cliffhanger chapter endings, however, pulled young readers through unrealistic stories and trite dialogue.

The Hardy Boys and *Nancy Drew* books are still published, although with updated characters and settings. Daniel A. Gross writes, "They're still here because their creators found a way to minimize cost, maximize output, and standardize creativity."[2] To standardize creativity is to squelch it.

Writing excellence is sacrificed on the altar of commercialism in a host of books linked to movies, video games, or superheroes. Such books, particularly beginning readers, suffer from unimaginative language and incoherent plots.

Simple language is necessary for younger readers, but we needn't abandon good writing. Geoffrey Trease asks,

> But must every children's book be written in semi-basic? It is obviously a matter of introducing unfamiliar words and phrases carefully, in context which make their meaning plain. And may we not, once in a while, permit ourselves a lovely flourish of sound which the child may enjoy without yet comprehending?[3]

Content concerns are also far-ranging. A simple picture book, featuring lovely language and beautiful illustrations, may promote an unbiblical concept. Even nonfiction is often laced with manipulative indoctrination. A first grade student may bring home a flyer advertising revisionist history as well as stories about vampires or aliens. Objectionable content increases in books aimed at older readers, especially those geared toward teens. Jill Carlson found, "Almost without exception, novels which reveal God's positive power are censored from library shelves. Into this vacuum, . . . authors [writing for teens] pour a torrent of books offering a narrow spectrum of other 'isms'—rationalism, occultism, and nihilism." She adds with emphasis, "*In the name of diversity, our kids are offered books channeling them into a humanistic dead end.*"[4]

The Young Adult genre includes hopeless dystopian and occult horror, but it is overwhelmingly weighted with "real life" fiction. In most of these books, teens struggle with problems ranging from trivial ones about appearance to weighty trauma like sexual abuse. No matter how minor the problem, self-centered protagonists see themselves as victims with a difficult life. No one understands these protagonists (especially parents), and they need to handle struggles on their own. God is absent or Christians are portrayed negatively. Scenes are graphic, but answers are few and hope elusive.

David Mills describes these "tawdry and sometimes depraved" books as appealing to the "worst in every teenager." He writes, "The hope presented in these book is one of two kinds . . . merely getting what you want . . . [or] surviving until college or adulthood."[5]

Such supposedly "realistic" novels fail to provide the ultimate answers found in the reality of Christ. Children should learn problem-solving skills, but must they figure out solutions to all problems on their own? We want them to love and trust parents and especially to love and trust God. Few books combine an engaging story with an authentic (but not moralistic) portrayal of godly parents and growing faith. This is especially true for boys. Because girls—as a whole—read more than boys, publishers often prefer a female protagonist. It can be difficult to find a well-written story about a boy living a normal life without superpowers or magic tools but exceptions do exist.[6]

Adults who care about what children read can become aware of concerns by considering perspectives. We should ask, "What is this book's view of the world?" Reading through a worldview lens helps bring content problems into focus.

But because appropriate content ought to be presented with literary excellence, we should also ask, "Is the writing good?" Many well-written books contain inappropriate content, but the opposite is also true. Countless books with unobjectionable material display poor writing. We want to be aware of both quality and content.

CHOOSING GOOD BOOKS

Considering quality and content helps us choose good books. Most people simply want to get children reading. The prevailing philosophy is that it doesn't matter what kids read as long as they are reading. But just as decent parents wouldn't feed children a steady diet of junk food, we shouldn't allow children to constantly consume books of poor quality and questionable value.

Literary quality is good writing. Sentences flow smoothly, and the occasional phrase sings. Figurative language is fresh and apt, appropriate to both content and reader. Interesting and authentic characters make progress. They do and say things to propel the plot gradually toward a satisfying resolution.

Worthwhile content promotes biblical values without preaching. Problems can be portrayed, but goodness and hope ought to illuminate any darkness. This is especially important in books for children, who must be guided to develop intellectual and spiritual maturity. Children's books should shine with hopeful content and sing with excellent writing.

Even if we keep those two primary aspects in mind, how do we pick a good book? Here are some bookstore and library browsing tips:

- *Consider the reader's interests and abilities.* Children become easily frustrated when trying to read something they find boring, especially if it is beyond their skill level. But they will put great effort into reading a book about their current passion.
- *Choose books with main characters a little older than the intended reader.* Books with younger characters may seem condescending. Books with much older characters are likely to be too mature for the reader.
- *Read the table of contents.* Chapter titles convey more about the story's progression than front cover pictures and back cover blurbs. They may even indicate if the conflict and resolution are appropriate for the reader and within value parameters.

- *Read the first page.* If the writing isn't engaging enough to draw you into the story, it probably won't capture a child's attention.

Most people these days shop online. A posting that allows viewers to look inside a book may show the table of contents and first page. Reading any page gives a glimpse of the writing.

Browsing a bookstore, scrolling a website, or perusing library shelves can be overwhelming. But many books and online sources provide assistance in choosing good books.

Gladys Hunt set the standard for thoughtful analysis and lists of suggested reading with her *Honey for a Child's Heart*. She and Barbara Hampton later wrote *Honey for a Teen's Heart*.[7] Elizabeth Wilson's *Books Children Love* (foreword by Susan Schaeffer Macauley) advocates Charlotte Mason's "living books" concept, which homeschoolers are rediscovering.[8] Helpful reading lists conclude Michael O'Brien's *A Landscape with Dragons: The Battle for Your Child's Mind*, although he reportedly did not compile them.[9] *How to Grow a Young Reader* profiles authors and assesses books.[10] In *Read for the Heart*, Susan Clarkson writes, "A good book, like any great piece of art, is an agent of awakening."[11]

It's easy to search Sarah Mackenzie's Read-Aloud Revival website for specific lists or download them by subscribing to the site's popular podcasts.[12] Janie B. Cheaney, author of several excellent books for children, contributes to Redeemed Reader, a website that rates children's books according to artistic quality and worldview.[13] This system mirrors our twofold concern for literary excellence and worthwhile content.

Three authors concur in wisdom that encapsulates choosing good books. Madeleine L'Engle wrote, "The only standard to be used in judging a children's book is: *Is it a good book?* Is it good enough for me? Because if a children's book is not good enough for all of us, it is not good enough for children."[14]

Her thoughts echo those of J. R. R. Tolkien and C. S. Lewis. Tolkien wrote, "Books written entirely for children are poor even as children's books."[15] And Lewis said, "I am almost inclined to set it up as a canon that a children's story which is enjoyed only by children is a bad children's story."[16]

That a good book for children ought to be one adults also enjoy implies parents should read good books themselves. Being a discerning reader and guiding children to become thoughtful readers are part of a lifestyle that integrates God's word and words.

INTEGRATED LIFESTYLE

Deuteronomy 6:6–9[17] forms the foundational text encouraging parents to adopt a comprehensive nurturing style that becomes second nature. We can convey truths to our children while sitting at home, putting them to bed, walking uptown, or driving in the car. The Deuteronomy 6 life is not constant preaching but an integrated lifestyle. We do not want to make parents feel guilty about shortcomings or become obsessed with moralistic instruction. We encourage gentle and spontaneous nurture, punctuated by Spirit-initiated moments.

Such moments help children discover God's truth, goodness, and beauty in what they read. Children learn to share characters' merits, question behavior, or recognize printed words that contradict the word of the Bible.

Modeling reading helps foster reading in children. Parents shouldn't limit reading until after kiddos are tucked into bed. Adults should feel free to share humor or insights from books with children. If children see how much adults enjoy reading, they'll want to emulate them.

An integrated home makes good books available. Think of how many books could be bought with half, or even a quarter, of what is spent annually on toys. Grandparents may be thrilled to receive book suggestions as gift ideas.

Why spend money on books when you can check them out from a library or download digital copies from the Internet? Because simply having books in the home provides children with a variety of lifetime benefits. A global study shows that the presence of books in the home increases not only literacy but also math and technology skills into adulthood. "Growing up with home libraries boosts adult skills in these areas beyond the benefits accrued from parental education, or [one's] own educational or occupational attainment."[18] Only eighty books will make a positive difference that continues to increase until about 350 books, an amount at which the benefits appear to level out.

Surrounding children with books has positive effects beyond literacy skills, but our goal supersedes attaining any particular skill set. Our primary aim exceeds even raising children who love to read. We invite parents to foster a Scout Finch attitude: "Until I feared I would lose it, I never loved to read. One does not love breathing."[19] This perspective sees reading as necessary as breathing.

READING ALOUD

Few activities foster family bonds and childhood development more than reading aloud. Parents shouldn't hesitate to begin reading to infants, perhaps even before they're born,[20] and shouldn't stop when children become teenagers. An integrated family captures moments for reading aloud (even when a toddler requests the same book for what seems the hundredth time), but we encourage families to aim for a daily routine.

According to one report, reading to children is the "single most important activity for building the knowledge required for eventual success in reading" and is a "practice that should continue throughout the grades."[21] Newer research indicates that reading aloud to children goes beyond developing language and literacy skills to shaping social and emotional development. One author writes, "The parent-child-book moment even has the potential to help curb problem behaviors like aggression, hyperactivity and difficulty with attention."[22] Who knew something as simple as reading aloud has potential for helping children be kinder, calmer, and more focused?

Our favorite benefit is fostering delight. Jim Trelease writes, "When we read to a child, we're sending a pleasure message to the child's brain. You could even call it a commercial, conditioning the child to associate books and print with pleasure."[23] Prolific author Sigmund Brouwer agrees: "Reading aloud from the time your children are very young will introduce them—whether reluctant or eager readers—to the *pleasure* of written words."[24]

Setting a regular time helps provide the security and routine children crave. Many parents find reading aloud works well as a wind-down interval before bedtime. The best read-aloud is a good Bible story book, which conveys the Bible's redemptive thread rather than disjointed or moralistic stories. Simple stories work best with younger children, but their attention spans may surprise you.[25]

We both love reading aloud. Having practiced it with our children and grandchildren for decades, we're eager to share some tips:

- *Create a circle of love and light.* Turn off lights in other rooms and shut down electronics. Encourage cuddling, but don't insist children sit still or on your lap. Some children listen better while coloring or playing quietly. Don't force teens to participate, but exude fun to woo them into the story and the family circle.
- *Revel in the reading experience.* Don't rush. Ask and allow questions. Let children linger over pictures or express their thoughts. Explain puzzling words or concepts. Don't be

self-conscious. Unleash the latent actor within you and read expressively.

- *Conclude before interest wanes.* Children begging for more sets the stage for your next reading session.

Parents may be eager to share childhood favorites, but don't be discouraged if your children fail to find them engaging. Perhaps interests and attention spans need to develop. Books with general appeal are best for listeners in a wide age range. If a book isn't working, simply try another.

When making the transition from picture books to short novels, Sarah Mackenzie suggests choosing ones with "short chapters, lots of dialogue, and memorable characters."[26] The best books for initiating a read-aloud routine engage listeners from the start with a well-written and entertaining story. Parents may want to avoid beginning with classics containing archaic language, long sentences, or unfamiliar words. Better choices might be a story about a loving but realistic family in a modern setting or a horse story or a simple mystery or a fun fantasy.

Some of our favorite read-alouds include the Little House books by Laura Ingalls Wilder. The narrative content contains little to distress but long descriptions of homemaking processes may be beyond younger children's imaginative grasp. The variety of English accents in the Redwall books by Brian Jacques makes them great fun to read aloud, but some scenes are quite suspenseful. Parents should be sensitive to personalities rather than age, as an older child with a more active imagination could be more easily frightened by danger than a younger sibling.

The Chronicles of Narnia is our favorite series for children, although we don't recommend it as a first read-aloud for young children. Lewis's lengthy sentences and intense action make it a better choice for children accustomed to following complex thoughts and who are mature enough for suspense and sadness.

Whenever parents or children pick up the Narnia series, we recommend beginning with *The Lion, the Witch, and the Wardrobe* and reading them in publication order.[27] Editions released in recent years often package sets with *The Magician's Nephew* as the first book because it tells how Narnia was created. But attempting to maintain chronological order is pointless because the events in *The Horse and His Boy* occur during the same time frame as *The Lion, the Witch, and the Wardrobe.*

A far more important factor is how the revised order deprives the reader of the magical delight as revelations unfold. How much better to allow children to discover Narnia's wonders and dangers alongside the four young Pevensies! Children may notice on their own how events or characters remind them of Christian truths, or parents may guide discussions with gentle questions. We encourage adults not to force allegorical discussions that steal a child's pure enjoyment. For example, you may want to refrain from announcing at the outset (as one mother did in a theater prior to the start of a movie adaptation), "Aslan is Jesus."

Far less allegorical, J. R. R. Tolkien's *Lord of the Rings* conveys providence and sovereignty in a complex narrative appropriate for older children and teens. The Christian perspectives of Tolkien and Lewis permeate their inspiring imaginative tales. But what about the best-selling series in history, the *Harry Potter* books by J. K. Rowling?

Christians differ on their opinion of the Potter books. The primary theme of self-sacrificial love's saving power resonates with many believers, who hear echoes of the Greatest Story. But some Christians view the series as dangerous to individuals and society as a whole.[28] Both believers and unbelievers value the series for its ability to engage reluctant readers with clever writing and exciting plots. We recommend reading and discussing the books with your children (instead of letting them read the series on their own). This allows the adult to ask questions, point out moral ambiguities, or provide guidance at appropriate moments.

CONTROLLING TECHNOLOGY

How can parents possibly find time for reading aloud in today's hectic society? The most effective way to gain minutes each day may be to cut down screen time—for both parents and children. But why is it so hard to put down the device and focus on reading? At least part of the reason is digital media's intentional design to keep people online.

In an article titled, "The Tech Industry's War on Kids," Richard Freed shows how psychology is used as a weapon against children through persuasive technology. He writes, "While persuasion techniques work well on adults, they are particularly effective at influencing the still-maturing child and teen brain." Tech companies develop individual user profiles and employ "brain hacking" and other "dark design" technologies to exploit young people's vulnerable emotional moments.[29] The problem with technology isn't merely that it's stealing children's minutes; it's stealing their childhood.[30]

Some people with ties to the tech industry are calling for change. It's telling that many industry executives restrict or prohibit their children's access to digital media. Parents need to be aware of their own susceptibility and put down the phone to be fully present in their children's lives. They should also protect their children from falling into unhealthy technology use as much as they would shield them from other forms of possible harm or addictions.[31] *The Tech-Wise Family* by Andy Crouch advocates a "full, flourishing"[32] lifestyle consistent with the integrated one we described earlier.

It may help to seek advice or relationships with people who share commitments to less technology and more reading. Grandparents may offer biblical wisdom. Like-minded parents might be found at church by chatting about children's books or in the community by attending library events. Children are in the home for only a short time (unless they become part of the growing population of young people who remain gaming in their parents' basement rather than joining the work force). It's worth extra effort to control screens instead of allowing screens to control the family.

HAPPILY EVER AFTER

Who doesn't love a fairy tale ending, when characters overcome conflict and begin living happily? Although we recognize the busyness and stress within today's families, we hope readers will find great joy in an integrated lifestyle that prioritizes reading. Because books play such a crucial role in shaping children's minds and perspectives, we encourage parents to fill their homes with good books and read regularly to their children. This becomes easier within communities of like-minded people to come alongside us in this great reading adventure.

We are realistic enough to realize that no one lives happily ever after on this earth. But we believe reading good books helps shape a spiritual perspective that will live happily in the hereafter.

12

Reading Creative Nonfiction

To Tell the Truth

ON JANUARY 26, 2006, author James Frey sat on the set of Oprah Winfrey's television show, attempting to answer her questions about fabricated parts of his memoir, *A Million Little Pieces.* Oprah had chosen it as a book club selection only months earlier, but now she exposed one falsehood after another as she grilled Frey about the time he'd spent in jail, how his girlfriend died, and if he had really received a root canal without painkiller. Regarding the dental procedure, Frey said, "Since that time, I've struggled with the idea of it—"

"No, the lie of it," Winfrey interrupted. "It's a lie. It's not an idea, James, that's a lie."[1]

Frey's book about overcoming addictions sold well when first published in 2003 but skyrocketed into the bestseller stratosphere following Oprah's endorsement in September of 2005. Early in January of 2006, the Smoking Gun website exposed multiple inaccuracies in Frey's book. For one thing, Frey had been in police custody for only a few hours, but he wrote of spending eighty-seven days in jail.[2] Only three days after the Smoking Gun report, CNN's Larry King confronted Frey about the memoir's falsehoods. Frey said, "To be honest, I still stand by the book as being the essential truth of my life. I'll stand by that idea until the day I die." Oprah called in near the end of Larry King Live to express her and her producers' support, saying that "the underlying message of redemption in James Frey's memoir still resonates with me. And I know that it resonates with millions of other people who have read this book and will continue to read this book."[3]

Only two weeks (but many irate responses from fans) later, Oprah invited James Frey back for her January 26 show, or better, showdown. In addition to lashing out at Frey, she apologized to listeners for her call to Larry King Live: "I made a mistake and I left the impression that truth does not matter. And I am deeply sorry about that, because that is not what I believe."[4]

Oprah Winfrey's waffling makes one wonder what she really believes about truth. And how can Frey claim the "essential truth" of a work containing so many falsehoods? As this anecdote demonstrates, people have different perceptions of truth in creative nonfiction. But shouldn't readers expect nonfiction to be true? In this chapter, we'll explore the crucial issue of truth in creative nonfiction. But first, we'll define the genre and delineate its traits and forms. After exploring the truth issue and describing scene recreation, we'll see how readers share in the author's curiosity. Finally, we'll conclude with specific tips for reading creative nonfiction.

WHAT IS CREATIVE NONFICTION?

The term "creative nonfiction" may sound like an oxymoron, but examining each word helps define the phrase. *Creative* refers to artistic craftsmanship. *Nonfiction* conveys its factual content. Creative nonfiction is sometimes called literary journalism, but it differs from newspaper or magazine articles. A more accurate way to describe the genre may be literary prose.

Lee Gutkind, an advocate for the identifier "creative nonfiction" and a popular authority on the genre, defines it as "true stories, well told."[5] Phillip Lopate, an academic expert and author, prefers the term "literary nonfiction." He summarizes the organizing principle as "tracking the consciousness of the author" and stresses its combination with a "highly intentional literary style." Lopate says, "Consciousness plus style equals good nonfiction." In a memorable turn of phrase, he refers to well-known nonfiction works as "glorious thought-excursions."[6]

Creative nonfiction shares many elements with story and fiction. Its characters progress through a coherent plot, complete with setting and dialogue. But it is a distinct genre with characteristic traits that set it apart from other genres.

TRAITS AND FORMS

Defining creative nonfiction has highlighted its two primary traits, while hinting at others. Artistic expression combined with factual content form the foundation of the genre. Three additional factors can also be considered characteristic of this genre: thorough research, personal presence, and reflective interpretation.

Artistic expression is a distinguishing component of creative nonfiction. Authors employ literary techniques and stylistic features to convey a story in an artistic manner. Alliteration or assonance makes language sing. Similes and metaphors help readers visualize details. Sentence types and lengths vary to create interest and match emotional moments. Such techniques (also found in poetry and fiction) can be used effectively to enliven nonfiction.

Factual content is another key feature of creative nonfiction, but this trait is shared with journalism rather than fiction or poetry. Just as newspaper reports or magazine articles are (or should be) about things that really happened, creative nonfiction is (or should be) about real people and true events. Some imaginative elements may be necessary. Names are often changed, dialogue may be recreated, or action compressed; however, the people, conversations, and events are not invented by the author. Creative nonfiction may be about real people or actual events in the past, but it is not historical fiction. And while it shares factual content with journalism, it is not news reporting.

Still, like good journalism, creative nonfiction is characterized by *thorough research*. Some authors practice what is called immersion research. They spend a great deal of time, perhaps months, alongside people in a specific profession or in a certain situation. They attempt to observe as unobtrusively as the proverbial fly on the wall in order to capture reality with vivid descriptions and accurate dialogue. Historical subjects require more painstaking and traditional research, but trustworthy authors who write about any subject or person will do their best to verify the truth of the story they are telling.

Another characteristic of creative nonfiction is *personal presence*. The author may be writing about his or her personal life, as in autobiography or memoir. An author also could write from a personal perspective about another individual or a general topic. Examples of the latter would be books or essays about food or travel. Although authors may reveal few private details in these types of books, their individual preferences appear as they relate impressions and assessments of restaurants or sights. Even if a creative nonfiction work is not primarily about an individual's experiences, the reader generally senses a real person's presence more in creative nonfiction than in other genres.

Such a strong personal presence leads naturally to *reflective interpretation*. This may be authorial commentary, which is likely to be sprinkled throughout autobiographies or memoirs as writers muse on how various events affected them. Structural elements are also part of the way an author interprets a story. The author chooses representative dialogue or specific events to lead the reader along a logical path toward the resolution or to illustrate the overarching theme. The "show, don't tell" maxim for fiction holds sway within specific scenes in creative nonfiction, but reflective telling is also obvious and acceptable. A work of creative nonfiction tells a true story in an artistic manner. It shows evidence of extensive research, but it is not a sterile account of bare-bones facts. A strong personal presence goes beyond merely relating events to reflecting on them and interpreting their meaning.

TRUTH OR CONSEQUENCES?

Because the official designation of creative nonfiction has been around only since the early 1980s, it seems like a new genre. But this type of writing has existed for at least as long as Augustine's *Confessions*, which were written between 397 and 400 AD. Other well-known examples in this genre include Henry David Thoreau's *Walden* (1854) and Isak Dinesen's *Out of Africa* (1937). A "memoir craze" that began in the 1990s made publishers eager for shocking stories to boost sales, which generated more controversy about differing views of truth. The Oprah Winfrey and James Frey anecdote illustrates how people define truth differently. Did either Oprah or Frey pay any consequences after the public showdown?

The Oprah Winfrey Show continued five more years, until 2011, when Frey returned during final episodes for mostly-congenial conversation. Four of Frey's books, including *A Million Little Pieces*, have become international bestsellers.[7] The high-profile spat apparently caused little long-lasting harm to the careers of either.

Some authors have paid a price for fabricating falsehoods in a book marketed as nonfiction. One author committed suicide after losing public favor.[8] A few people responsible for well-known fakes have gone to prison.[9] Sometimes a publisher offers payments to duped readers or recalls copies, especially when a memoir's author is exposed as being someone completely different than as represented in the book.[10] Some authors lose their reputation or support,[11] but many nonfiction authors whose work is riddled with falsehoods appear to get away with it. Some even profit.

An author worth mentioning is John D'Agata, who's a vocal proponent of taking liberties with facts in the name of art. D'Agata is notable primarily due to his influential position as the Director of the highly-ranked Nonfiction Writing Program at the University of Iowa.

After a magazine rejected an article for its inaccuracies, D'Agata submitted it to another. There it ran the fact-checking gauntlet of an unpaid intern named Jim Fingal. The original process took less than a year, and Fingal wrote a hundred pages documenting inaccuracies in D'Agata's essay. At some point, the two men decided to write a book about the process. Their interaction turned into a seven-year collaboration that produced *The Lifespan of a Fact*. The book depicts blocks of D'Agata's original article, with Fingal's research comments and questions in the margins, interspersed with email exchanges between the two men. But the book does *not* portray their actual interaction. Fingal describes the Jim and John in the book as "characters enacting a parallel process" and admits to "dramatizing it a bit." D'Agata calls the book "an exaggerated farce" in which he and Fingal "knowingly amped up the hostility of our comments."[12] The book appears to be a platform for D'Agata's views.

You'd expect such a book to quickly move off the radar of public consciousness. But in 2018, *Lifespan of a Fact* opened as a Broadway show, starring Daniel Radcliffe of Harry Potter fame in the role of Fingal. Apparently, both writer and fact-checker are experiencing popular success with few—if any—consequences.

The heart of creative nonfiction's problem lies within the hearts of its authors. They have differing views of truth. It may seem obvious that inaccurate facts are untruths, but some nonfiction authors believe accurate facts are not as important as artistic writing. They feel certain inaccuracies enhance the story's artistry. They excuse what they consider minor untruths in order to create a work of art, which they believe conveys a greater or more essential truth. A common belief is that art has no limitations; it should be experimental. The trouble comes when unlimited experimentation crosses an invisible line into intentional deception.

D'Agata thinks "it's art's job to trick us" and "lure us into terrain that is going to confuse us [or] perhaps make us feel uncomfortable and perhaps open up to us possibilities in the world that we hadn't earlier considered."[13] We agree that great literature can open our minds to new possibilities, but we don't believe nonfiction should intentionally manipulate or confuse the reader. While some poetic license may be necessary in creative nonfiction, it has limits. It ought to be restricted to true facts. D'Agata seems to view the only criteria for drawing a line between truth and artistic license as being when a fabrication causes harm. In *Lifespan of a Fact*, the D'Agata character claims, "I have taken some liberties in the essay here and there, but none of them are harmful."[14]

Hannah Goldfield, who checks facts for *The New Yorker*, takes issue with his assertion. She writes:

> What D'Agata fails to realize is that not only are these liberties indeed harmful—even if only to the reader, who is trusting the writer to be accurate in his or her description of what exists or took place in reality—they are also completely unnecessary to creating a piece of great nonfiction. The conceit that one must choose facts or beauty—even if it's beauty in the name of "Truth" or a true "idea"—is preposterous. A good writer—with the help of a fact-checker and an editor, perhaps—should be able to marry the two. . . . Altering and cherry-picking details is an easy, hollow

game for a writer. The challenge, and the art, lies in confronting the facts—all of them, whether you like them or not—and shaping them into something beautiful.[15]

We agree. The nonfiction author doesn't have to choose between facts or beauty. The trustworthy nonfiction author combines both by presenting true facts in an artful manner.

Due to memory's elusive nature and everyday conversation's banality, total recall is rarely possible or even desirable. William Giraldi writes, "Readers of memoir understand that total accuracy is not possible; they ask only for no calculated distortions. They ask for a moral reckoning, morality fertilized in style, and for imaginative assertions that do not contradict the facts."[16] Writers may imaginatively recreate scenes, but they should not mislead readers by creating imaginary scenarios.

Phillip Lopate believes nonfiction writers should try to be "as honest as our courage permits. Honest to the world of facts outside ourselves, honest in reporting what we actually felt and did, and finally, honest about our own confusions." As he sees it, the nonfiction author's challenge is "to take something that actually happened, to oneself or to others, and try to render it as honestly and compellingly as possible." He adds, "My own feeling is that, all things considered, and whenever possible (it's not always possible), I would rather employ the actual facts in a nonfiction piece, because there is something magical and uncanny about the world that is given to us."[17] Creative nonfiction, more than any other genre, highlights the veracity of the old adage about truth being stranger than fiction. We live in a fascinating world, populated by interesting individuals who do incredible things.

Lee Gutkind stresses the need for truth, accuracy, and fact checking in creative nonfiction because "honesty and credibility are the bone and sinew, the essential irrefutable anchoring elements of nonfiction." The bottom line is his maxim and one of his book titles: *You Can't Make This Stuff Up.*[18]

SCENE RECREATION

Memory usually does not recall every detail with perfect clarity, and different people recall the same event in various ways. Unless a conversation is recorded, it's impossible to remember word-for-word dialogue from the past. For these reasons, readers can expect nonfiction authors to recreate scenes and dialogue. But they can also expect it to be done as accurately as possible.

Let's consider a personal example. When I (Glenda) collaborated with Uriah Courtney on his memoir about his wrongful incarceration and subsequent exoneration,[19] we selected a few scenes from his childhood to begin early chapters. We did this to illustrate his love for nature and adventure as well as to show how small steps and a desire for thrills began taking him down the path leading to his arrest and wrongful conviction.

Uriah had written his memory of when he and a friend were exploring a storm tunnel under a San Diego freeway and the batteries in their flashlights died. Imagining how it would have all played out, I added dialogue and description to the factual information he had provided. When Uriah read the scene, he said, "Wow! I didn't know Glenda was there with us."

Recreating scenes and dialogue to reflect actual events and conversations is entirely different from relating events and conversations that never happened.

CURIOSITY

The fiction writer is compelled by a desire to tell an imaginary tale, but the nonfiction author has a compulsion to relate a true story. What fuels this compulsion is the author's curiosity. A nonfiction author is innately curious about the incredible things in the world and its amazing people. Each individual, endowed with an eternal soul, has their own unique story. It is the nonfiction author's privilege to share a slice of a person's life with the world. So many fascinating places, occupations, or events exist that the nonfiction author never runs out of interesting subjects.

Robert Root says, "The writer chooses nonfiction as a medium because of a desire or a need or a drive to understand a portion of the world and to record and respond to that understanding." He calls this the "nonfiction motive" and believes the center of nonfiction is "the point where the nonfiction motive emerges."[20]

Phillip Lopate says the nonfiction author's curiosity "sounds more tepid than obsession, but it's a lot more dependable in the long run." He adds:

> You follow a strand of curiosity and pretty soon you've an interesting digression, a whole chapter, a book proposal, a book. The solution to entrapment in the hothouse of self is not to relinquish autobiographical writing, as though we had to buy into the anti-memoir backlash that says memoirs are self-absorbed navel gazing. . . . No, the solution is to expand the self by getting it to interface in curiosity with more and more parts of history and the concrete world."[21]

Here Lopate captures the antidote to sensational and self-absorbed memoirs. In well-written nonfiction, authors looks beyond self to observe history and the world with curious interest.

And as Lopate addresses the problem of portraying nonfiction's inevitable conclusion, he hints at the reader's curiosity: "In fact, inevitability is to be avoided in essays for as long as possible. The form must be kept open, the lines of inquiry left receptive to new curiosities."[22]

Nonfiction may come to a predetermined conclusion, but it can be written in a way that stimulates the reader's curiosity. The author and reader share in a desire to explore humanity's curious inclinations.

READING RECOMMENDATIONS

Whether readers prefer to label this genre as creative nonfiction, literary nonfiction, or literary prose, we hope you now understand it and its controversies better. Because it's different from the other genres we've discussed in this book, it requires some unique reading tips.

- Enjoy the literary skill of a well-told true story.
- Expect accurate facts, but be aware that some authors intentionally use inaccuracies for what they view as the greater artistic purpose.
- Recognize how the elusive nature of memory means that different people recall the same events differently.
- Realize that scenes with dialogue may be recreated and don't expect word-for-word accounts of past conversations.
- Expect to sense a strong personal presence, complete with reflective interpretation.
- Allow yourself to share the author's curiosity.
- Consider how overarching truths might apply to your own life.

It may seem as if sensationalism has fueled publishing's memoir craze in recent decades. The more sordid details an author confesses, the more sales are likely to soar. And the controversy about truth and honesty may make one wonder if creative nonfiction is even worth pursuing.

But the genre has much to offer readers and, as noted earlier, it took root in fertile spiritual soil. William Giraldi reflects on how the Western autobiographical tradition began with Augustine: "In his *Confessions*, to confess does not mean a self-glorification dressed up as gaudy, pretended self-debasement—all that vaunting humility in the midst of another identity crisis—but rather a surrender, a giving over of the self to an eminence, an Other, in an effort to achieve the searing of grace."[23]

Reading creative nonfiction can be a fascinating exploration of a true subject. The reader walks beside the writer in discovering answers to humanity's innate curiosity. Creative nonfiction, no matter how much of an oxymoron the phrase may sound, can even be a vehicle of surrender to the searing power of God's grace.

Reading the Bible as Literature

Words of Delight

C. S. LEWIS STATED that "the Bible, since it is after all literature, cannot properly be read except as literature; and the different parts of it as the different sorts of literature they are."[1] This often-quoted statement serves as this chapter's epigraph, summarizing and suggesting its theme. The subject of reading the Bible as literature breaks down naturally into four topics: (1) what the Bible as literature does *not* mean, (2) what it *does* mean, (3) *how* we can read the Bible as literature, and (4) *why* we should read the Bible as literature.

WHAT DOES THE CONCEPT OF THE BIBLE AS LITERATURE *NOT* MEAN?

Before we can fully embrace the idea known familiarly as "the Bible as literature," we need to be relieved of possible anxieties. These fears deserve to be taken seriously. When we examine the issues, we find that possible objections turn out to be misconceptions. Four of these fallacies are perennial.

An initial misconception, especially for people unaccustomed to considering the Bible's literary aspect, is to suspect this concept as a modern and liberal notion. But the idea itself is neither modern nor inherently liberal. The concept began with the writers of Scripture, who show mastery of literary technique on nearly every page. These authors sometimes use technical literary terms such as chronicle, song, parable, apocalypse, and epistle. We also can easily dispel the misconception of the idea as inherently liberal. Such towering theological stalwarts as Augustine, Luther, and Calvin did not doubt that the Bible possesses literary qualities. When we read literary commentary on the Bible, we find the same range of liberal and evangelical leanings found in other types of biblical commentary. Reading and analyzing the Bible as literature begins where any other study of the Bible should begin—by accepting as true everything the Bible itself declares about its unique status as the word of God.

Secondly, to describe the Bible as literary does not imply that it is fictional rather than factual. Although fictionality is common in literature, it is not an essential ingredient. The properties that make a text literary are unaffected by whether the material is historically accurate or fictional. A text is literary whenever it displays literary qualities. There is an unwarranted assumption abroad, including in some evangelical circles, that a high degree of patterning and conscious artistry in a biblical text signals it as fictional.

Additionally, reading the Bible as literature need not lead a reader to pay attention only to the literary qualities in the Bible to the exclusion of other aspects of it. Three types of material converge in the Bible—historical, theological, and literary. That very combination makes it impossible to read the Bible *only* as one of these. To neglect any is to distort the Bible's nature. More often than not, history and theology are packaged in a literary format, with the result that there *are* no theology and history without the literary form in which they are embodied. In this sense, it is appropriate to speak of the primacy of the literary mode in the Bible.

Finally, people unaccustomed to thinking of the Bible as literature sometimes object to what seems to be an attempt to place the Bible on the same level as English and American literature. But to say that the Bible is literature is simply an objective description of the form in which Scripture comes to us. There is no intention either to elevate or demote the Bible. If we approach it using ordinary methods of literary analysis, the Bible elevates itself and reveals its unique spiritual quality and power. Despite all the traits Scripture shares with other literature, it never seems just like that literature. As English poet Samuel Taylor Coleridge correctly stated, "[T]he words of the Bible find [us] at greater depths of [our] being" than any other book.[2]

It would be tragic if we allowed ourselves to be deterred from the literary study and enjoyment of the Bible by objections that turn out to be fallacies. We do not need to abandon the special status and spiritual reverence we accord to the Bible in order to read it in keeping with its literary nature.

WHAT DOES IT MEAN THAT THE BIBLE IS LITERATURE?

The traits making a written text literary comprise a long list. There are correspondingly many things that make the Bible a literary anthology. The following discussion should therefore be understood as a selective list of the Bible's most important literary qualities. Much more could be said. An important preliminary point is that these literary qualities are exactly the same ones that characterize literature in general. Any standard handbook of literary forms and techniques provides the correct categories and definitions for the Bible as literature.[3] Although we discuss literary traits elsewhere in this book, we need to state some here because most people do not adequately understand how they apply to the Bible.

We can profitably begin at the level of content or subject matter. The subject of literature is human experience, rendered so concretely that we live the experiences in our imagination. Truthfulness to life and human experience is the first level of content we encounter in a work of literature, in the Bible as well as beyond it. At this point we need to heed Flannery O'Connor's principle that "the whole text is the meaning, *because it is an experience*, not an abstraction."[4]

The story of Cain is a mere sixteen verses (Gen. 4:1–16), but the list of recognizable human experiences it embodies keeps expanding: sibling conflict, domestic violence, harboring a grudge, feeling rejected, anger at having gotten caught, refusal to repent, making a wrong choice and living with the consequences, guilt, exile, and so on. Psalm 23 shows the same experiential approach to truth in a poetic mode. As we work through the poem, we do not first of all grasp ideas with our mind but instead follow a shepherd through his daily routine, experiencing the actions that a shepherd performs and picturing a succession of settings.

As a work of literature, the Bible initially puts us in touch with universal human experience. It is not primarily a book of ideas the way a theology book is, though we can always extract themes or ideas from a work of literature after we have relived the text at an experiential level. Literature is incarnational; it embodies its content in a way that gets us to share an experience—the feelings of being in love in the Song of Solomon, for example. How much of the Bible meets this literary criterion of "showing" rather than "telling" (embodiment or enactment instead of abstraction)? An earlier chapter mentioned 80 percent, and the percentage is higher with a generous application of the principle.

If the Bible's literary nature can be defined by its experiential *content*, we can also define it in terms of the *forms* expressing that content. Through the centuries, the most common way to identify a text as literary is by its genres (literary types). The human race has long recognized some genres as expository and others as literary. Expository discourse conveys information directly and abstractly (examples are reports, journal entries, and some essays). Literary genres include story or narrative, poetry, satire, visionary writing, proverb, and epistle. The Bible is one of the most copious anthologies of diverse literary genres and forms in the world, and their presence easily demonstrates that the Bible is a literary book.

A second aspect of literary form in the Bible is a wide-ranging quality called artistry, with which we automatically associate beauty. This can extend to a global level with the beginning-middle-end structure of a story, or the careful construction of a poem around the principle of theme-and-variation. Consider how Psalm 1 turns the prism of the blessedness of the godly person in such a way that we contemplate various facets of that unifying subject. Verbal beauty permeates the Bible, producing the most aphoristic book we know, filled with memorable statements we easily retain. Rhetorical patterning is a form of artistry, seen in Matthew 5:2–10, where every beatitude follows the same pattern of (1) pronouncement of blessing, (2) naming of a group, (3) a reason for the blessing that starts with the formula *for*, and (4) stating a promised reward. For example: "Blessed are the poor in spirit, for theirs is the kingdom of heaven" (Matt. 5:3).

Another aspect of the Bible's literary style or form consists of special language resources that set off a literary passage from everyday expository prose. The most obvious examples are figures of speech, such as imagery, metaphor, simile, allusion, and personification. These make up the very language of poetry, but in the Bible they are not limited to the poetic sections. They are present on nearly every page and especially prominent in the discourses of Jesus and the epistles, as well as the book of Revelation.

What does it mean that the Bible is literature? It means that it presents human experience for our contemplation, is packaged in a wide array of literary genres, is replete with artistry, and uses literary resources of language.

HOW CAN WE READ THE BIBLE AS LITERATURE?

Many people (including biblical scholars) assent at a theoretic level to everything we have said about the Bible's literary nature, and then when they read and teach the Bible, they ignore what they believe in theory. They revert to conventional ways of handling the Bible instead of using methods of literary analysis. Paying lip service to the literary nature of the Bible has been a gigantic missed opportunity, equivalent to preparing a meal and then refusing to sit down to eat it.

The obvious and simple answer to the question of how we can read the Bible as literature is that we need to *do justice to* the literary qualities the Bible possesses. It is as simple as that. Our approach in the following discussion is to explore what actions are required of readers in light of the specific literary qualities we have ascribed to the Bible as a literary book.

At the level of content, literature is the voice of authentic human experience. Stories and poems put actual human experience before us to contemplate and share. This requires us to recognize and name the human experiences in the text we are reading. Because the Bible is a sacred book dealing with spiritual reality, it is easy to conclude incorrectly that it does not deal with such down-to-earth experiences as farming and cleaning the house and being robbed and fishing. When Jesus told his parables, he typically said his subject was what the kingdom of heaven was like. But the terms in which he revealed this truth were the human experiences named above. We can read the Bible as literature by allowing it to immerse us in human experience as a way of clarifying it for us. That is what literature does, and it is what the Bible as literature does.

Literature is known by its distinctive genres or kinds of writing. The corresponding activity this requires is to allow our awareness of the diverse genres to guide our encounter with a given text in the Bible. When we read a story, we need to apply the usual narrative considerations of plot, setting, and character. When we read a poem, we need to identify the images and figures of speech, and then discover the meanings embodied in them. We need to operate on the premise that a prophetic oracle of judgment is a piece of satire. As such, it possesses an object of attack, a vehicle in which the attack is embodied, and a stated or implied satiric norm or standard of correctness by which the object of attack is being condemned or ridiculed.[5]

Another trait of literature is that it is artistic and a source of beauty in our lives. It is the product of creativity and technical skill. It offers something in the same category as listening to a piano recital or visiting an art gallery or strolling through a formal garden. To read the Bible as literature is to receive its artistry and beauty, taking time to recognize these aspects of a text and accepting their intended effect of enjoyment. The writer of Ecclesiastes includes in his philosophy of composition the statement that he "sought to find words of delight" (Eccles. 12:10). To read the Bible as literature is to notice and relish the delight we receive from the Bible's words and the larger compositions made out of them.

As you looked at this book's table of contents, you might have expected that the chapter on the Bible would somehow be an alternative to the literature discussed in the other chapters. The truth is the reverse. Our goal is to bring to bear on the Bible what this entire book discusses. We would handle the Bible so much better if we would read and interpret it in light of what we already know about literature generally. A great deal of damage has been done to our understanding of Scripture by practices that seal off the Bible in a world remote from the rest of our lives, including our literary experiences. Martin Luther desired "that there shall be as many poets and rhetoricians as possible, because I see that by these studies, as by no other ones, people are wonderfully fitted for the grasping of sacred truth and for handling it [by implication, the Bible] skillfully and happily."[6]

WHY SHOULD WE READ THE BIBLE AS LITERATURE?

The quick answer to the question of *why* we should read the Bible as literature is that we cannot read it fully *except* as literature. Because most of the Bible is literary in nature, we cannot avoid interacting with its literary features. We cannot read a story in the Bible without interacting with its plot, setting, and characters. We cannot assimilate a poem without encountering its images and figures of speech. People who are oblivious to these literary aspects of biblical texts may *think* they are getting by without literary analysis, but either they are performing literary analysis intuitively and unconsciously, or they are not really interacting with the Bible but with a substitute, probably in the form of context or "background information" or ideas someone has extracted from the Bible and passed on to them. Because the Bible is not a collection of directly stated ideas, *some* type of analysis of literary form is required before we can glean what the Bible says.

A second reason why we should read the Bible as literature is because doing so opens the door to experiencing the fullness of a text, as opposed to various and common types of reductionism. The starting premise for reading a passage in the Bible is to assume that everything the author put into the text is important and worthy of our attention and admiration. The details of setting in a story are there for a purpose. The parallelism of biblical poetry and some of its prose did not appear by accident but by design. Literary analysis is based on the practice of close reading of a text. It assumes that everything present in the text is important, no matter how remote it may *seem* (but probably is not) from the text's main purpose. This stands as an alternative to the reductionism extremely prominent in evangelical circles, namely, reducing every Bible passage to a set of ideas.

Reading the Bible as literature also opens the door to reading and teaching the whole Bible. If we are geared to read only idea-oriented expository prose, we do not know what to do with literary passages, especially ones belonging to unfamiliar genres. The solution to the problem is to acquaint ourselves with the Bible's range of literary genres, which is approximately the same as what is covered in high school and college literature courses.[7]

Another reason to read the Bible as literature is that this approach respects the author's intention. Evangelical biblical interpretation (hermeneutics) has championed the idea of authorial intention as the key concept, but it has not applied the concept widely enough. It stands to reason that whenever a biblical author entrusted his message to a literary form, he *intended* us to read the resulting work in a literary manner. To read in keeping with an author's intention means to read and interpret a text in light of its literary qualities.

Many additional answers to the question of "why" can be adduced, but we have space for only one more. Reading the Bible as literature offers a fresh experience of the Bible. The things that make our recreational reading a source of enjoyment can be transferred to our Bible reading. Most people who catch a vision for the literary approach to the Bible uniformly speak of how it rejuvenates their interest and joy in Bible reading and offers new angles of vision. Adding a literary dimension to Bible reading not only improves the accuracy of the enterprise but also carries Bible reading beyond duty to delight.

PART 3

———————

RECOVERING THE
ART OF READING

14

Recovery through Discovery

LIKE MANY ENGLISH WORDS, *recover* has multiple meanings. People recover when they enjoy renewed health after a time of illness. Another meaning is to find lost treasure. Recovering reading encompasses both those aspects. The general health of reading has declined in recent decades, and reading is a treasure worth recovering for the lasting value of its many pleasures.

The first part of this book showed how reading is becoming a lost art. The second one provided rationale for reading literature and offered coaching on how to enjoy several different genres or categories. This chapter begins our final part on recovering the art of reading. Because subsequent chapters explore specific aspects of the quest in depth, this chapter simply provides you with a coherent overview of a game plan for recovering artful reading.

Our plan follows the path taken when we are ill or lose something valuable. We first must recognize our poor health or realize the treasure is missing. After that, we can adopt a positive attitude and decide to do something about it. Then we implement helpful strategies toward recovery, trusting the Great Physician for healing and the Good Shepherd who finds the lost.

Similarly, the initial step in recovering reading is discovering the problem. We then discover personal perspectives to facilitate more artful reading. We read artfully by discovering truth, goodness, and beauty in literature. This helps us discover good books. Artful reading can enhance our spiritual life or even lead to discovering the Good News. The road to recovery lies through discovery.

DISCOVERING THE PROBLEM

This book's first chapter showed how thoughtful reading of good books seems to be waning. People may be spending more time scanning screens, but they are spending less time reading literature.

Many people have expressed concern over how Internet use affects the brain and about technological methods that manipulate users. While screen use can be addictive and damaging for any age, teens are especially susceptible to manipulation and addiction. Boys tend to get caught up in gaming, while girls usually vie to become popular on social media. Adults or young people who succumb to the screen's siren song often ignore family members and enriching activities like reading.

Our losses encompass more than squandered time and stunted brains. We're losing depth and wisdom, perhaps even a part of ourselves that jeopardizes our very souls. Losing thoughtful reading causes multiple losses for our culture and for each of us as individuals. Once we discover and acknowledge the problem's existence, we can adopt perspectives and take steps to recover artful reading.

DISCOVERING PERSPECTIVES

We begin to recover reading by nurturing positive perspectives within ourselves and our children. While other chapters discuss specific attitudes in more detail, we can summarize a comprehensive perspective by identifying three general categories. Individual readers can think of themselves as perusers, partners, and participants.

On its simplest level, a *peruser* is someone who reads. And reading is essential for recovering this lost art. The more we read, the better readers we become. Rather than view ourselves as unliterary people, we can think of ourselves as readers.

To peruse can also mean to read carefully and attentively. Instead of attempting to conquer a mountain of books on someone's list of great literature, we immerse ourselves into the story before us with open minds and wide eyes. When we read attentively, we become more aware of the work's artistry and increase our joy.

Artful reading takes more time than scanning. But rather than stressing about not having time to read, we can think in terms of having freedom to read. Instead of wasting precious minutes on meaningless activities, we can remind ourselves of our ability to make conscious choices. We have the freedom to choose reading's pleasure and refreshment.

A reader is also a *partner*, primarily with the author. A book on a shelf is inert. The writer has poured hours and effort into creating artistry and meaning for the reader's benefit, but its power and meaning flow only when someone opens the book and reads.

Writers and readers partner in the book's conversation. Annie Murphy Paul writes that readers "establish an intimate relationship with the author, the two of them engaged in an extended and ardent conversation like people falling in love."[1]

Most readers will never meet authors of the books they enjoy, but they can partner in more concrete community with fellow readers. We can find like-minded readers in our churches, local libraries, or bookstores. We can join or form book clubs or online discussions.

A reader is additionally a *participant*. Other chapters discuss at length how a reader participates in a literary work's art by receiving and responding to it. But a reader also participates in civilization's ongoing conversation.

The entire body of literature reflects humanity's hopes, goals, and thoughts throughout history. Literary works throbbed with civilization's heartbeat from the dawn of recorded history through its faint pulse during the Middle Ages to its contemporary erratic beat.

Literature distills the accumulated wisdom and beauty of the ages into a form available to any reader. In Tolkien's *The Two Towers*, Sam Gamgee speaks about "old songs and tales . . . that really mattered . . . [and] stay in the mind."[2] Readers share and contribute to this continuing conversation.

No individual can conceive or encounter everything in one lifetime, but through literature we learn from many lives. Gene Edward Veith Jr. writes,

> When ideas and experiences can be written down, they are, in effect, stored permanently. People are no longer bound by their own limited insights and experiences, but they can draw on those of other people as well. Instead of continually starting over again, people can build upon what others have discovered and have written down.[3]

Literature multiplies experiential knowledge and shares timeless meaning. Readers have the amazing opportunity to participate in humanity's ongoing conversation.

DISCOVERING GOOD BOOKS

Earlier chapters described characteristics of specific genres and later chapters will explore literary excellence and reading good books. At this point, we want to focus on discovering or choosing those good books.

Why do we close a book, sigh, and think, "That was a good book!"? What makes us wish we could keep reading it? The characters stick in our minds as we go through the motions of daily duties. Good books make us think. It's been said, "The book to read is not the one that thinks for you, but the one which makes you think. No book in the world equals the Bible for that."[4]

We long to read good books again, and they can be enjoyed repeatedly with increasing delight. C. S. Lewis called the desire to reread "a good test for every reader of every kind of book."[5]

But the desire to reread shouldn't guide all our book choices. We should expand our horizons into new genres and authors. Some readers stick to books they view as safe. Books that won't surprise or upset them. The kind found in church libraries or Christian bookstores turned coffee shops. While an increasing number of works within the Christian market show spiritual subtleties and literary skill, many others are overtly evangelistic and aesthetically poor.

Each reader has to recognize personal limits. Someone who struggles with specific temptations or anxiety or depression does well to avoid books that could trigger problems, especially when going through a difficult season. But readers in general shouldn't limit themselves to banal books that never cause uncomfortable feelings or expand the spirit. These novels fail to acknowledge either life's pain or its beauty. Reading fluff that generates warm fuzzies is like eating cotton candy. A steady diet of spun sugar would be far from healthy.

Some Christians err too far in the other direction by promoting gritty realism, which teems with disturbing images and language. Of course, we should avoid pornography and graphic violence, no matter its claims of redemptive value. We need to discover a balance.

An artful reader may read dark fiction depicting the biblical reality of broken people living in a fallen world. Genuinely realistic fiction, however, should be pierced by glimmers of redemption's light. The author depicts characters who are neither unbelievably perfect nor unnecessarily debased. The reader expects imperfections and depictions of sin but recognizes redemptive aspects. Fiction can be realistic without being vulgar, evangelistic without being didactic, and beautiful without being esoteric.

DISCOVERING THE TRUE, GOOD, AND BEAUTIFUL

We've presented the true, the good, and the beautiful as foundational in shaping our perspective for reading literature. Plato is credited as the originator of the triad, but we believe it reflects a more ancient source: the Ancient of Days.[6] Long before Plato instructed students in his philosophies, God taught his people about his truth, goodness, and beauty. God himself and his word provide a basis for an aesthetic encompassing the true, the good, and the beautiful.

These three elements are interwoven with each other and reflect characteristics of God. Clyde Kilby wrote: "Beauty, truth, and goodness are not one entity and therefore are not to be totally equated; yet the entire history of thought indicates that they are to be closely related. The believer will see them related, not only to each other but to that Ultimate Beauty, Truth, and Goodness at the apex of his pyramid, even the Lord God Almighty."[7]

"All truth is from God," John Calvin wrote.[8] God speaks the truth (Isa. 45:19), and the sum of his word is truth (Ps. 119:160). Jesus identified himself as the truth (John 14:6) and asked the Father to sanctify his people in the truth, which is his word (John 17:17). When we read, we want to ask, "How is it true?"

Jesus declared that no one is good except God alone (Mark 10:18, Luke 18:19). God's name is good (Ps. 52:9), and everything he created is good (1 Tim. 4:4). In six successive days, God spoke into existence light, sky, land and plants, heavenly bodies, fish and birds, and animals. Each day God saw every element of creation doing what it was created to do, and he viewed it all as good. Then God formed the first man and woman as his image-bearers, endowed with eternal souls, intelligence, speech, and moral responsibility. After this crowning point, God indicated creation's completeness and perfection by seeing everything as "very good" (Genesis 1). Our Creator God sets the good, even the very good, as an artistic standard. A second way to evaluate literature is to ask, "How is it good?"

But the true and the good are not sufficient criteria for artistic excellence. As Kilby wrote: "To believe in God involves accepting Him as the sovereign perfection, not only of truth and goodness, but also of beauty, thus establishing the highest possible conceptions of excellence."[9] Only faith in a sovereign God enables us to form an artistic paradigm that is correct, honorable, and admirable.

The Bible teems with depictions of God's beauty, details for beautiful worship items, and the beauties of creation. God shines forth from the perfection of beauty (Ps. 50:2), and the psalmist longs to spend all his days gazing upon the beauty of the Lord (Ps. 27:4). Articles for worship were crafted skillfully from valuable and colorful materials "for glory and beauty" (Ex. 28:2, 40). Multiple psalms extol the way creation proclaims God's glory and sovereignty (i.e., Psalms 8; 19; 95; 96). Romans 1:20 assures us that the entire cosmos declares God's glory so effectively that no one is without excuse. The *Belgic Confession* calls the creation a "most elegant book."[10] Beauty in our world reflects the beauty of God himself. In reading literature, we can ask a third question, "How is it beautiful?"

DISCOVERING THE GOOD NEWS

Biblical standards for truth, goodness, and beauty apply to all people in all cultures, whether or not they acknowledge God and his word. In recent decades, literary anthologies have expanded to include much literature from outside the Western tradition. These literary works help us empathize with people whose history and experiences are far different from our own. Why have various cultures developed in such diverse ways? The Bible is the primary factor in shaping perspectives that respect God's law and value human life and dignity.

Vishal Mangalwadi comprehensively supports this claim in *The Book That Made Your World: How the Bible Created the Soul of Western Civilization*. He relates a fascinating account of how he came to a biblical understanding of values. Alone in the darkness one night, after the electricity had gone out, he muses: "Standards of beauty, as of morals, indeed differed from culture to culture and age to age. Did that make all values subjective? Even in the twentieth century, we had entire castes in India whose socially sanctioned profession was to steal. Was stealing then merely cultural preference, or was it bad in itself?"

He continues, "Sitting in that dark room, my mind was illuminated by the little phrase, 'And God saw that the light was good.' It gave a credible explanation of why we make value judgments:

> *Moral judgments:* This is good; that is evil.
> *Aesthetic judgments:* This is beautiful; that is ugly.
> *Epistemological judgments:* That is true; this is false."

Mangalwadi reflects on how Genesis "explains beauty" in the God-planted garden with pleasant trees and "describes human choices and actions that God said were not good. Could it be that we make value judgments because they are intrinsic to what it means to be a person (like God), as opposed to being mere animals?"

He concludes, "I began to get excited about the Bible because it provided me with explanations. It made greater sense of who I was—a godlike person with a capacity to know, experience, and enjoy goodness, beauty, and truth."[11] Scriptural truth opened Mangalwadi's eyes to the good news of human value and the Bible's timeless standards for making value judgments.

The Bible is the infallible word of God, but it is also literature. Many works of literature can help readers discover the good news. Reading poems or novels or fantasy or nonfiction enriches our lives, including the spiritual component. Reading can bring us closer to God, or may even be the vehicle God uses to draw us to saving faith in him.

Our journey to recover reading begins with acknowledging the problem and implementing positive perspectives. It progresses through the discovery of good books, which reflect (or remind us of) biblical standards. Scripture shapes cultures that embrace each person's worth and make accurate value judgments. Artful reading of good literature enriches even our spiritual lives.

15

Truth in Literature

PILATE ASKED JESUS, "What is truth?" (John 18:38). Philosophers have debated the famous question throughout history, and Pilate didn't recognize the incarnate truth standing before him. Christians know truth as an objective reality based on the Bible. But as discussed in chapter 12 on creative nonfiction, the topic of truth in literature can be complex.

We should realize that ideational or conceptual truth is not the only category of truth that exists. Truth comes to us in forms other than ideas. In the following discussion, such words as *knowledge* and *understanding* help supplement the word *truth*. But before we explore forms and assess literature's truth claims, we should become aware of certain fallacies.

FALLACIES ABOUT TRUTH IN LITERATURE

It's helpful to begin by clearing the field of four common fallacies. They are:

1. Literature by definition tells the truth.
2. All literature tells the truth.
3. Literature's usefulness depends on its ideational truth.
4. Works of literature make no truth claims.

Fallacy 1: *Literature by Definition Tells the Truth*. This fallacy rests on the truth that works of literature embody themes or ideas. Many people incorrectly equate ideas with truth. Ideas can be either true or false. It confuses categories to equate ideational *content* in literature (the presence of ideas) with intellectual *truth*. The confusion is prevalent, and many literary scholars have added to it in efforts to promote their favored discipline.

Fallacy 2: *All Literature Tells the Truth*. The premise here is that all literature asserts a common truth. For example, a literary scholar claims, "[W]e may say of the greatest pagan and Christian poets that they 'are folded in a single party.'"[1] This ecumenical inclusiveness usually is an attempt to avoid criticizing a much-loved author or work. But such protectionism is unnecessary because we can reject one aspect of a work while embracing other aspects.

Two facts disprove the notion that all literature tells the truth. First, truth itself is not contradictory, so not all the ideas in literature can be true. We do not need to read many literary works to sense how authors contradict each other in their ideas about life, their moral outlooks, and their worldviews. Second, much literature written through the centuries has not espoused a Christian worldview and value structure, so we cannot make a blanket statement about literature as a whole telling the truth.

Fallacy 3: *Literature's Usefulness Depends on Its Ideational Truth*. Many of the exaggerated claims about truth in literature spring from a desire to refute utilitarian arguments against literature. Through the centuries, a twofold formula bequeathed by the Roman author Horace has governed defenses of literature. Whatever specific terms are used, the dual formula is that literature is pleasurable (yielding a hedonistic defense of literature) and useful (yielding a utilitarian defense of literature). Because the second criterion trumps the first one in our modern era, defenders of literature are busy scrambling to prove that literature is useful. This maneuver quickly introduces the concept of truth into the mix, as the usefulness of literature is said to depend on the truth we find there.

But we cannot allow our desire to defend literature against its detractors to lead us into incorrect statements about literature. Nor do we need to. As earlier chapters have demonstrated, multiple good defenses of literature exist. Among other considerations, truth manifests itself in different categories. Even when literature promotes truth as Christians understand it, the usefulness of literature does not depend solely on ideational truth.

Fallacy 4: *Works of Literature Make No Truth Claims.* This is the exact opposite of the previous fallacies. It is the product of philosophical skepticism. Often it is part of an aesthetic philosophy that goes by the name of "art for art's sake," which claims that literary works are purely artistic objects whose sphere is beauty but not truth.

Several considerations counter this viewpoint. The first is that authors themselves claim to advocate truth in their works. William Wordsworth said poetry's "object is truth."[2] Novelist Joyce Cary asserted that "the great writers are obsessed with their theme," defined as a firm conception of "what is right and wrong."[3] Flannery O'Conner believed that "the basis of art is truth."[4]

Leading literary critics agree. One of them believes "the rule of significance" is the primary convention of literature, by which he means that we should read books "as expressing a significant attitude to some problem concerning man and/or his relation to the universe."[5] And literary scholar Gerald Graff states two good reasons for accepting the view "that literary works make assertions. Briefly put, the arguments are that authors intend assertions and readers can scarcely help looking for them."[6]

REPRESENTATIONAL TRUTH IN LITERATURE

Literature is a hybrid form. With the sister arts of painting and music, it shares artistic form and beauty. But because literature consists of words, it also has a foot in philosophy. Most people assign literature to philosophy's realm and assume that literary truth is ideational only. Literature *does* embody and assert ideas, but its distinctive contribution to the realm of truth does not lie here.

We can profitably begin by exploring the parallel between literature and the nonverbal art form of painting. What type of truth would we ascribe to a landscape by John Constable? Not ideational truth but representational truth. Representational truth is truthfulness to reality and human experience. If a work of literature or art *presents* or *portrays* life accurately, it can be said to be a *truthful* representation of human experience and the external world. It is an embodiment of the way things are and can be said to tell the truth about life as we experience it.

Representational truth is a category not ordinarily associated with the concept of truth, so a leading task of those who teach and write on the subject of representational truth is to educate the public in the matter. Ideational truth is not literature's specialty; representational truth is. Before literary authors can offer an interpretation of life in the form of implied ideas, they need to *portray* life.

The case for the representational truth's primacy in literature will seem more plausible if we unpack its dimensions. The literary author's chief gift is the ability to observe life accurately, including the inner world of emotions and spiritual experience as well as the outer world of people, actions, and objects. Overwhelmingly, storytellers and poets tell us the truth at this observational level. The classical tradition viewed literature as an *imitation* of life, and even after that terminology dropped out of vogue twenty centuries later, the concept has remained.

How do we assimilate the representational truth of literature? We join the author in contemplating life. The author stared at life first-hand and portrayed it in words. As we read a story or poem, we look at the world with the author, experiencing it secondhand. We need to keep reminding ourselves this includes the inner world of thought and feeling. Seeing life accurately is a form of knowledge, which we can call right seeing and feeling. Useful synonyms are *understanding* and *awareness*. Literature *raises our awareness* about various aspects of life and the external world, so we might think of truth in terms of *being aware*. Seeing things accurately ranks high on the list of knowledge worth having. *Not* seeing things accurately is a huge handicap to carry through life.

We can clarify by considering Jesus's parable of the good Samaritan (Luke 10:30–34). The story itself avoids abstract or conceptual truth. The lawyer asked Jesus to define *neighbor* ("And who is my neighbor?" 10:29), and Jesus refused the direct invitation. Instead he told a story in which all meaning is incarnated in character and action. As we read or listen to the parable, we *see* what neighborly behavior is, and we *feel* its various aspects. We become *aware* of what it means to be a neighbor and also what it means to avoid being a neighbor. Jesus's story teems with truth, but it is not conveyed abstractly or conceptually.

IDEATIONAL TRUTH IN LITERATURE

Ideas are present in literature and are an important part of literary experience. We do not initially encounter them as we read, but it is important to give ideas their due attention in our reflection on a literary work. We can enjoy literary works that simply entertain, but such books seem shallow compared to ones that make us think. British fiction writer Graham Greene divided his stories into the categories of "entertainments" and "novels," and the distinction holds true to our experience of literature generally. Both categories can have a place in our reading.

Literature's embodied ideas are not stated as ideas in the works themselves. Ideas are indirectly shown instead of directly told. If an author veers toward the telling side, we intuitively sense the literary nature becoming diluted. Our task as readers is to infer embedded ideas. Making intellectual sense of a story or poem might be thought of as moving from the work itself to meaning. This interpretive task falls on the reader because the writer does not hand over ideas as a list.

We can move with confidence from text to theme, if we follow some simple guidelines. We need to start with the story or poem, which presents human experience concretely. What is the work about? The more substantial the work, the longer the list. In addition to *presentations*, authors offer implied *interpretations*. What does the work convey about the presented experience? We can think of a reader's division of duties as determining (1) the experience a work presents, and (2) what the work implicitly says about that experience. The terms *topic* and *theme* are commonly used for these two elements.

Consider the following helpful tips. First, the process described above will take a wrong turn if we do not thoroughly interact with the text of a story or poem. Correct interpretation depends on our reliving the text so we genuinely know what we need to interpret. Second, most of the time we are not searching for *the one right* formulation of topic and theme. The whole bent of literature is to do justice to the multiplicity and ambiguity of real life, so our tendency should be to see a plurality of topics and interpretive angles. Third, authors preside through their works as travel guides. They employ devices of disclosure to nudge readers in the right interpretive direction.

ASSESSING LITERATURE'S TRUTH CLAIMS

We can enjoy a literary work's beauty and representational truth at face value. But ideas require the further step of assessing the work's truth claims. Believers do this in light of our biblical convictions, a process which Christian critics and schools refer to as the integration of literature with the Christian faith.

As used in an academic context, to integrate means to bring the data of a discipline into dialogue with the Christian faith, with the further understanding that the Christian faith serves as the standard of truth. The process of literary analysis begins in the same way for every reader—by reliving the text as fully as possible. We initially determine what the author embedded and intended in a work, and then we complete the task by comparing those claims to our own framework of truth. Modern poet and critic T. S. Eliot is the definitive source on the subject. Here is his oft-quoted statement: "Literary criticism should be completed by criticism from a definite ethical and theological standpoint. . . . It is . . . necessary for Christian readers to scrutinize their reading, especially of works of imagination, with explicit ethical and theological standards."[7] In this comparative process, we place a literary work's truth claims beside what the Bible and Christian doctrine say about the same subjects.

This extra-literary exercise moves us beyond literature into the separate realm of Christian belief. Secular perspectives or twisted teaching too often warp our spiritual views. Like the Bereans, we must examine the Scriptures to see if the ideas presented and our own thoughts are true (Acts 17:11). This intellectual process may require online research or looking up concepts in theological or religious books to reach a deeper understanding of Christian doctrine. The most profitable process humbly ascertains what the Bible and Christian doctrine assert. Then we can construct a dialogue between Christian truth and the truth claims of a literary work (or an author's corpus of writings) to see where the writer has hit the bull's-eye of truth or missed the target completely.

We shouldn't feel intimidated about judging an author to have missed the mark. Francis Schaeffer has said "as Christians, we must see that just because . . . a great artist portrays a world view in writing or on canvas, it does not mean that we should automatically accept that world view."[8]

An additional reason why we should be unapologetic about disagreeing with some truth claims in a work is that there are almost certainly other elements that we can affirm. We can appreciate skill of composition, artistic beauty, an accurate and clarifying portrayal of life, and maybe even some of the author's ideas. As an addendum, we also need to scrutinize Christian authors from a biblical and doctrinal vantage point; they are not infallible and do not always get everything right.

Literature may or may not tell the truth at an ideational level. But it can serve as a stimulus to our thinking about matters of truth and error. Readers who compare literature to biblical doctrine will find their knowledge of Christian truth greatly expanded over the course of time.

As we look at the total landscape of literature from a standpoint of Christian truth, we can picture it as existing on a continuum. On one end is explicitly Christian literature. At the other pole, we find the literature of unbelief. The literature of common human experience (which can also be considered the literature of clarification) forms the middle of the continuum. As the common wisdom of the human race, it clarifies the human condition to which the Christian faith speaks. While not explicitly Christian, it is congruent with Christianity. It may even have been written by a Christian.

Readers may also find it helpful to envision two overlapping circles. The left one represents Christian belief. The right one expresses truth as asserted by other religious and ethical systems. There is a middle overlapping body of truth that we can call inclusively Christian, meaning that it includes Christianity and other systems of belief. The non-overlapping part of the left circle represents exclusively Christian belief, not shared by other systems, and the non-overlapping part of the right circle represents anti-Christian truth claims.

CONCLUDING WITH SIMPLICITY

We began this chapter by describing the topic of truth in literature as complex. As we conclude, we offer balance by affirming the ideas embodied in literature as simple. They convey the ideas of common humanity. In the high art of the sonnet, Shakespeare relates how time flies. William Wordsworth's poetry shows nature as beautiful and healing to the human spirit. Homer's *Odyssey* describes home and family as worthy of our devotion.

No wonder Renaissance poet Sir Philip Sidney called the literary author "the right popular philosopher," meaning how literature presents the simple, bedrock ideas by which the human race orders its affairs.[9] Novelist Walker Percy claimed literature tells the reader "something he already knows but which he doesn't quite know that he knows" and shows "people the deep human truths which they already unconsciously know."[10] When we ponder the literature we read, we often feel that we have come home to the truth.

16

The Moral Vision in Literature

OSCAR WILDE ONCE declared that "there is no such thing as a moral or an immoral book. Books are well written, or badly written. That is all."[1] His statement codifies the modern view of morality in literature. Before the twentieth century, people universally accepted literature's moral aspect and viewed it as the contributing factor to literary significance. People regarded the accuracy of a work's moral vision as part of its greatness, and they understood that a leading goal of literature was to move a reader to better behavior. But at the end of the nineteenth century, the modern view created a great gap between it and the older view. C. S. Lewis reflected the traditional perspective in saying, "the ethical is the aesthetic *par excellence*."[2] In other words, the moral is the best artistic expression. A genuine Christian faith excludes no aspect of life from moral responsibility and judgment, even reading.

Reaching a correct understanding of literature and the moral life requires careful attention to specific issues, but the overall strategy is simple. Three factors determine whether our literary reading is moral or immoral: the subject matter of a literary work, the moral perspective embodied within it, and the work's moral effect on a given reader. Once we understand the three-fold strategy, we can apply its principles to become moral readers.

Before exploring our central topics, we need to define morality and discuss how it operates in the reading life. Morality deals with human actions, especially between one person and another. Since narrative (including drama) is the genre that most fully portrays human conduct, this chapter most obviously pertains to stories. To extract a moral vision from lyric poetry requires a more active interpretive hand, but some of this chapter's content carries over to poetry.

What readers regard as moral or immoral depends on the ethical system they as individuals accept as correct. For Christians the Bible determines what is moral and immoral. In the foundational triad of the true, the good, and the beautiful, morality claims the good as its province. Identifying the system of virtues and vices being advocated in a narrative helps determine the moral vision of a literary work.

SUBJECT MATTER

Literature's moral vision begins at the level of subject matter. By its nature, literature puts models of behavior before us. Sometimes a work depicts moral actions, and sometimes it presents examples of immoral actions. We need to proceed thoughtfully here, because the mere portrayal of bad behavior does not automatically indicate immoral literature. The best example is the Bible, which presents continuous examples of immorality without becoming an immoral book.

We also need to avoid the opposite pitfall of viewing the literary portrayal of immoral action as having *no* moral implication. Plato was partly wrong in his claim that when literature depicts immoral conduct "the contagion *must* pass" from the characters in a story to a reader, with the implication the effect is automatic.[3] But we agree with Plato that the contagion *can* and often *does* infiltrate a reader's thinking and behavior. How this happens deserves careful consideration.

When we read literature and view movies, we encounter images (broadly defined to include action and characters) that we absorb with our minds and emotions. These images become the furniture of our imaginations. Some images naturally refine and redeem and sanctify. In a noble treatise of literary theory, Renaissance poet Sir Philip Sidney noted how some literature encourages the will "to that which deserveth to be called and accounted good."[4] The effects of other images are coarse, cheapening, and degrading. In Sidney's words, such literary works "infect the fancy [an old word for *imagination*] with unworthy objects."[5]

Over the course of time, we become the sum of our indulgences, including the books we read and the movies we watch. If we habitually fill our minds with images of sex, we become obsessed with it and begin to objectify people. If we continuously read and watch acts of violence, we become numbed to brutality. When characters or actors exhibit positive examples of generosity or compassion, we are moved to emulate these virtues. The strategy of literature is to give form to our feelings and impulses. These feelings and impulses are a mixture of good and bad, waiting to be encouraged or discouraged by outward stimuli. Some literary subject matter awakens the wrong impulses, such as condoning every form of self-expression or unrestraint or sexual license or defiance of traditional moral standards. Other literature encourages good impulses, such as honesty or courage or self-control or compassion. Additionally, the more we expose ourselves to portrayals of immoral attitudes and conduct, the more normal they seem. We may condone, promote, or even embrace immorality. On the other side, when we see virtuous behavior in a story or drama, we find our desire to be virtuous strengthened.

Although literature's subject matter can be influential, the depiction of human depravity or virture is not the only factor. It depends on what the work as a whole does *with* the depravity or virtue that is portrayed.

MORAL PERSPECTIVE

The perspective built into a literary work is generally a more reliable guide to its moral vision than subject matter alone. When writers portray models of behavior, they suggest an attitude toward such conduct. Even authorial silence about an event—for example, a straightforward account of dishonesty or adultery with no apparent consequences—can imply the author's approval. Writers employ calculated strategies to influence readers to approve of some things and disapprove of others. Authors additionally use devices of disclosure to shape a reader's approval pattern.

T. S. Eliot wrote: "When we read of human beings behaving in certain ways, with the approval of the author, who gives his benediction to this behavior by his attitude toward the result of the behavior arranged by himself, we can be influenced towards behaving in the same way."[6] Literary authors can influence our moral thinking and conduct through the behavioral models they put before us, through the way they arrange outcomes of behaviors, and through the embedded attitude toward the behavior and its results. Another literary scholar has similarly noted that "a novelist selects both what he represents and how he represents it."[7]

If we understand how works of literature embody perspectives toward the subject matter being depicted, we can identify moral literature and immoral literature. Moral literature "recommends moral as opposed to immoral behaviour."[8] A story or poem can incarnate a moral perspective by many different methods:

- making the good appear attractive or ultimately satisfying (even though there may be a price tag for doing the right thing)

- showing that immoral acts do not bring ultimate satisfaction
- displaying models of moral behavior in a way that makes the reader wish to imitate them
- generating final sympathy for moral characters
- exposing the self-destructive nature of evil
- including foils (something showing contrasting qualities) to immoral behavior as a way of showing the power of choice to resist evil
- unmasking the personally or socially destructive consequences of evil

Moral literature does not avoid evil as a subject, but it finds ways to discredit it.

Immoral literature is the opposite of these things. It recommends immoral behavior for our approval. It does so by:

- making immoral acts attractive
- valorizing immoral characters
- denigrating moral characters and actions
- portraying evil as something that brings satisfaction
- omitting moral characters and behavior to serve as a foil to immoral ones
- treating immoral acts with a comic tone that prompts a reader to acquiesce in something immoral
- depicting immoral acts as something irresistible
- treating immoral acts as normal

Writers incorporate perspectives in their works both by the nature of the models they choose to depict and the attitude they imply toward the characters and actions portrayed. Samuel Taylor Coleridge's comment about moral tone provides a good summary: "Shakespeare always makes vice odious and virtue admirable, while Beaumont and

Fletcher do the very reverse—they ridicule virtue and encourage vice: they pander to the lowest and basest passions of our nature."[9]

THE HEART OF THE MATTER: A READER'S RESPONSE

We've considered the moral tendencies within a literary work in the dual form of subject matter and the embedded perspective toward that subject matter. But these two aspects of literature are not the most crucial determinants of a work's morality or immorality. Our claim here may seem surprising; however, the depicted experiences and the author's attitude do not produce automatic results. Books themselves have never committed murder or adultery; they have never stolen or lied. Nor have books performed moral feats of honesty or compassion or love. Literature becomes moral or immoral only as it is assimilated by a reader and translated into thoughts or acts. Even reading the Bible does not automatically produce moral behavior.

We encourage thinking of readers and reading experiences as being moral or immoral, more than labeling works of literature. It is not wrong to speak of books, plays, and poems as embodying a moral or immoral tendency, as long as we realize that the reader's response is the ultimate moral determiner. Moral readers can resist prompts toward immorality in such a way as to make the reading experience a moral one. The medieval storyteller Boccaccio wrote that literary authors "are not corruptors of morals. Rather, if the reader is prompted by a healthy mind, not a diseased one, they will prove actual stimulators to virtue."[10] We reiterate the key criteria: "if the reader is prompted by a healthy mind, not a diseased one."

No good reason exists for immersing ourselves in literature that portrays immoral behavior and recommends immoral attitudes. We have good reason to worry about readers with an insatiable appetite for such literature. Unless we know how a reader is assimilating a specific work of literature, however, we should be slow to judge. When a friend or family member consumes literature glorifying immoral attitudes or acts, we should compassionately explore how or why it is being assimilated.

BECOMING A MORAL READER

If we accept the foregoing premises, we recognize the crucial element in literature and morality as the individual reader. Our thoughts now turn to our own reading experience. How can we become moral readers?

The first step is to refuse to be intimidated by modern society's claims regarding literature and morality. A common current declaration of the secular academy is that literature does not possess a moral dimension. Ordinary readers in the culture at large put that assumption into practice. But the claim about literature as beyond moral considerations is easily refuted. The author of *The Moral Measure of Literature* correctly writes that moral standards "are as relevant to literature as they are to life itself. . . . If the subject matter of literary art is the full range of human values, then ethical principles are always relevant."[11] In a similar vein, a Shakespeare scholar asserts that "if all deliberate action has a moral bearing, Shakespeare's description of the moral world is but a name for his collected works."[12]

Books and movies always evoke a response of approval or disapproval toward the material presented. Personal response has a potential to be either moral or immoral. Reading literature is not a merely external event such as viewing a landscape. Instead it is an internal event like eating and digesting food. Just as the food that we ingest affects our physical health for good or ill, the moral input that we take in affects our moral being. The indifference of contemporary society to the morality of literature is simply an extension of its indifference to ethical standards in general. Most non-Christians go to the latest movie or read a current bestseller without a thought about the work's morality. Christians, however, resonate with Plato's statement about literature's effect: "Great is the issue at stake, greater than appears: whether a person is to be good or bad."[13]

Convinced of literature's potential for moral or immoral influence in our lives, we need to scrutinize and monitor the moral effect of what we read or view. For Christians, the best form of censorship is self-imposed. It begins with awareness of how our literary experiences influence our thinking and behavior. If a work of literature is prompting us to immoral thoughts or actions, we either need to stop reading the book or exercise stronger control over its influence. Literary works are moral and immoral persuaders, but as readers we need not be convinced against our will. If you find your moral control relaxing, you need to strengthen your resolve.

Instead of viewing this topic solely in terms of resisting literature's immoral effects, we should also remember to consider the positive side. We can respond in ways that enhance literature's moral influence. Karen Swallow Prior writes about literature's potential for morality: "Literature embodies virtue, first, by offering images of virtue in action and, second, by offering the reader vicarious practice in exercising virtue."[14] Vicarious experience can actualize in daily living.

Most readers do not perceive literature as a potential ally in living morally because our education and culture do not train us to look for its moral dimension. Being aware of literature's moral ingredient is the first step. We need to identify the nature of both moral and immoral literary examples. Having named the virtues and vices displayed in a work, we should resolve to imitate the virtues and repudiate the vices. This is not, as sometimes claimed, a simplistic approach to literature; it is demonstrably how literature works.

But how do we know what moral and immoral behavior is? Chapter 15's section on assessing literature's truth claims described comparing the ideas in a literary work to what the Bible says on those same subjects. We also need to exercise this comparative process to assess the moral claims in a work of literature. The more our literary excursions send us to the Bible, the better we expand our grasp of Christian ethics.

Oscar Wilde's claim that "there is no such thing as a moral or an immoral book" falsifies both the nature of literature and what happens when we read. Literature portrays human conduct, both good and bad, and it does so from an embedded perspective. While subject matter and perspective play a part in the moral effect of literature, the ultimate determiner of moral influence rests with readers. In this way, reading becomes a sphere for developing and practicing moral discernment.

17

Beauty in Literature

MY MOTHER AND I (Glenda) once sat at the kitchen table, reading
the biblical directives found in Exodus 28 for the construction of the
priestly garments. Gold and fine linen were "skillfully worked" with
blue, purple, and scarlet yarns into colorful vestments. An onyx stone,
engraved with six names of the sons of Israel, was secured to each
shoulder of the high priest's ephod by gold filigree. Two chains of pure
gold, twisted like cords, connected the set stones. The breast piece,
connected to the ephod's shoulders with gold rings and twisted chains,
gleamed with twelve gems, each engraved with the name of a son of
Israel. The rainbow of colors included yellow topaz, red carbuncle,
green emerald, blue sapphire, white diamond, purple amethyst, and
aquamarine beryl. The hem of the priest's blue robe featured gold bells
between pomegranates woven from blue, purple, and scarlet yarns.
Coats and caps for each priest were worked in fine linen, and sashes
were embroidered with needlework. Fastened to the front of Aaron's
turban was a plate of pure gold, engraved with the words: "Holy to
the LORD" (Ex. 28:36).

After reading these vivid descriptions, Mom and I paused thoughtfully. She said, "It's easy to see how people got the idea for wearing
their Sunday best to church." It is indeed.

Beauty matters to God. In his directions for constructing the tabernacle and the items associated with worship, God prescribed the finest materials and expert craftsmanship. His instructions reached their epitome when it came to the intricate and colorful construction of the priestly garments. Before giving their specifics, God declared their purpose was "for glory and for beauty" (Ex. 28:2). And after describing the detailed designs, God reiterated that twofold purpose (Ex. 28:40).

While we finite humans cannot fully comprehend the symbolism of the valuable materials and their specific designs, one thing we know with certainty is that the priestly garments were intended for beauty as well as God's glory. We understand that God deserves glory, but how often do we consider a biblical perspective of beauty?

The two previous chapters examined the true and the good. This chapter explores this foundational triad's third aspect: beauty. Just as truth belongs to the intellectual realm and goodness to the moral realm, beauty belongs to the aesthetic realm. Beauty is a crucial characteristic of art. It is what makes objects, including literature, artistic. A written work could be good and true, but without beauty it is not art.

A definition of beauty may be elusive, but we can begin by looking at what God says about it. A biblical basis will help us shape a balanced perspective and appreciate beauty's significance, which then will lead us to an exploration of the artistic experience and beauty's expression.

GOD'S BEAUTY

How should we understand the glorious and beautiful twofold purpose of the priestly garments? God certainly did not intend people to worship by focusing on a human's glory or a garment's beauty. The only appropriate worship focus is God himself. The excellence and artistry of the garments symbolized God's perfection and beauty. The priests' garbed splendor generated an awareness of God's beauty, which resulted in his glory. The people also enjoyed the visual beauty as a gift God bestows to humanity in the world.

God is the source of all beauty and is himself beautiful. Zechariah 9:17 extols these attributes of the Lord: "For how great is his goodness, and how great his beauty!" We can imagine supreme goodness, but how can we comprehend the beauty of the God who is "immortal" and "invisible" (1 Tim. 1:17)?

When David desires to dwell in God's house and "gaze upon the beauty of the LORD" (Ps. 27:4), it is God himself he longs to see. The beautiful elements of the tabernacle were not worship-worthy in themselves but pointed to "the perfection of beauty" in which "God shines forth" from Zion (Ps. 50:2). God's "strength and beauty" are apparent "in his sanctuary" and believers should worship the Lord "in the splendor of holiness" (Ps. 96:6, 9).

Scripture's references to God's beauty seem an attempt to express the inexpressible. These texts teem with mystery that will be fully revealed only when our "eyes will behold the king in his beauty; they will see a land that stretches afar" (Isa. 33:17). It is as though beauty does not define God, but God defines beauty.

CHRISTIAN PERSPECTIVE

While unbelievers and Christians can agree on many aspects of beauty, secular philosophies will only lead us astray. As Clyde Kilby says, "Clear as a trail through the forest may appear, it is valueless if it leads in the wrong direction, and this I think is inevitable when beauty is separated from Ultimate Beauty."[1] Our concept of beauty is rooted in the biblical view of God as beautiful and as the source of beauty.

Various cultures throughout history have viewed beauty differently. Modern definitions pull from the past or simplify beauty's meaning to merely individual opinion or taste. But because God conveys eternal truth about beauty in his word, the beautiful has an absolute aspect that transcends cultures and historical periods. Christians need not accept either past or modern worldly concepts, including the popular idea that beauty is whatever a particular culture in a certain time thinks. We can embrace a balanced and biblical perspective of beauty that is timeless.

Because beauty is such a crucial element of art, our understanding of it cannot be separated from our artistic perspective. Kilby provides helpful direction. "Aesthetics, of course, is not Christianity any more than beauty is God. Genuine Christianity will never make the mistake of which non-Christians are sometimes guilty, that of substituting art for God," he writes. "Beauty, then, is not king but only prime minister. Not a servant, it nevertheless delights to serve because of its concinnity with the king and his entire kingdom."[2] Although I (Glenda) had to look up "concinnity," I wanted to use this quotation because the word applies perfectly to our discussion. *Merriam-Webster* defines concinnity as "harmony or elegance of design especially of literary style in adaptation of parts to a whole or to each other."[3] Beauty serves God and his kingdom in an honored and lofty position by creating harmony and elegance within artistic creations and literary works.

Kilby further notes how a Christian perspective "avoids either of two unwarranted extremes: the elevation of beauty to equality with God and the degradation of it to pretty ornamentation, without essential value."[4] Earthly beauty is neither the divine nor mere decoration.

Between those opposite ends of the spectrum, too few Christians can articulate a clear perspective about beauty. Some view it as the esoteric province of high art aficionados and, therefore, beyond the scope of ordinary people. Perhaps you've heard (or said), "I don't know anything about art, but I know what I like." While tastes and expertise vary, anyone can see and enjoy beauty in artistic works. Knowing God's emphasis on beauty in his word persuades us of the importance of developing a balanced and biblical perspective.

BEAUTY'S SIGNIFICANCE

A common adage proclaims beauty as being in the eyes of the beholder, which seems true to a certain extent. After all, different people see things differently and have varying tastes in art, music, and literature. Some viewers find the vibrant colors and bold strokes of impressionism most appealing, while others prefer realistic portraits or reverential landscapes. Some people listen to classical music, while others turn to a modern rock station. When it comes to literature, some readers consume Agatha Christie's cozy mysteries, while others mull over Flannery O'Conner's startling stories.

Although people have different tastes, true beauty has timeless and lasting significance. John Keats famously wrote, "A thing of beauty is a joy for ever," but he didn't end his poem there. He noted how its "loveliness increases" and removes the pall from "our dark spirits." He spoke about the beauties of nature and then referred to literature by saying,

> All lovely tales that we have heard or read:
> An endless fountain of immortal drink,
> Pouring unto us from the heaven's brink.

He then wrote that all essences of beauty "haunt us till they become a cheering light / Unto our souls" and how "they always must be with us, or we die."[5]

Keats viewed beauty as generating joy and having eternal significance. The meaning of something beautiful increases in our minds over time and lifts our spirits. Beautiful literature provides an endless supply of heavenly nourishment. The essence of beauty speaks to our very souls, staying with us and increasing our joy. Indeed, Keats sees beauty as such a crucial aspect of life that unless we are always aware of it, we are as good as dead.

We have seen the biblical link between God and beauty. The poem by Keats aptly conveys the significance of beauty to the human spirit. It delights more than the beholder's eye; it delights the very soul.

GOD AS ARTIST

God is the ultimate artist. In the beginning, he created the cosmos by the word of his mouth and two humans through his personal touch. The man and woman lived in a garden, where God had caused trees to spring up that were both fruitful and beautiful (Gen. 2:9). The Creator viewed creation and its creatures as very good, which conveys an aesthetic as well as a moral judgment. As both artist and observer, God produces and enjoys beauty.

Kilby associates spiritual and artistic vision. "Vision in art and vision in religion are both directed outward and upward," he writes. "The Christian believes that the creative impulse itself is derived from the great Creator Artist, who first brought form out of chaos, who made man in His own image, and who is Himself beautiful."[6]

Excellent literature reflects the beauty God placed in the cosmos. William Wordsworth described the beauty authors craft into their works for the reader's pleasure as "an acknowledgement of the beauty of the universe."[7] God emphasizes beauty in his world as well as in his word.

As God's image-bearers, people reflect his creativity when they make artistic works. And the importance of the written word in the Christian faith stresses the need to apply a biblical perspective about beauty to the literature we read.

ARTISTIC EXPERIENCE

Both the artist and the viewer experience art. All people, Christians and unbelievers, share the basic aspect of pleasure in the experience of art. But Christians experience beauty more profoundly.

What does the human artist experience when producing an object of beauty? Any writer will testify to the delightful feeling when words flow and form themselves into text that seems right. Such writing does not come easily or often for most of us. But feelings of satisfaction and pleasure assure the writer when the work is going well and help the author determine when it is finished. Olympic medalist Eric Liddell famously credited God with making him fast, and said, "When I run, I feel his pleasure." Anyone who uses God-given gifts for God's glory feels pleasure. It's the joy of knowing you are doing the very thing God created you to do.

What happens when we view beauty? Although an observer can experience a wide range of emotions, the most basic—like the experience of the artist—is pleasure. This is true of natural beauty like a sunset's vivid layers of orange and purple reflected in a shimmering lake or dawn's rosy glow turning mountain tips pink. But it is also true when observing the creative work of artists: the sublime heights of an Albert Bierstadt landscape, the powerful animation captured in a Frederic Remington bronze sculpture, the memorable characters in a Charles Dickens novel, or the grasp of human nature reflected in the poetic genius of William Shakespeare's plays. Such works of art generate pleasure in anyone, but because Christians view beauty with the soul as well as the eye, they experience art more deeply. Believers may even hear echoes of Eden.

Patrick Francis Mullany, writing as Brother Azarias, effectively expresses this particularly Christian phenomenon. When we perceive a thing of beauty, he explains, a feeling of pleasure "possesses our soul." He describes this perception as a "recollection slightly awakened" and compares it to the feeling "that passes over us on recognizing an old friend after a long absence." We recall the prototype of "perfect implanted in our natures" by God's creative act, and we recognize "a dim reflection" of the original "standard within us," which awakens our aesthetic sense.[8] In these ways, he sees both *recollection* and *recognition* in beauty.

Kilby also believes Christians experience art more profoundly. He says beauty "may become for the Christian believer a more thrilling experience than for the unbeliever. The beauty of a Turner landscape or a Rembrandt still life contains for him a double beauty—the hand of the artist and also the hand of a personal and loving God."[9] Anyone can admire an artist's skill, but believers recognize the Giver of both the artist's skill and the viewer's pleasure. Whether or not the artist acknowledges God, it is the Lord who endows talent and enables a creative person to accomplish artistic work. Christian viewers receive beauty as a gift from the One who knows us intimately and delights to generate joy in our souls.

A Christian aesthetic sense includes a feeling of reverence, a term Roger Scruton employs in his description of breath-taking works "like Botticelli's *Birth of Venus*, Keats' *Ode to a Nightingale* or Susana's aria in the garden in Mozart's *Marriage of Figaro*. Such works are sometimes described as 'ravishing', meaning that they demand wonder and reverence, and fill us with an untroubled and consoling delight."[10] Where is wonder and reverence most properly directed? Who quiets our souls and consoles us with delight? Scruton doesn't answer these questions, but the object of the Christian's reverence is the ultimate artist, God. He alone is the truly awesome source of genuine consoling delight.

ARTISTIC EXPRESSION

Just as artist and viewer both experience pleasure in art, they also share in its expression. Leo Tolstoy wrote, "Art is an activity by means of which one man, having experienced a feeling, intentionally transmits it to others."[11]

Brother Azarias believes expression is crucial to beauty because "expression alone in every beautiful object . . . has power to awaken the sense of the beautiful in the soul." The success of the artist "depends upon his power of infusing expression into his work," while "the secret of our pleasure in admiring his production" is how it is "modeled after the eternal and uncreated ideal in the Divine Mind."

Echoing 1 Corinthians 13:12, Azarias continues: The "Divine Artist" who "fashioned the universe, also infused therein a trace of His own beauty—a reflection of Himself, once clear and serene as the undisturbed lake of crystalline waters; but since the fall, it is a mirror that has been cracked, broken, and bedimmed."

He describes how God communicates through physical beauty:

That which speaks to us in Nature is behind the hill and dale and starry sky, on which we fix our gaze. It is the ideal which the Cosmos actualizes. He who holds in His Divine Essence the types after which the physical world and we are created, has established between us and it this harmony and sympathy.

God mirrors himself in creation and uses beauty to facilitate harmony between divinity and humanity. Due to this close link, Azarias defines the beautiful as "the expression of the Word." Paraphrasing Thomas à Kempis in *The Imitation of Christ*, he writes: "From one Word are all things, and this one all things speak."[12]

Although Scruton wrote an entire book on the subject of beauty, he admits that in the aesthetic context, words behave "more like metaphors than literal descriptions." The reason for this is because we are not simply describing an object. "We are giving voice to an *encounter*, a meeting of subject and object, in which the response of the first is every bit as important as the qualities of the second." Here Scruton conveys the joint aspect of expression for both artist and viewer, noting how the mental process contributes to emotional responses. He believes the logical act of making a judgment about beauty "orders the emotions and desires of those who make it." He writes, "It may express their pleasure and their taste: but it is pleasure in what they value and taste for their true ideals."[13] We can feel free to like certain works of art or books without being able to articulate why we like them. But our pleasure in beauty should not be divorced from value judgments about it as well as truth and goodness.

Artist Makoto Fujimura believes art must properly express the relationship between God and humanity. "Art needs to be an expression of how God defines us rather than an expression through which we define God," he says. "We must seek and express our identity in Christ, rather than expressing our identity in ourselves." The more Christian artists fulfill God's calling within biblical parameters, the more freely they express their art. "We are created to be creative," adds Fujimura, "and we have stewardship responsibilities that come with that gift. The more we find fittingness in the God given responsibility, the more freedom we will find in our expression."[14]

The true ideals of beauty for a Christian shine forth from our glorious and beautiful God. As the source of beauty, he bestows this gift to humanity for our pleasure and the spiritual stirring of our souls.

GLORIOUS AND BEAUTIFUL

Jesus declared Mary's anointing of his feet "a beautiful thing" (Matt. 26:10; Mark 14:6). The Bible shows her act as characterized by humble adoration and sheer extravagance.

Fujimura calls Mary "the quintessential artist" and says, "The arts parallel this act of pouring the expensive perfume." As a practitioner of an ancient Japanese technique in which he crushes semi-precious stones for pigments, Fujimura is well acquainted with costly materials.

"The extravagance of the materials used only contrasts the poverty of my heart," he says. Questions related to expense should not be formulated in terms of *why* but *to whom*. "We are either glorifying ourselves or God," he says. "And the extravagance can only be justified if the worth of the object of adoration is greater than the cost of the extravagance."

The minerals in his pigments function "like prisms, and they refract, more than just reflect," he says. "I use them not just because they are beautiful, which they are, but because they have this wonderful lineage. They symbolize God's spiritual gifts to people [and] were embedded . . . in the garments of the high priest."[15] Like the priestly garments described at the beginning of this chapter, Fujimura's art is for God's glory and for beauty.

BEAUTIFUL WORDS

This chapter has discussed many thoughts about the elusive concept of beauty, beginning with God's beauty and exploring how that ultimate beauty guides our perspective about beauty's significance. God's status as the ultimate artist contributes to our understanding of the artistic experience and artistic expression. God's prescription for glorious and beautiful priestly garments served as this chapter's bookends. At this point we want to crystallize ways readers can view beauty in literature.

We do that by offering the following broad guidelines:

- Because the concept of beauty derives directly from God and his word, it is not exclusively the province of high-art aficionados or literary experts. Every reader should seek and enjoy beauty in literature.
- Literary beauty reflects God's beauty and reminds us of his perfections as well as humanity's original and future states.
- We see beauty in literature when we recognize its artistry and experience pleasure.

- While any reader can enjoy artistic writing, Christians may experience more profound levels of meaning.
- The most beautiful literature glorifies God rather than humanity.

When reading any literary work, every reader can enjoy the way its beauty provides personal pleasure. Christian readers, however, can also experience beauty on spiritual levels that point to God. In the words we read, we often see dim reflections of the One who created by his word and the Living Word, Jesus Christ.

18

Discovering Literary Excellence

WE BOTH SHARE a fondness for our hometown of Pella, Iowa. We also appreciate the slogan on the city's police vehicles: "Committed to Excellence." We strive for excellence in what we write, and we love discovering literary excellence in what we read. We view writing and reading well as practical applications of biblical teaching.

Philippians 4:8–9 encourages believers to not only *think* about any excellence but also to *practice* excellent things. God calls us to ponder and produce what is excellent. Shouldn't all Christians, like Pella's police, be committed to excellence? But what is literary excellence, and how can we discover it?

Good writing includes a host of techniques and elements. Attempting to explain them all in this chapter would be like trying to describe every ingredient and recipe for many full-course meals; therefore, we can offer here only a limited selection of literary appetizers.

We believe it's more important for readers to recognize and enjoy excellent writing than to name and define techniques. Rather than present a litany of technical terms, we'll provide literary clips and brief commentary under general themes related primarily to narrative literature. Like any well-constructed plot, we'll start at the beginning and work through the middle to the end. Our survey will include brief looks at specific voices and poetic elements.

BEGINNINGS

A well-written beginning introduces characters, grounds readers in the setting, and shows the conflict the characters face. While writing styles vary, authors attempt to capture reader attention from the start. Some succeed better than others.

Jane Austen (1775–1817) wrote during the lifetime of Sir Walter Scott (1771–1832), but their styles are almost polar opposites. Scott doesn't start the actual story of *The Heart of Midlothian* until the second chapter, which begins with an agonizing paragraph of 178 words in five convoluted sentences that drone on in vague and repetitive language. All the reader learns is that the plot will probably involve class distinction and a public execution in Edinburgh.

Contrast such a ponderous paragraph to this snappy initial sentence in *Pride and Prejudice*:

> It is a truth universally acknowledged, that a single man in possession of a good fortune, must be in want of a wife.[1]

Austen's one-sentence paragraph is a masterpiece of satire, succinct and packed with information. That every rich unmarried man must want a wife is hardly a universally-acknowledged truth. We can guess this will be a lively and ironic tale about how financial considerations play into matrimonial pursuit, particularly in that time and culture.

It takes little imagination to realize *White Fang* by Jack London will be an entirely different sort of book:

> Dark spruce forest frowned on either side the frozen waterway. The trees had been stripped by a recent wind of their white covering of frost, and they seemed to lean towards each other,

black and ominous, in the fading light. A vast silence reigned over the land. The land itself was a desolation, lifeless, without movement, so lone and cold that the spirit of it was not even that of sadness. There was a hint in it of laughter, but of a laughter more terrible than any sadness—a laughter that was mirthless as the smile of the sphinx, a laughter cold as the frost and partaking of the grimness of infallibility. It was the masterful and incommunicable wisdom of eternity laughing at the futility of life and the effort of life. It was the Wild, the savage, frozen-hearted Northland Wild.[2]

This will obviously be a dark story of difficult survival in a harsh setting. While readers shiver at the cold scene and foreboding imagery, they can appreciate the paragraph's artistry. Notice how many words either begin with "f" (alliteration) or repeat its sound within or at the end of the word (consonance). The soft "f" sound seems like a breathless and insistent whisper in the silent and frozen landscape, which reinforces the hint of ironic laughter. Notice also the repeated vowel sounds (assonance) in the phrases "seemed to lean toward each other," as well as in "lone and cold." While short vowel sounds can speed up and lighten the mood of a text, long vowels sounds (as used here) tend to slow down a passage and make its mood more serious.[3] London uses these aural devices sparingly and separates them with enough text to avoid distracting readers from the grim setting.

The setting itself appears an agent of relentless evil, totally devoid of emotion. The ironic images of silent laughter, grim infallibility, and futile life convey hopelessness. The frowning forest, leaning trees, and smiling sphinx contribute to the overarching personification of the sinister Northern Wild. The final sentence exults in the wildness and savagery of its frozen heart.

In contrast to that cold and hard heart, *The Awakening of Miss Prim* occurs within a warm and vibrant village. The book's second paragraph describes the village this way:

> To visitors, San Ireneo de Arnois looked like a place that was firmly rooted in the past. Old stone houses with gardens full of roses stood proudly along a handful of streets that led to a bustling square full of small shops and businesses, buying and selling at the steady pace of a healthy heart.[4]

The reader easily envisions a colorful and busy village, pulsing with life. The last phrase paints a broad stroke in this picturesque landscape of community wellness. It's a marvelous metaphor for financial prosperity and security, but it goes deeper to imply how communal peace may be related to the spiritual state of the human heart.

Good beginnings draw readers into the story. Even if characters aren't initially admirable, they ought to seem authentic and do or say believable things. The reader starts to care about them, and wants to discover how their struggles will resolve.

HEARING VOICES

When we begin reading, we hear the voice telling the story. In nonfiction, the narrator is usually the author. The persona relating a poem may be the author but is often an imagined speaker. In fiction, the narrator is rarely the actual author.

Alan Bradley's novels about adolescent sleuth and chemistry genius, Flavia de Luce, provide a striking example of author and narrator disparity. Bradley was sixty-nine when his first book about the fictional eleven-year-old girl was published. He had no interest or training in chemistry, but Flavia was a competent chemist with her own lab. He found murder gruesome, but the discovery of a corpse excited Flavia.

Despite such differences, Bradley captured her cheeky (sometimes irreverent) attitude and realistic adolescent reflections. Readers may cringe at Flavia's interactions with her sisters, but her intense emotions reveal deeply-buried bonds within the unusual household.

Flavia's picturesque similes pique reader interest from the first book's initial sentence:

> "It was as black in the closet as old blood."[5]

Content draws the reader into the dark closet and propels continued reading. Repeated vowel and consonant sounds lend artistry to the frightening image, and "blood" appears in the ending position of power.

Flavia later answers a question from her father and then relates:

> I shot him a broad smile, a smile wide enough to present him with a good view of the wire braces that caged my teeth. Although they gave me the look of a dirigible with the skin off, Father always liked being reminded that he was getting his money's worth. But this time he was too preoccupied to notice.[6]

This paragraph accomplishes more literary work than its delightful dirigible imagery. It conveys Flavia's voice and age. It gives a first glimpse of her propensity to ingratiate herself to adults (usually to obtain information in solving a mysterious murder). The powerful verb "caged" expresses her age-appropriate feelings about wearing braces. The striking image of a skinless dirigible helps establish the novel's setting in 1950, while hinting at Flavia's somewhat ghoulish interests. The imagery's surprise is balanced by the mundane observation about her father getting his money's worth. Only her father is too preoccupied to notice Flavia, a sad reality the reader will frequently see in these narratives.

By the time the tenth novel about Flavia was published, Bradley was eighty years old and Flavia is the twelve-year-old partner in a detection agency. She has matured in many ways but still occasionally exhibits childish thoughts and behaviors. Although Flavia and her household have undergone significant changes, her voice remains familiar. When a solo at her sister's wedding touches her keenly, she experiences difficulty breathing. She reflects,

> Great music has much the same effect upon humans as cyanide,
> I managed to think: It paralyzes the respiratory system.[7]

Because readers recognize Flavia's exaggerations and understand a few matters that go over her young head, she occasionally functions as an unreliable narrator. Other narrators in literature, however, are consistently unreliable. Stevens, the aging butler in *The Remains of the Day*, epitomizes professional dedication and discretion, but the reader soon senses omissions in his selective reflections. His memories ebb and flow around repressed emotions like a carefully choreographed dance. Author Kazuo Ishiguro brilliantly reveals truth to the reader, while peeling away the layers of protection and denial Stevens has wrapped around himself.

While a first-person point of view is generally considered the most intimate, a skillful author can bring the reader into the minds of multiple characters through an omniscient third-person point of view. Few authors surpass Leo Tolstoy for revealing reflections of various characters. With the precision of a brain surgeon, he lays open the self-satisfied thoughts of a shallow person or the convoluted agonies of a deeply-troubled soul. In one paragraph, he moves seamlessly between the perspective of Anna Karenina to that of her lover:

> Looking at him, she felt her degradation physically and she could not utter another word. He felt what a murderer must feel when he looks at the body he has deprived of life.[8]

Sharing a character's thoughts, without setting them off in italics or quotation marks, lends first-person immediacy without distraction to a third-person account.[9] Jane Austen was an innovator at this unobtrusive weaving technique. It is obviously not the narrator, but Emma herself forming intentions regarding Harriet Smith:

> *She* would notice her; she would improve her; she would detach her from her bad acquaintance, and introduce her into good society; she would inform her opinions and her manners. It would be an interesting, and certainly a very kind undertaking; highly becoming her own situation in life, her leisure, and powers.[10]

The reader senses impending doom for Emma's arrogant interference.

A skillful author intentionally uses a particular perspective or shifts between them to engage readers and tell the story most effectively. The next time you read a book, listen to its voices.

MIDDLE MATTERS

The middle of a well-written plot keeps the reader turning pages as characters and events progress. Forward movement is often checked by roadblocks or setbacks. Minor conflicts may resolve, but suspense builds in the primary struggle as literary hints propel the plot forward and pave the way for believable resolution.

Jane Eyre, one of literature's most beloved young women, progresses through life-changing conflicts from childhood to marriage. Many people recognize the book's beginning: "There was no possibility of taking a walk that day." And its ending: "Amen; even so come, Lord Jesus!" Oh, wait. Perhaps you're thinking it ended with, "Reader, I married him."[11] Almost! But that famous quotation is only the *first line* of the last chapter. The final line is from a letter St. John Rivers wrote to Jane. These first and last lines function as bookends to Jane's progression from a self-centered child to a mature woman, content in a marriage brought about by divine intervention.

In a day when many modern romances portray young women initially noticing a man's physical appearance and pursuing him on such a shallow basis (even novels by Christian authors), the developing relationship between Rochester and Jane stands out as a refreshing contrast that reflects better ideals. Their acquaintance grows through the mental stimulus of invigorating conversation. Rochester first appreciates Jane for her mind: "Not three in three thousand raw schoolgirl-governesses would have answered me as you have just done."[12] This recognition encourages her: "The ease of his manner freed me from painful restraint: the friendly frankness, as correct as cordial, with which he treated me, drew me to him."[13] Intelligent conversation and easy camaraderie awaken Jane's sense of well-being and feelings of physical attraction. She says, ". . . my bodily health improved; I gathered flesh and strength. . . . And was Mr. Rochester now ugly in my eyes? No, reader: gratitude, and many associations, all pleasurable and genial, made his face the object I best liked to see."[14] Rochester's manner and conversation have helped Jane bloom intellectually and physically.

In contrast, St. John Rivers squelches her. She confesses, "I fell under a freezing spell."[15] When she nearly succumbs to his pressure for a loveless marriage, she prays for guidance. God intervenes in a supernatural experience, sending her to the only place that ever seemed like home. She rejoices in an equal and exceptional marriage: "I know what it is to live entirely for and with what I love best on earth. I hold myself supremely blest . . . because I am my husband's life as fully as he is mine. . . . My Edward and I . . . are happy."[16] The literary skill in telling Jane's progression from misery to happiness delights readers.

POETIC NOTES

We both love poetry. We believe even a passing acquaintance with its techniques helps anyone become a better writer and reader. Accomplished authors incorporate poetical devices throughout prose compositions. An author who develops an ear for sensory harmony and connotation (implied meaning) may not consciously consider technique but chooses certain words over others simply because they sound better or carry more literary weight.

Poetry pulses with images and is fueled by the power of its economy. It generates concrete pictures in the reader's mind and conveys a great deal in few words. Excellent prose can do the same things. Consider this gem from *Anna Karenina*: "He went down, trying not to look at her, as though she were the sun, but he saw her, as one sees the sun, without looking."[17] Even taken out of context, the reader recognizes how much this woman (Kitty) means to this man (Lenin).

Effective figurative language connects the author's word choices with the reader's mental images and emotions. Roger Scruton writes, "Figurative uses of language aim not to describe things but to connect them, and the connection is forged in the feeling of the perceiver." After listing multiple literary devices as ways the connection may be made, he says, "Sometimes a writer places two things side by side, using no figure of speech, but simply letting the experience of one leak into the experience of the other." He concludes, "That is the kind of transformation at which metaphors aim: dead metaphors achieve nothing, but living metaphors change the way things are perceived."[18]

Anthony Trollope wrote this lively metaphor: "He was the finest fly that Barchester had hitherto afforded to her web; and the signora was a powerful spider that made wondrous webs, and could in no way live without catching flies."[19] The spider and fly metaphor immediately brings the scene's dynamic to life.

"The Love Song of J. Alfred Prufrock" contains this apt metonymy (a part of something representing the whole): "I should have been a pair of ragged claws / Scuttling across the floors of silent seas."[20] The phrase "a pair of ragged claws" represents the entire crab. The image powerfully conveys Prufrock's feelings of uselessness and disconnection.

Here's how Charles Dickens describes the arrival of a cold morning: "The day came creeping on, halting and whimpering and shivering, and wrapped in patches of cloud and rags of mist, like a beggar."[21] He begins with personification and ends with a clarifying simile. Dickens apparently wants to make sure the reader envisions a specific image that contributes powerfully to the mood and story.

In order for any literary device to be effective and beautiful, it should be *fitting* and *fresh*. It must be appropriate to the style, subject, and narrator of the story. It should convey an image or idea in an original manner but in a way that makes sense and doesn't interfere with the story's flow. The best techniques do double duty, sharpening the reader's focus and conveying layered meaning. Readers recognize an effective technique when they notice *and* delight in it.

THE END

Cliché or not, everyone knows that all good things in this world must come to an end, even the most delightful and engaging book. Authors may revise repeatedly, but they finally reach a point when they know it's time to type those magic words: The End.

Only it's not really the end. A good ending leaves readers pondering the story. Its characters initially accompany us on the drive to work or stand beside us as we cook dinner. We wonder what might happen to them next. We imagine how the story might have ended if certain events hadn't occurred, or if characters had made different choices. We may even consider what we need to change in our own lives. Not every conflict must be completely resolved in every story, but good endings provide sufficient resolution that readers feel satisfied rather than cheated.

Although definite endings are common and preferable in children's books, endings in novels and short stories are often ambiguous. The reader is left to puzzle out possible resolutions. A prime example is Katherine Manfield's short story, "Bliss." After a shocking revelation near the story's end, the reader joins the young wife in wondering: "Oh, what is going to happen now?"[22] Ambiguous endings leave the reader with many questions.

Some great endings tie in with the story's beginning. Seeing the author's craft in this circular construction can be a delightful surprise. Larry Woiwode once described this recognition as "bumping your head back on the beginning" and cited *Middle Passage* by Charles Johnson as a good example.[23] The book's first sentence reads: "Of all the things that drive men to sea, the most common disaster, I've come to learn, is women."[24] The book's end echoes the beginning with surprising circumstances and reversals. Changed characters and unanticipated events make circular constructions delightful and satisfying rather than boring or predictable.

RECOGNIZING EXCELLENCE

God himself is the epitome of excellence. He calls his image-bearers to consider and create that which is excellent.

We discover literary excellence when we notice elements of skillful writing. Well-written plots engage interest from the beginning, show progression through the middle, and conclude with a satisfying ending. A skillful author crafts the best voices to tell the story and uses figurative language artfully.

A survey of literary excellence could include much more than we covered in this short chapter, and we have discussed many additional aspects in other chapters. If you wish to learn more about literary elements, you can seek out technical books or conduct online searches. We hope readers already familiar with the topic have enjoyed this brief refresher. Most of all, we hope we've whetted every reader's appetite for literary delights.

19

Freedom to Read

HERE, AS WE NEAR the end of our quest to recover the lost art of reading, we address a question you probably have wondered since picking up this book: "How in the world do I find more time to read?" It's a valid concern. Most people feel they're too busy, busier than they'd like to be. Kevin DeYoung reflects:

> How did we all get this way? I've yet to meet anyone in America who responds to the question 'How are you?' with the reply, 'Well for starters, I'm not very busy.' I suppose there must be a six-year-old somewhere out there who doesn't 'have anything to do' and some dear folks at the nursing home who could use a few interruptions, but for almost everyone in between there is a pervasive sense of being unrelentingly filled up and stressed out.[1]

We may want to read more, but even the thought of doing one more thing overwhelms us. Most of us could probably manage our time better or increase our reading competency. But the ultimate answer won't be found in implementing a particular time management system and certainly not in signing up for a speed reading course. We will only begin to find a solution when we view the question differently. Rather than stressing about the tyranny of time and the pressure to do more, we can embrace a biblical perspective of rest and celebrate our freedom to read.

BIBLICAL REST

Having grown up in a Dutch ecclesiastical tradition, we both are well acquainted with the "Protestant work ethic." We were taught to work hard and not waste time. People with similar backgrounds or demanding careers may consider rest as being lazy or unproductive. But biblical rest applies to every person and is God's gift for a full and rich life.

God established rest as a divine ordinance at creation, and he promises eternal rest after Christ's return. Between these two great bookends of cosmic history, he prescribes rest as a weekly practice *and* a daily attitude.

From Genesis to Revelation, from creation to re-creation, God reveals his will for us regarding rest. At the dawn of history, God established a rhythmic pattern between work and rest. He blessed the seventh day and made it holy because on it he rested "from all his work that he had done in creation" (Gen. 2:1–3). God ceased from his creative work, but his rest was not idle or meaningless. He contemplated and delighted in his "very good" and beautiful world (Gen. 1:31). Rest included an element of refreshment for both God and his people (Ex. 31:17; 23:12). God enjoyed fellowship with Adam and Eve not only on the seventh day but also in the cool of each evening (Gen. 3:8).

The poetry of Ecclesiastes extols the ebb and flow of life's rhythms, reminding us that everything is beautiful in its time. The Psalms and prophets are replete with references to rest such as Psalm 37:7, "Rest in the LORD" (KJV). A biblical perspective encourages balance between work and refreshment.

When Christ came in the fullness of time, he overturned not only the money-changers' tables but also the pharisaical view of Sabbath. After religious readers raised an outcry, Jesus said, "The Sabbath was made for man, not man for the Sabbath" (Mark 2:27). Sabbath rest is a gift for humanity, not a burden of external rules. Jesus invites all who labor and are heavy laden to come to him and find soul rest. How? In the counter-intuitive act of taking upon ourselves his yoke and burden. But they are easy and light, and plowing beside him, we learn to mirror his gentleness and humble heart (Matt. 11:28–30). If we won't bow our necks to Christ's yoke, we remain chained to sin. Galatians 5:1 tells us, "For freedom Christ has set us free; stand firm therefore, and do not submit again to a yoke of slavery." Each day we're either going to wear sin's choking yoke of slavery or Christ's easy yoke of freedom.

Jesus set an example for regular rest by frequently going off to pray and rest in solitude. He encouraged his disciples to do the same: "And he said to them, 'Come away by yourselves to a desolate place and rest a while.' For many were coming and going, and they had no leisure even to eat" (Mark 6:31).

The author of Hebrews draws parallels between the Israelites entering the promised land and the entrance of all believers into their eternal rest. Hebrews 4:9–10 says, "So then, there remains a Sabbath rest for the people of God, for whoever has entered God's rest has also rested from his works as God did from his." This text ties together God's creation ordinance, our regular practice of rest, and our hope for eternal rest.

We cannot find genuine rest apart from God. Augustine famously wrote, "You awake in us a delight at praising You; for You made us for Yourself, and our heart is restless until it finds its place of rest in You."[2]

Christians avoid falling into legalistic patterns when they recognize how a Sabbath perspective is a matter of the heart. Mark Buchanan explains what he means by Sabbath: "I also mean an attitude. It is a perspective, an orientation. I mean a Sabbath heart, not just a Sabbath day. A Sabbath heart is restful even in the midst of unrest and upheaval. It is attentive to the presence of God and others even in the welter of much coming and going, rising and falling. It is still and knows God even when mountains fall into the sea."[3]

A biblical view of rest honors God's command to keep the Sabbath holy, develops a Sabbath heart daily, and anticipates our eternal Sabbath. The answer to Question 103 of the Heidelberg Catechism beautifully ties together the aspects of Sabbath keeping, describing Sunday as "the festive day of rest" and calling us to rest from sin "every day" of our lives, "and so begin in this life the eternal Sabbath."[4]

Because we both have spoken and written extensively about the concept of rest and the importance of leisure time, we easily could expand this chapter into another book! But we'll leave you to explore more of our thoughts on those subjects elsewhere,[5] sharpening our focus here on the subject of reading.

Biblical rest is valid and necessary. Mirroring God's initial rest, ours may celebrate the beauty of nature or any accomplished artistic work, including a good book. Biblical rest embraces a view of leisure as freedom in Christ to use spare moments to be refreshed with meaningful rest, which certainly includes our freedom to read.

FREEDOM TO CHOOSE

Even in our busy and tightly scheduled lives, we have freedom to make choices regarding time. Rather than considering leisure as unnecessary idleness, we can choose to view it as required refreshment. Instead of thinking of recreation as meaningless play, we can remind ourselves of its original meaning of re-creation. And as an alternative to stressing about how to fit reading into a hectic schedule, a person can choose to think, "God gives me freedom to read."

This switch in mental gears immediately relaxes tension and calms thoughts. Instead of viewing reading as one of many neglected duties, reading appears a delightful opportunity. Rather than becoming frazzled by our failures to read, we embark on a quest for the hidden treasures of reading refreshment.

Our culture talks a lot about managing time, but we can't actually manage time itself. We can only choose how to spend moments. Most of our 24 daily hours must be devoted to work, sleep, and family commitments. But many minutes are more fluid, and we have a choice about what we do during them. We can choose to scroll through Facebook posts or play a video game or watch a TV show. We can choose to wait nervously for our dental appointment or become frustrated at the long line at the DMV. Or we can choose to read. We have freedom to choose how we spend many of our minutes.

God gives us exactly 1,440 minutes each day, which we can neither extend nor reduce. We can't prolong a relaxing day at the beach or shorten a painful day at the hospital. Each of us has a single finite life on this earth. How will you choose to spend each minute of what poet Mary Oliver calls "your one wild and precious life?"[6]

TIME THIEVES

Thieves of time are different for each person. But the most insidious and common ones have a screen. The first step is to become aware of how many minutes are spent daily on digital media. A certain amount of time online is necessary for research or communication, but important work too easily bleeds into scrolling social media or following distracting hyperlinks. An hour passes before we're even aware of it.

Tracking time spent on meaningless pursuits helps us identify time thieves. Some people keep a chart open on their computer desktops to note when they begin and end a distraction or down time. Others use time-tracking apps or set up the Screen Time app on their iPhone. Some of us prefer old school methods like jotting numbers in a planner or desk calendar or setting alarms or timers. A clock that chimes the number of hours audibly signals time's rapid progression and doesn't depend on user effort (aside from being wound occasionally). What works for one person isn't practical for another, but each of us can try to recognize the meaningless activities eating up our time.

Identifying time thieves helps us arrest their influence in our lives. We can ask ourselves, "Do I really want to spend time on this?" We can remind ourselves of the things we'd rather be doing—like reading.

Track down your time thieves. If you prefer to spend even a few precious minutes reading, exercise your free will and freedom to do so.

DON'T LEAVE HOME WITHOUT A BOOK

Many minutes each day consist of flexible time. We can read quite a bit while waiting for flights or appointments, commuting by public transport, or even during pauses in sporting events.

Several baseball fans have snapped pictures of Stephen King, undoubtedly one of America's highest-paid writers, reading between innings at Red Sox games. If this famous author takes a book with him to a ballgame, we needn't feel shy about reading any time or anywhere. Picking up car keys can be a visual reminder to grab a book. We never know when we might have to wait somewhere or have a few free minutes. Capturing elusive moments to read can become a game as compelling as the popular Pokémon Go.

POWER OF HABIT

We all know the power of habit. Bad habits are hard to break, and good ones are difficult to develop. Incorporating reading into your daily routine can help reading become a good habit. Twyla Tharp writes, "Over time, as the daily routines become second nature, discipline morphs into habit."[7]

It may be helpful to set a designated reading time, like when you wake up or when you go to bed. Perhaps you could swap an hour of reading for binge watching a show. A helpful strategy may be to make a commitment, perhaps determining to read a certain number of pages or minutes each day. Starting small boosts your chances for success with this strategy. Too much sets one up for failure, while too little can always be increased. Setting an attainable goal makes the commitment more likely to become a habit.

Check your daily schedule for small blocks of time during which you could read, such as while waiting for coffee to brew or for dinner to cook. Reading for even a brief time yields cumulative benefits. If you consider the average reading speed is 250 words per minute, and the average book contains 250–300 words per page, most people could read a page per minute. Because book chapters generally average between 3,000 and 5,000 words, it's possible to read an entire chapter in only ten or fifteen minutes. Think about ways you can harness the power of habit to foster what we've referred to as the "Scout Finch" attitude, when reading is as integral and natural a part of life as breathing.

READING CHALLENGES AND COMMUNITIES

Participating in a reading challenge may be a great way to kick start your reading habit. Tim Challies and Redeemed Reader offer annual challenges for adults and children respectively.[8] Readers choose from commitment levels and use charts to track progress. These challenges expand reading interests with options in various genres while still allowing for personal tastes with open-ended choices. Both websites offer tips and suggestions for developing the reading habit.

Thousands of people use online communities such as Goodreads or Pinterest to set yearly goals or share what books they're reading.[9]

Some people prefer to create a personal challenge and track their progress in a journal or on note cards. Challenges can be as private or public as you like.

In addition to online reading networks, readers can find camaraderie and accountability within local communities. Nearly every public library hosts book clubs or programs to encourage reading. Forming your own book club can be as simple as discovering two or three other interested people, agreeing to read a certain book over the next month, and then meeting to discuss it. A quick online search will yield many suggestions for how a book club functions. Readers should explore available options and move on if the first attempt isn't a good fit. As you can choose how to spend your moments, you can choose how you prefer to read in community.

AUDIO BOOKS

Audio books are a legitimate method of "reading" in many circumstances. Listening to a book can make miles fly by on long commutes or business trips. It can even eliminate the dreaded "Are we there yet?" question on long stretches of family vacations. Shared listening may actually lead to an eager, "May we hear more?"

Audio books can be used at home as well. Time-consuming tasks like taping and painting a room pass more quickly while listening to an engaging tale. A gripping mystery makes monotonous handwork, such as knitting or crocheting simple patterns, far more enjoyable. While exercising on an elliptical or treadmill, it's generally easier to listen to audio than read a bouncing book. Audio files are also a good way to tackle works that seem insurmountable in physical form, such as our frequently-mentioned *War and Peace*.

Some readers or recordings are better than others. If you encounter a poor recording or a narrator who's difficult to understand, try another version. When you find favorite readers, look for other work they've done. Jayne Entwistle superbly reads the Flavia de Luce books from Random House Audio.

Audio books can be purchased as CDs or downloaded from suppliers such as Audible Books, which charge a monthly free. Most libraries carry CD copies of books on the shelves but also make many more available for free through digital apps. Recently manufactured vehicles even support digital technology.

It may be tempting (especially for a student whose thesis is due the next day) to simply watch the movie version of a book. While excellent video productions exist, many bear little resemblance to the actual books on which they're based. For multiple reasons, a book is almost always better than its cinema depiction. Because movies must appeal to the masses and fit tighter time constraints, they tend to stress or create action and then skip the slow (but sometimes most meaningful) parts of a book. It's also difficult to surpass personal imagination. Additionally, movies can't capture the nuances and flow of delightful language. The *Jeeves and Wooster* productions (based on P. G. Wodehouse's Jeeves stories) may be fun to watch, but the viewer misses Jeeves shimmering into a room or Bertie climbing into the outer crust of an English gentleman.

While listening to a book is an excellent and viable option in many circumstances, it isn't the preferred method of "reading" for either of us. We love the feel and smell of a physical book. One can underline striking sentences, jot notes in margins, or festoon a work with sticky notes. Reading words on a page allows the reader to pause for reflection, to reread difficult concepts, to linger over lovely language or savor beautiful phrases. Reading pages imprints words better in the memory. Readers can recall the approximate location of a sought-after reference, if it was on the left or right page, and about how far down on the page it appeared. While a person misses all these physical benefits with an audio book, we heartily endorse any form of reading—including listening.

ABOUT TIME MANAGEMENT

We noted earlier that it's impossible to manage time itself, and we stressed how perspective was more important than specific methods. But we don't want to dismiss the genuine need some people have for incorporating time management strategies. Many books or online resources exist on this topic. Some sources suggest ideas that may seem too complicated to implement or inappropriate for your particular situation. But others might be helpful. Each person's situation is unique, and various personalities benefit from different approaches.

People desiring practical assistance in setting priorities or getting organized might benefit from *Do More Better* by Tim Challies.[10] He guides the reader through an assessment process that includes figuring out what God is calling you to do in every area of your life. He suggests writing out mission statements, which can be helpful in determining how and where to invest your time. And if you're interested in using digital tools, he walks you through implementing a few applications.

Rather than advocating a highly-structured organizational plan, Kevin DeYoung's *Crazy Busy* explores heart issues that contribute to the feeling of busyness. Here is DeYoung's convicting final paragraph: "It's not wrong to be tired. It's not wrong to feel overwhelmed. It's not wrong to go through seasons of complete chaos. What is wrong— and heartbreakingly foolish and wonderfully avoidable—is to live a life with more craziness than we want because we have less Jesus than we need."[11] Clinging to Jesus as our highest priority helps us view the many elements of our busy lives with a biblical perspective.

Our greatest fear in this chapter is that we may have inadvertently burdened anyone with additional pressure. We want to come alongside readers with cheerful encouragement. Remember how God calls us to rest and re-creation. Try framing the matter of *time to read* as *freedom to read*. You are free to choose how to enjoy the limited minutes of your wonderful and precious life.

20

Reading Good Books

IN 2018, THE PUBLIC BROADCASTING SERVICE (PBS) launched "The Great American Read," which allowed readers to vote daily for their favorite titles on a list of one hundred books.[1] Titles ran the gamut of literary expression from American potboilers to British classics, from twisted sexual depictions to epic love stories, from hopeless dystopian fantasy to inspiring contemporary realism. While literary gems appeared on the list, many titles promoted ungodly living and unbiblical worldviews, and a few books had even been broadly denounced as poor writing.

Adam Kirsch analyzed the list in a *Wall Street Journal* article appropriately titled, "The Way We Read Now." His conclusion included this insight: "For one thing, it seems clear that American readers don't care very much about good prose. 'The Da Vinci Code' and 'Fifty Shades of Grey' are regularly cited as examples of terrible writing, but both were mega-best sellers, and both find a place among the top 100."[2]

The PBS list seemed to confirm the need to recover the art of reading in today's culture. People have different tastes, of course, but shouldn't Christians want to read good books artfully? Building on the material presented in previous chapters, this chapter will explore how to read well and assess books.

We will begin by encouraging ways to become better readers. Then we'll discuss ways to read, from reception through slow and thoughtful reading. Understanding the act of artful reading leads to explorations regarding bad and good books.

Reading good books well increases our pleasure. The reluctant reader becomes more confident and motivated. The busy person discovers increased peace and joy. Even people who regard themselves as voracious readers may benefit from assessing how and what they read.

BECOMING BETTER READERS

How does one become a better reader? The short answer is simply to read. Anyone gets better at something with practice. Athletes participate in scrimmages. Musicians and singers rehearse daily. Reading is a lifelong skill that improves the more we do it.

The previous chapter encouraged adopting a "freedom to read" perspective to help us view reading positively. Although we may capture moments for reading in almost any location, we enter more fully into the reading experience by dedicating blocks of time to it. Rather than frittering away disappearing minutes on social media or binge-watching a show, try designating an hour or two for reading.

It's difficult to change deeply-engrained habits. We may feel our brains badly need a break from mental activity, and reading is just too much effort after a stressful day. But it helps to view dedicated sessions as recreational reading in the true and original sense of the word: re-creational. Re-creational reading renews the human spirit. Scrolling aimlessly through Facebook posts tends to generate negative feelings such as envy or anger or despair. Wouldn't you rather renew your spirit through reading?

Considering yourself a reader enhances dedicated sessions. Adults who struggled to read as children may still view themselves as poor readers. Most of us fill so many roles in our busy lives that "reader" is crowded out of our identities. But thinking of yourself as a reader will help to generate confidence and to prioritize the activity.

Creating a conducive environment with minimal distractions reinforces positive perspectives and experiences. Release current concerns with a deep breath and relax into a comfortable chair. Make sure good lighting falls on the pages of your open book. Clive Thompson beautifully describes this experience: "I love nestling into a chair at night with a paper book, reading in a room that's pitch black except for a single lamplight pooled on the page, a chiaroscuro of concentration. When we fold ourselves into these literary yoga poses, it's a ritual of physicality; we are communicating to ourselves, 'I am a reader.'"[3]

We become better readers by reading more and adopting positive attitudes. Dedicated sessions in favorable settings help us enter more fully into the experience of artful reading.

RECEIVING

Artful reading begins with receiving. A visitor to the National Gallery of Art in Washington, D.C., pauses to gaze at striking masterpieces, noticing colors and style. Someone attending a National Symphony Orchestra concert at the Kennedy Center sits quietly and listens intently to the music. Literature can be received in much the same way as visual or musical art.

Readers may find it difficult to think of reading in terms of receiving. Too many of us have been conditioned to read as if we're wielding a tool, trying to make it "do" something for us.

C. S. Lewis famously encouraged readers to *receive* art rather than use it. When we are "busy doing things with the work," he wrote, "we give it too little chance to work on us. Thus increasingly we meet only ourselves." He encouraged us to "begin by laying aside as completely as we can all our own preconceptions, interests, and associations."[4]

The "true reader" receives literature by initially suspending personal thought processes and being open to the work's art.

Could it be that so many of us are poor readers because we're poor listeners? Our human nature makes us preoccupied with ourselves during a conversation. How many of us interrupt a speaker to share our own thoughts or experiences? Even if we wait until the other person pauses, we're often so focused on our planned response that we don't hear parts of what the other person says. Similarly to how we should actually listen to another speaker, we should listen to a book's author.

Listening means paying attention. Lewis wrote, "And if it is worth while listening or reading at all, it is often worth doing so attentively. Indeed we must attend even to discover that something is not worth attention."[5]

Receptive readers are alert to the work's artistry. They notice beautiful language and experience the emotions of the characters. Just as tourists who rush through the National Gallery of Art receive little enjoyment from its many masterpieces, fast readers sacrifice pleasure. For most people, reading attentively requires slowing down.

READING SLOWLY

In chapter 1 we noted the intimidating length of *War and Peace*. "I took a course in speed-reading," Woody Allen once said, "and was able to go through *War and Peace* in twenty minutes. It's about Russia."[6] This humorous quip demonstrates how much we miss by reading quickly.

Educator Charlotte Mason wrote: "It is a sad fact that we are losing our joy in literary form. We are in such haste to be instructed by facts or titillated by theories, that we have no leisure to linger over the mere putting of a thought. But this is our error, for words are mighty both to delight and to inspire."[7] Artful reading is possible only when we read slowly enough to appreciate beauty and savor phrases, experiencing pleasure and renewal.

Slow reading at our leisure leads to fulfillment. Susan Hill describes slow reading as "deeply satisfying" and then contrasts reading speeds:

> Fast reading of a great novel will get us the plot. It will get us names, a shadowy idea of characters, a sketch of settings. It will not get us subtleties, small differentiations, depth of emotion and observation, multilayered human experience, the appreciation of simile and metaphor, any sense of context, any comparison with other novels, other writers. Fast reading will not get us cadence and complexities of style and language. It will not get us anything that enters not just the conscious mind but the unconscious. It will not allow the book to burrow down into our memory and become part of ourselves, the accumulation of knowledge and wisdom and vicarious experience which helps to form us as complete human beings. It will not develop our awareness or add to the sum of our knowledge and intelligence. Read parts of a newspaper quickly or an encyclopaedia entry, or a fast-food thriller, but do not insult yourself or a book which has been created with its author's painstakingly acquired skill and effort, by seeing how fast you can dispose of it.[8]

Hill beautifully and comprehensively captures the differences between fast and slow reading. Slow reading allows us to become aware of character depth as well as literary expressions and style. Language and concepts seep into our subconscious minds to shape us and expand our wisdom.

Annie Murphy Paul writes, "The combination of fast, fluent decoding of words and slow, unhurried progress on the page gives deep readers time to enrich their reading with reflection, analysis, and their own memories and opinions."[9] Slow reading allows us to read artfully.

READING THOUGHTFULLY

It may seem as if we are giving conflicting advice: suspend your thought processes, but read thoughtfully. This makes sense if we think of reading imaginative literature as having an element of progression. We suspend our own preconceptions in order to receive the work. We read it slowly and attentively, soaking up its beauty and immersing ourselves in the story. As we read receptively, we notice things. We delight in the author's artistic skill. Because everyone has a right to be heard before being judged, we allow the author to speak to us as we listen.

As our reading progresses, we recognize patterns or recurring motifs. Concepts begin to emerge, and our thought process becomes more comprehensive. A reader should not determine the work's meaning too early in the reading. Lewis cautioned against early assessments that interfere with reception: "Then the pencil gets to work on the margin and phrases of censure or approval begin forming themselves in our mind. All this activity impedes reception."[10] Christian readers, especially, should not be impatient to discover meaning or wrestle religious significance from stories. Assessing meaning, particular in fiction or poetry, belongs chiefly *after* reading a work.

In contrast to imaginative literature, nonfiction often requires thoughtful reading throughout. We may want to note the author's main thesis from the start and look for ways it's supported in the rest of the work. No matter what literary genre we're reading, we frequently discover beautiful language or a well-expressed idea we want to ponder or remember.

Some people underline or highlight or scribble notes and questions in margins (unless, of course, the book is borrowed from a friend or the library). Perhaps you grew up viewing books with such respect that dog-earing or marking—even with a pencil—seems like desecration.

Many people festoon books with sticky notes. They may even jot key words on the notes to help them find references later. Some people find it helpful to write reflections in a journal as they read.

Every person is a unique individual, and what works well for one reader may not be effective for another. Notations may help a reader develop slower and more attentive reading habits. Many people employ physical aids for nonfiction but feel they detract from the pleasure of reading fiction.

Each reader should approach every book with a receptive mind. Reading attentively naturally develops into increasingly thoughtful reading, whether it is aided by physical notation or not.

Even if a book isn't immediately engaging, it's a good idea to give it a chance to prove itself. Some people recommend setting aside an hour or ninety minutes for an initial reading. This allows the reader to become grounded in the story and acquainted with the characters. Also many people advocate a "50-page rule": Read at least fifty pages to see if it captures your interest.

If you're simply not enjoying the book, try another one. We all go through seasons, and a book that doesn't appeal to you at one point in your life may become a favorite later.

Completing a book shouldn't be like finishing a meal with your mother haranguing you about starving kids in China. It's okay to be picky. Don't waste time by slogging through poorly-written, immoral, boring, or unhelpful books. Contrary to deeply-ingrained beliefs, you don't have to read the whole thing. Feel free to put down a bad book!

BAD BOOKS

C. S. Lewis defines a prime example of a bad book according to the way it can (or perhaps better, cannot) be read: "The ideally bad book is the one of which a good reading is impossible. The words in which it exists will not bear close attention, and what they communicate offers you nothing unless you are prepared either for mere thrills or for flattering daydreams."[11] A bad book not only defies good reading, but it also offers little genuine pleasure.

Walker Percy famously and succinctly wrote: "Bad books always lie." About what? "They lie most of all about the human condition, so that one never recognizes oneself, the deepest part of oneself, in a bad book." Listen for echoes of Lewis as Percy expands on his frequently-quoted definition: "And even when a bad book gives its own sort of pleasure, either a pastime of diversion and adventurism, or the titillation of voyeurism, it leaves a sour taste in the mouth, like a hangover from bad Bourbon."[12] Percy's descriptions of warped pleasure, like the "mere thrills" and "flattering daydreams" of Lewis, bring to mind the kinds of books that capitalize on humanity's baser instincts.

Many contemporary authors follow a popular model of making something happen every five pages. A bomb explodes and body parts rain down or a sexy young man turns into a vampire. Anything can happen, but some kind of action must occur frequently to tickle a sense of thrill or adventure.

Much commercial fiction, especially in the romance genre, is thinly-veiled pornography. Percy differentiates literature and pornography in this way: "Literature is an 'I-you' transaction in which symbols are used to transmit truths of a sort. Pornography is an 'I-it' transaction in which you become an 'it,' an organism manipulated by stimuli."[13] Authors and readers should avoid graphic descriptions of sexual actions or gratuitous violence. This kind of writing objectifies its characters as well as the reader.

God created human beings as image-bearers with value, dignity, and responsibility. Clyde Kilby writes that "by believing man a re-sponsible creature before God, Christianity upholds the adequate presentation of life as a sufficient aim for art rather than either the deifying or sentimentalizing of man on the one hand or the brutalizing of him on the other."[14] A biblical view of humanity and the arts helps writers and readers find balance.

Lewis writes, "The best safeguard against bad literature is a full experience of good; just as a real and affectionate acquaintance with honest people gives a better protection against rogues than a habitual distrust of everyone."[15]

GOOD BOOKS

Like other artistic preferences, people have different tastes in literature. What one person recommends as a good book may not be enjoyed by another individual. As in all art, however, we can apply certain standards.

In previous chapters we explored many elements of good books, which needn't be repeated at this point. But as we talk about reading good books, we can make some general observations and share the wisdom of experts.

C. S. Lewis defines a good book as one that "permits and invites" good reading. He adds: "It is not enough that attentive and obedient reading should be barely possible if we try hard enough. The author must not leave us to do all the work. He must show, and pretty quickly, that his writing deserves, because it rewards, alert and disciplined reading."[16] Although Lewis initially focuses on a good book as permiting and inviting good reading, he explains that attentive reading ought to be rewarded quickly. What reward is he referring to?

Pleasure. Lewis believes the entire work should generate enjoyment. He writes, "Every episode, explanation, description, dialogue—ideally every sentence—must be pleasurable and interesting for its own sake."[17]

Walker Percy also prioritizes pleasure as the measure of a good book. He writes, "The first rule of thumb, of course, is pleasure. A good book gives the reader pleasure, the sort of deep, abiding pleasure he likes to come back to."[18] Percy makes it clear that he's not talking about superficial gratification but a pleasure profound enough to woo the reader back.

One of the best marks of a good book is if it stands up to multiple readings. Lewis famously defined an unliterary person as someone who reads books only once. Such people view a book they've already read as "dead, like a burnt-out match, an old railway ticket, or yesterday's paper"—a thing used up. "Those who read great works, on the other hand, will read the same work ten, twenty or thirty times during the course of their life."[19] Even after multiple readings, a well-written book will delight the artful reader with new discoveries as well as familiar favorites. Although we know how the story ends, we never grow weary of the way it's told. How is this possible?

Roger Scruton believes we come back to good books because the story is presented through the senses to the mind. He admits we are more interested in what is being said than in the "sensory character of the sounds used to say it." But if stories were "simply reducible" to their information, it would be "inexplicable" for us to constantly return to the words, reading over favorite passages, "allowing the sentences to percolate through our thoughts, long after we have assimilated the plot." The story's "sensory features" unfold in "anticipation and release" in our perception. "To that extent a novel is directed to the senses—but not as an object of sensory delight, like a luxurious chocolate or a fine old wine. Rather as something presented *through* the senses, *to* the mind."[20]

When teaching college classes, I (Leland) frequently describe this characteristic of good literature as "bifocal" (see, for example, chapters 4 and 6). We look through the sensory details and images of the work to real life.

Lewis wrote, "Unless you are really trying to look through the lens you cannot discover whether it is good or bad. We can never know that a piece of writing is bad unless we have begun by trying to read it as if it was very good and ended by discovering that we were paying the author an undeserved compliment."[21]

Scruton urges the reader to consider "any short story by Chekhov." He writes, "Chekhov's art captures life as it is lived and distils it into images that contain a drama, as a drop of dew contains the sky.[22]

Recall how Percy identified bad books as those lying "most of all about the human condition, so that one never recognizes oneself, the deepest part of oneself." Conversely, a good book allows readers to identify with universal truths and experiences that resonate within their very souls. This is what Percy calls "telling the truth."[23]

In his inimitable way, Lewis sums up reading good books: "But in reading great literature I become a thousand men and yet remain myself. . . . Here, as in worship, in love, in moral action, and in knowing, I transcend myself; and am never more myself than when I do."[24]

A GOOD BOOK

We both were pleasantly surprised when first place in the 2018 Great American Read was announced as *To Kill a Mockingbird*. Harper Lee's multi-layered novel about racial injustice and growing up in the Deep South during the 1930s has been widely recognized as a good book since it won the Pulitzer Prize for fiction in 1961. The book is a global favorite, having been translated into over forty languages with more than forty million copies sold worldwide.

It's easy to see why many people love the book. Lee depicts the complexities of racial injustice through the childhood eyes of narrator Scout Finch, an impulsive tomboy and avid reader. Keen insights about growing up within Southern culture and empathizing with marginalized people are woven seamlessly into the story's fabric. The title reflects an evocative and effective metaphor that neatly ties its themes together: To shoot a mockingbird would be a sin. The book's popularity gives us hope for recovering our culture's lost art of reading.

Calling and Creativity

NO BETTER PERSON could introduce a discussion about calling and creativity than the biblical character, Bezalel. Exodus 31:1–6 relates how God called and equipped him to his artistic task. God called Bezalel "by name" and "filled him with the Spirit of God, with ability and intelligence, with knowledge and all craftsmanship, to devise artistic designs, to work in gold, silver, and bronze, in cutting stones for setting, and in carving wood, to work in every craft" (vv. 2, 3–5). God also appointed Oholiab "with him" and tells Moses, "I have given to all able men ability, that they may make all that I have commanded you" (v. 6). These verses demonstrate four specific things about creativity and the creative person's calling.

God calls the individual by name. God called Bezalel to the artistic work of creating items for worship. The fact that God calls the artist by name signifies both the individual's distinctive character and God's intimate knowledge of the person.

God inspires the individual through the Holy Spirit. God "filled" Bezalel with the Holy Spirit. Being filled with the Spirit implies a permeating and continuing presence. The Christian who writes may struggle in many ways. In fact, the more important a work for Christ's kingdom, the more intense difficulties the author will likely face. But the believing writer is inspired and upheld by the Holy Spirit's indwelling.

God equips the artist with specific gifts. God endued Bezalel with inherent talent and a keen intellect, but he also gave him comprehension and skillfulness to design and fashion worship objects in a wide variety of materials and applications.

God provides supportive people. The Lord appointed an assistant to come alongside Bezalel. God gave all the workers the ability and desire to do excellent craftsmanship. Most artistic work takes place in isolation, but networks and friends lighten a writer's load. And all artists need supporters to promote and purchase their work.

These four areas guide us as we explore our calling and creativity as readers and writers. This chapter discusses the concept of calling, views of creativity, and the mystery of inspiration. Then it examines factors involved in the creative process. The chapter concludes with explanations of promotional work and ways others can encourage and support authors. Understanding these concepts helps readers embrace and enjoy their partnership with authors.

WHY WRITE?

Journalists get paid, often per word or article, and technical writers usually earn an hourly wage or salary, but the literary writer receives income through one of the loveliest words in the English language: royalties.

While writers appreciate the income the word represents, the reality may not be quite what many people imagine. Some envision the author, dashing off a book in a few spare moments here and there, then sitting back to enjoy a guaranteed lifelong wealth stream. A few select authors have become millionaires and some earn thousands each year, but many writers don't earn a living wage from royalties. The majority require a second income (like that of a spouse or a teaching career) if they want to eat daily and pay bills monthly. For most authors, the sad truth is that one cannot live on royalties alone.

The time writers devote to their work might be considered abusive in a business situation. Dedicated authors may be at their keyboard early in the morning or late at night, perhaps working more than sixty hours a week. An author usually spends months, even years, slogging away at one manuscript.

Typing "The End" signals the beginning of the long and excruciating process of "shopping" the manuscript. Authors may spend hundreds of dollars and many days attending conferences. With fear and trembling, they scramble for brief appointments with editors or agents, during which they try to sell themselves and their work in ten minutes or less. If the author is fortunate, the editor may ask for a complete proposal and sample chapters. Months later, the author will most likely receive a rejection. But sometimes the publisher expresses an interest. Weeks or months pass. After the proposal makes committee rounds, the publisher either rejects the concept or—happy day!—offers a contract. The author may even receive an advance. An advance isn't a gift or bonus; it's simply a portion of the anticipated royalties paid ahead of time. The author will not receive any royalties until the publisher has earned back the advance money. If that eventually happens, the royalty checks finally begin to arrive. They may show up once every six months, and the amount may be only enough to buy a pizza.

Author royalties are often less than a dollar per book sold, sometimes only pennies. If authors figured out how much money they've earned per hour on a book, they'd probably curl into a fetal ball and cry.

Obviously, literary authors aren't in it for the money. So why in the world do they write? The answer is simple: they have to. Their sense of calling is so compelling, it's as if they have no choice.

This sense of calling is more than an awakened desire. Similar to the calling to ministry, the artistic calling is a God-ordained obligation to perform a specific kind of work. God chooses individuals, whom he knows and loves, and compels them to write. The serious author views writing as a calling, not a hobby.

Unbelieving authors also experience a strong compulsion to write, which they acknowledge as something within themselves or some mysterious influence they can't really explain. But Christians who write can look to the biblical account of Bezalel to understand how God calls them by name.

Calling by name implies God knows the writer intimately. He knows the individual's distinctive character because he endowed it upon that person. Just as God called prophets and apostles to their respective task before they were born,[1] God ordains writers from the womb. They may not be aware of his call or able to practice it until late in life. They may need to acquire much learning and life experience before beginning a writing career. But God formed them with the innate imagination and necessary talent for writing. And write they must.

What about readers? Do they have a calling? Yes. Every person has a calling to read. At this point, such a claim shouldn't seem shocking. Reading continues civilization's conversation and contributes to personal pleasure and spiritual renewal. Christians are people of God's word and are called to read it as well as other literary words.

WHAT IS CREATIVITY?

Creativity is using one's imagination to create an original and artistic work. Note the individual words: *imagination, create, original, artistic,* and *work*. Creativity involves each of those important aspects. The writer employs inherent imagination in crafting something that is both original and artistic. Work is not only the finished product but also the effort used in the process.

Two different traditions about the writer's work have existed side by side in Western history. One (which can be traced back to Plato and the biblical prophets) stresses content over form and sees the writer primarily as a seer with superior insight. This tradition emphasizes spontaneity and inspiration by divine forces. The other tradition (traceable back to Aristotle and the biblical author of Ecclesiastes) stresses form and technique over content and regards the writer as a maker. This tradition emphasizes the self-conscious element in literary creativity.

Christianity has developed its own variations on these two viewpoints. One tradition regards the Christian writer as a creator or maker, as an image-bearer of God. The other Christian tradition views the writer as the agent of God. We both see these two views as complementary parts of a comprehensive perspective, although we give greater weight to the aspect of artists as sub-creators. As God's image-bearers, people have creative abilities. They imagine and make, crafting quilts or sculptures, cakes or paintings, blog posts or fiction. They also are God's agents, realizing they can do nothing without the Spirit's inspiration and equipping.

Dorothy L. Sayers saw the artist as image-bearer, who shares aspects of God's creativity. She wrote, "When we turn back [in the Bible] to see what [God] says about the original upon which the 'image' of God was modeled, we find only the single assertion, 'God created.' The characteristic common to God and man is apparently that: the desire and ability to make things."[2]

Larry Woiwode warns against an inflated view of the writer as creator:

What writers face in the most searing revelation is this: I am the God of this creation. That is the original and ultimate fall. It doesn't help that contemporary writing workshops tend to teach young writers that the ultimate attribute, that of creator, can pass one-on-one to *you*—transforming the rankest beginner into a mini-god. Seasoned writers recognize the trait and realize they must be metaphorical servants to the work at hand.[3]

These quotations from Sayers and Woiwode help us shape a balanced and comprehensive perspective about creativity. Writers can embrace the honor of their creative calling as God's sub-creators, while recognizing how their human frailties and limitations make them totally dependent servants of the Lord. We need both the Spirit's indwelling and his inspiration.

How does this apply to readers? People are image-bearers with creative abilities, in whatever way those skills manifest themselves in individuals. Even people who consider themselves as all thumbs when it comes to craftsmanship possess cognitive creativity. We construct castles in our minds and build bridges in relationships. When we read, we share in the experience of literary creativity.

INSPIRATION

When we consider writing, inspiration can mean different things. The author's inspiration may be something generating an idea, or it may be circumstances facilitating the process. But we're speaking here primarily of the action of a higher force compelling the writer. While compelling may sound forceful, creativity is anything but. It shimmers with ethereal mystery.

We're not talking about the same kind of divine inspiration God used to write the Bible. No authors we know presume their work is the infallible word of God. But you might say writers experience something that dimly echoes divine inspiration.

The etymology of "inspiration" points to the biblical meaning of God breathing or "in-spiriting" Adam to life and men to write his word. In Middle English, the word continued to convey divine guidance. Today's definitions include enlivening or motivating in more general ways; however, we're exploring the sense of inspiration in the mysteries of artistic composition.

Spontaneity and openness factor significantly into inspiration. A famous quotation by Madeleine L'Engle speaks of creativity as "riding the wind." But seeing it in context shows her caution against completely discarding human intellect:

> In the act of creativity, the artist lets go the self-control which he normally clings to and is open to riding the wind. Something almost always happens to startle us during the act of creating, but not unless we let go our adult intellectual control and become as open as little children. This means not to set aside or discard the intellect but to understand that it is not to become a dictator, for when it does we are closed off from revelation.[4]

Writers don't check their brains at the door and become mere recorders of revelation, but they do need to subdue their internal editor or tyrannical logic in order to freely receive inspiration.

Words sometimes seem to come from nowhere and flow onto the page with brilliant precision. But such moments are rare gifts. Authors can't sit around and wait for inspiration to hit. Even when it does strike, inspiration by itself is not enough to complete an artistic creation. The artist must have the inclination and experience to receive the revelation and then perform the work.

THE PROCESS OF CREATIVITY

If creativity could be pinned down, it would be as lifeless as a skewered beetle on a display board. But creativity is as vibrant and elusive as a beautiful butterfly flitting in the sunlight. Its shimmering wings glint tantalizingly and then fold—as if in grateful prayer—when the creature briefly alights on a burst of color.

Authors implement a great variety of rituals or practices, hoping to woo the muse into their minds and wrest the words onto the paper. But these are mere externals, not the internal process. While the creative process can't be presented in a neat little formula, we can identify contributing aspects.

Bret Lott's progression comes close to describing the process without removing its energy or mystery. Lott calls *wonder* and *reverence* the "twin dynamos that generate the art of writing." He adds, "To look at something without wonder and reverence . . . is to dismiss *deliberation*; dismissing deliberation eliminates the possibility for *reflection*; to eliminate reflection is simply and fully and sadly to reject the possibility of *discovery*."[5]

In workshops on creativity, I (Leland) identify an anatomy of ingredients that enter the creative process: memory, observation, imagining, reading, discovery, synthesis, revision, self-expression, design, and perseverance. It's important to note these factors converge with the God-given talent and inspiration already mentioned.

Memory stores the author's reservoir of images, words, experiences, feelings, and sensory perceptions. Most of the time, authors draw from this pool unconsciously. The reality of memories accumulated over the author's lifetime renders verisimilitude to the writing.

Observation is frequently called the writer's eye. Writers observe intensely and thoughtfully. They think, "What does that remind me of?" or "How would I describe that?" They might simply wonder, "Where is that woman going and what will she do when she gets there?" Or an author may look at a high school choir and feel staggered by the weight of all their combined souls' glory.

Imagining, in earlier years, referred to as *inventiveness,* means making things up. Writers employ vivid imaginations, which come to expression when they translate the movies or images in their minds into words on paper.

Reading provides a constant supply of words and knowledge into the author's mind. But it also continually hones the writer's skill by showcasing effective and beautiful styles or techniques.

Discovery delights writers and is a key element in the creative process. Even when crafting nonfiction from a comprehensive outline, authors do not know exactly how the work will turn out. They may be surprised to discover beautiful phrases or unifying threads. Characters in fiction frequently shock the author by what they say or do. Plots take unexpected turns, motifs pop up, or unplanned themes develop. On the shelf directly above Glenda's monitor is a sticky note that says: "I have to write to discover what I have to write."

Synthesis means the ability to see how the various parts connect and make them come together into a coherent whole. Whether the work is factual or imaginative, it is full of details the author must meld into one meaningful unit.

Revision is an often overlooked necessity. The first version of a work isn't called the rough draft for nothing. Writers are exhorted to revise, revise, and then revise again. How often? Until the author knows the work is complete. Writers have an intense desire to get it right. They keep working until they know they've done their best to capture the elusive leprechauns in their mind.

Self-expression reflects the writer's perspective, personality, style, and voice. It is the power of introspection and the ability to recognize what specific thoughts and reflections have universal implications.

Design forms the trellis upon which the work grows and flourishes. It is the idea and the plan. Without a supportive framework, thought vines would curl into thin air and droop unnoticed on the ground.

Perseverance marks the successful writer. Creative people must have the power of concentration and be willing to invest a huge amount of time and effort into their work. If a writer doesn't sit in the chair and put fingers on the keyboard, the work won't be written. Fingers may rest on those keys or dance a tango, but the author must place them there—day after day after day. Another sticky note above Glenda's monitor says: "Begin to write by writing."

SUPPORT YOUR FAVORITE AUTHORS

For the most part, writing is a solitary task. Except for the occasional conference or retreat, writers spend the majority of their time cloistered alone. Perhaps more than most other occupations, writers need fellow believers to come alongside them. Supporting your favorite authors can take a variety of forms, and none of them are difficult or costly. But before getting into specifics, we want to depict a bit of the writing life's promotional aspect.

Having grown up in a small Dutch Reformed enclave, we both carry deeply-engrained aversions to self-promotion. We also believe God has called us to write and feel compelled to whole-heartedly obey that call. For these reasons, we would much rather spend time writing than engage in any aspect of marketing. The reality of the writing life in this day and age, however, requires that every writer apply effort to promotion. Publishers won't take a chance on an author who isn't willing to put some work into marketing a book.

You may recall the earlier description of the long process required to write a book and secure a publisher before beginning to receive regular royalties. But no royalties will appear if the book doesn't sell. And selling it is primarily the responsibility of the author. The amount of marketing undertaken by the publisher depends in general on how large and equipped the publisher is but also on how large a platform a writer has. The writer's platform is the author's visibility. The more books written and sold, the more online activity via social media and blog posts, the more speaking engagements scheduled, the larger the platform. Some authors enjoy all these marketing efforts, but many would rather write. Even authors with large platforms and well-known publishers can expect to expend time and energy in marketing efforts.

Why should readers care about the author's marketing efforts? Because authors aren't actually doing all that work exclusively for personal gain. Yes, we all need to eat. But at the back of the author's mind throughout the writing and marketing process is you, the reader. Writers truly do it all for you. We want to offer you something valuable, something you can take to heart, something that touches your soul. Writers care about their invisible partner, the prospective reader. Shouldn't readers care a bit about authors?

Readers can assist favorite authors in marketing efforts. How? Buy their books! Purchase copies for yourself and give books as gifts. Spread the word by telling other people what you liked about a book and by encouraging them to buy it. Consider writing book reviews. Reviews on websites such as Amazon and Goodreads are crucial in driving sales and boosting ratings. And posting a review is easier than you might imagine. When writing a review, be sure to address the book itself. Mentioning that you know the author or that "Aunt Glenda is a nice person" isn't helpful. Better to say how the author has a knack for writing realistic dialogue and creating believable characters or commend the engaging writing or plot. Be honest and specific by stating what you enjoyed or took away from your reading. Raving vaguely about a book being the best you've ever read won't convince many potential buyers to put it into their online carts.

Readers can also support their favorite author in less concrete ways. Anyone can pray for or with authors. Writers appreciate Christian brothers and sisters who follow the biblical injunction to rejoice with those who rejoice when a big project is complete or when a contract is signed. And writers especially need those who weep with those who weep when the words won't come as deadlines loom or when a rejection crushes their spirits.

The simple courtesy of thoughtful reading is a primary way people support authors. In fact, artful reading strengthens the invisible bond of shared creativity between author and reader. Nicholas Carr explains:

> The bond between book reader and book writer has always been a tightly symbiotic one, a means of intellectual and artistic cross-fertilization. The words of the writer act as a catalyst in the mind of the reader, inspiring new insights, associations, and perception, sometimes even epiphanies. And the very existence of the attentive, critical reader provides the spur for the writer's work. It gives the author confidence to explore new forms of expression, to blaze difficult and demanding paths of thought, to venture into uncharted and sometimes hazardous territory."[6]

The author writes in the hope of stimulating the reader's mind and generating enjoyment. But authors don't know how a book has affected anyone unless someone tells them.

We encourage you to consider ways you can support the Christians you know who write good quality work. No one expects a mechanic or a plumber or a hair stylist to perform their services for nothing. Everyone agrees teachers and ministers and doctors ought to receive a living wage. Why does it seem that authors are expected to provide their work for so little financial compensation? People who think nothing of the price for coffee drinks or restaurant dinners often hesitate to spend money on books. Perhaps they think (as one of us once heard someone say), "Why should we buy any books? We can go to the library and get whatever we want to read." The current trend toward minimalism is admirable, but we hope readers realize the value of physical books in the home and in their hands.

The account of Bezalel shows us that God values artists and equips them for their often difficult artistic endeavors. It also demonstrates how he provides partners in their calling and creativity. We hope this chapter generates within you a desire to embrace your calling and creativity as readers who partner with writers.

22

Literature and the Spiritual Life

Over and Above

INTRIGUED BY THE MANY references to *War and Peace* that cropped up during research for this book, I (Glenda) decided to assuage my guilt for never having read it. I captured winter evenings by doubling time, knitting or crocheting while listening to an audio version. While I often marveled at Tolstoy's literary genius, I was struck most profoundly on a spiritual level.

Contrary to Woody Allen's reported quip, *War and Peace* is not merely about Russia, although Tolstoy portrays the vast panorama of Russian culture across country and city landscapes almost as a beloved character. The novel isn't even about Russians, as much as the reader comes to care about characters caught in the inexorable chaos of war and victimized by societal hypocrites during peace. What many critics and reviewers miss is the novel's overarching exploration of human free will and the sovereignty of God. The book conveys a surprising and convicting spiritual influence.

In a famous statement about how Christians should judge the literature they read, T. S. Eliot spoke of how they need to apply standards "over and above those applied by the rest of the world."[1] We both embrace the principle of "over and above" in our reading of literature as Christians. Beyond simply being artful readers, we can enjoy reading at a spiritual level. The secular world experiences the literary quest for the true, the good, and the beautiful on a human plane only. But if we deliberately relate the true, the good, and the beautiful to God, these three aspects become part of the spiritual life and far more significant than mere enlightened humanism.

We believe the spiritual life is a "value added" component in the reading life. Throughout this book we've given prompts on how to read literature from a Christian viewpoint, but here at the end we want to incorporate those prompts into a summarized game plan for reading literature as an active part of spiritual life.

This chapter integrates the main points of our book under the motif of *finding*. Our unifying format of *finding* certain features of the spiritual life in literature implies that Christian readers should be active in *seeking* those features while reading.

FINDING GOD IN LITERATURE

Finding God is the primary task of everyone born into the human race. This calling includes multiple dimensions, but the one that towers above all others in importance is finding God as Lord and Savior of one's life. This comes in the form of either a conscious turning to God—a conversion—at a specific moment in time, or a gradual assent of the mind and heart to believe that God exists and is Lord of all and one's personal Savior.

Can literature be the actual agent God uses to bring a person to conversion? If we are skeptical, it is probably because we have not encountered people who trace their Christian conversion to reading specific works of literature. Considering the following five testimonials will be both enlightening and edifying.[2]

Someone joining Tenth Presbyterian Church in Philadelphia began his written testimony with the statement, "I was led to the

Lord by John Milton." He went on to explain that while reading *Paradise Lost* he felt within himself an "unholy alliance" with the character of Satan. He realized he was a sinner, "cried out to the Lord to save [him]," and found his prayer answered a week later.[3]

A professor of English who was raised in a liberal Protestant church repudiated his faith when he entered college. He recounts how "God drew me to him (unbeknownst to me at the time)" through four novels recommended to him by secular friends. He "was saved [through the influence] of Graham Greene and Evelyn Waugh [rather than] a preacher."

A young woman was brought into a personal encounter with Jesus leading to her conversion as a result of a two-hour reading of what would seem to be an unlikely agent of salvation—J. D. Salinger's novel *Franny and Zooey.*

Simone Weil, who became a famous French mystic, had long treasured and recited George Herbert's poem that begins "Love bade me welcome." Weil testified that "during one of those recitations . . . Christ himself came down and took possession of me."[4]

A political refugee from China, who had been imprisoned for involvement in the freedom uprising of 1989, read Milton's *Paradise Lost* during his eventual college education in North Carolina. The result was that he "accepted the Christian gospel and it changed [his life]."[5]

Other people testify to how literature brought them back to belief after having drifted from it. One of these stories comes from a college student who found himself bereft of his childhood faith in the gospel. His girlfriend (and eventual wife) suggested he read C. S. Lewis's Chronicles of Narnia series. While reading *The Silver Chair,* this person "put [his] faith back in Jesus Christ." His fuller account is that "as I read *The Silver Chair* I encountered the presence of the living God."

These are striking instances of finding God in literature. We should neither sensationalize them nor underrate them. As vehicles for conversion or recommitment, they are on a par with reading the Bible or listening to a sermon or conversing with a Christian in a coffee shop. Although the Bible is God's inspired word, he can choose any hearing of the word or reading of any words to bring spiritual renewal in a person. Just as the literary imagination often heightens human experience to help us see issues with greater clarity, the anecdotes we have cited prove with more-than-ordinary clarity that we can find God in literature.

Assured *that* this can happen, we can consider *how* it happens. First we need to recognize how large a proportion of English and American literature sprang from Christian cultures. To this we can add the literature written by Christians even in the secular modern era. Because most of this literature is God-centered and biblical, it is no wonder we find God in it. Even secular readers or scholars would encounter God in their ordinary reading or literary analysis of it. For a reader who wishes to find God in literature, the task consists partly of choosing literature with God in the picture.

At this point, it is useful to review the paradigm of a continuum on which we can place literature as a whole. At one end we find the *literature of Christian affirmation.* In the middle we have the *literature of common human experience* (literature that expresses the shared wisdom of the human race while stopping short of explicit Christian references), and at the other end is the *literature of unbelief.* Even if the literature of common humanity does not bring God explicitly into its picture of reality, it is easy for a Christian reader to supply the God who is there but not acknowledged in the work itself. If a nature poem stops short of ascribing the beauty or benevolence of nature to God, a Christian reader can still ascribe it to God. Such literature provides the materials for finding God, with the responsibility for doing so residing with the reader.

What about the literature of unbelief? Can we find God in it? If we are sufficiently active in supplying our own Christian convictions, we can. Just as in ordinary life a person can be present in our awareness even when absent, and often because of that absence, so too we can sense the existence of God even in literature that fails to acknowledge him. The literature of unbelief creates a vacant space, which a Christian reader correctly sees as needing to be filled by God. In the very act of protesting the omission of God, we find God—not in the work but in our interaction with it.

FINDING SPIRITUAL NURTURE IN LITERATURE

God is the essence of the spiritual life. Finding him is the greatest treasure, and after he is found, he remains at the center. As Christians we desire all of life to be part of our spiritual existence. We want the events of our lives, including our literary experiences, to nurture our spiritual life in Christ. Because it *is* a life, it needs to be fed. How can literature feed us spiritually?

Again it will be helpful to begin with a few testimonials. One of these came from a former student (of Leland's) who has suffered from chronic fatigue syndrome throughout her adult life. She received spiritual direction and sustenance from Milton's sonnet on his blindness.[6] After the poet contemplates the narrowing of life's options due to physical disability, he concludes that "they also serve who only stand and wait." This poem "really struck a chord" with the sufferer. She professes to have "remembered and reminded [herself] as well as others" of Milton's aphoristic line about waiting on God. The poem has nurtured her spiritual life, and she has used it to minister to others.

This same sonnet has been a beacon for a career missionary. He claims that Milton's line about standing and waiting "was a source of strength to me during our twenty years in Japan," as well as later when waiting for a position to open up.

Another of Leland's students recalls a year in college that she characterizes as "a difficult one in regards to spiritual struggle," even though she was a believer. She attributes a great breakthrough to an assigned reading in Book 3 of Milton's *Paradise Lost*, where God the Father and God the Son engage in an exalted dialogue to determine how to resolve the plight of fallen humanity. The dialogue ends with the Son's offer to undertake the redemption of the human race. The student "had never been so genuinely moved by literature before." Although she professed "a great love for literature," this reading experience was different "because I knew that what I was reading was so much more." She described the result as "a new dimension to my Christianity, and I am becoming fuller in the Lord."

Clearly, literature can provide spiritual nurture on life's journey. The case for literature's spiritual influence does not rest on these testimonials, but they encapsulate what is possible. They can serve as a model and incentive to us in our own literary sojourns. Among other uses, they can prompt us to desire spiritual uplift in our reading and, in light of that, make better choices in what literature to read (though spiritual edification is not the only criterion that should govern our choice of reading material).

Before we proceed to consider how literature can provide spiritual nurture for daily living, we should recall the idea of the Bible as literature. At least three-fourths of the Bible is literary in form. In other words, literature is the most customary vehicle for conveying truth in the Bible. People who undervalue the spiritual potential of literature tend to assume that the literary forms of the Bible are different from literary forms in literature generally, but this is a false assumption. A story is a story, and a poem is a poem. Each format operates exactly the same in the Bible and beyond the Bible. Furthermore, it is incorrect to separate the content of the Bible from the form in which it is expressed. When a person embraces the truth of the Bible as presented in a story or poem, the vehicle has been the story or poem, not some illusory free-floating truth separate from a literary vehicle. Our argument is that *of course* literature can be a channel by which spiritual nurture enters our lives. The Bible proves it.

Literature achieves its spiritual influence in ways parallel to those in the preceding section about finding God in literature. Christian sustenance comes most naturally when we read the literature of Christian affirmation. Here the process is the same as when we read the Bible. The Victorian enthusiast for literature Matthew Arnold overstated the case when he said that literature as a whole, regardless of its ideational perspective, tells us the truth about "how to live,"[7] but we can affirm Arnold's formula with the literature of Christian affirmation. Such literature is a spiritual guide first through the examples of characters and events it places before us. With literature, including the literature of the Bible, an author presents us with positive examples to emulate and negative ones to avoid. To say (as debunkers do) that this is a simplistic view of literature is beside the point; it is how literature works. In addition to presenting examples of character and action, literary authors use devices of disclosure and authorial assertions and persuasive strategies to prompt readers' responses. Christian authors point us down a spiritually correct path.

With the literature of common human experience and the literature of unbelief, spiritual nurture requires a more active stance from us. Sometimes we need to add something to a picture that is not wrong but simply incomplete—as with a story that elevates domestic values as a human experience only. At other times, we need to exercise corrective action to counter what a work is prompting us to believe or emulate. In the very act of countering and correcting what is being urged upon us, we can be strengthened in our spiritual commitment. Additionally, when we compare literature that is devoid of spiritual truth to the truth that we have in our Christian faith, we are led to gratitude for our riches in Christ. Interacting with the literature of unbelief can thus become a spiritual exercise.

FINDING THE TRUE, THE GOOD, AND THE BEAUTIFUL IN LITERATURE

An appropriate final consideration about how literature nurtures the spiritual life is to think of reading experiences as valuing what God values. What does God value that literature provides? The true, the good, and the beautiful. This familiar triad, first formulated by the Greek philosopher Plato, underlies most philosophic discourse, including perspectives on literature and the arts, even when the triad is not explicitly named. Philippians 4:8 is a biblical version of the paradigm: "whatever is true, whatever is honorable, whatever is just, whatever is pure, whatever is lovely, whatever is commendable, . . . think about these things." How can literature help us find the true, the good, and the beautiful?

We can understand literature's truth as a component of the spiritual life within the context of the Bible's teaching about truth. The following ideas summarize that teaching:[8]

1. Because God is the source of all truth, we can think of truth as God's possession.
2. God reveals his truth in two primary ways—in the Bible (special revelation) and in human reason, human thought, and nature (natural revelation).
3. Because truth conflicts endlessly with error in our fallen world, people must search for truth in order to find it.
4. Whenever we find truth, we must embrace it and walk in it.

As we apply these "truth principles" to reading literature, we can add the application that *all* truth, wherever we find it and whatever its secondary source, is precious to a Christian.

Literary truth divides itself into two categories, in keeping with literature's nature. Representational truth is truthfulness to human experience. Literature "holds the mirror up to nature" or life, as Shakespeare summarized the classical view of literature.[9] Reading puts us in touch with bedrock human experience. Literature keeps calling us back to the enduring elements of life—to nature, family, people and their relationships, human fears and longings, and institutions such as country and church. As the Bible itself demonstrates, God has placed us into this world with the intention that we will understand it and, to the degree to which it is good, embrace it. To live well and responsibly, we need to know the truth about ourselves, our fellow humans, and our world. God expects us to possess this body of truth, and it is part of the spiritual life.

The other type of literary truth is ideational truth. In the nature of literature, authors not only portray human life in the world but also offer an interpretation of it. Not all ideas embodied and asserted in works of literature are true. When they are false, God expects us to discern error, repudiate it, and counter it with the truth. That too is part of the spiritual life. But much literature offers us true ideas, and embracing this truth is to share God's delight in it. Moving with accuracy among the truth claims of literary works is a way of "walking in the truth" as part of the spiritual life (3 John 4).

As God values what is true, he equally values what is good. In literature, the good falls within the sphere of morality—human conduct, especially as manifested in personal relationships. God is both the chief exemplar of goodness and the origin of it among people. The goal of Christians is to behave in a moral way, but we need to know the difference between virtue and vice before we can live virtuously.

Although the Bible is our ultimate sourcebook, we find a testing ground in moving vicariously among examples of moral and immoral conduct in the pages of literature.

The moral life begins with intellectual knowledge of what is good, but a second aspect is moral influence that prompts us in actual living. Literature is a leading source of moral influence in the lives of readers. The influence flows partly from examples of good and bad behavior, and partly from moral ideas promoted directly and indirectly. Authors carefully design systems of influence to prompt our approval and disapproval. For literature to be a channel of good entering our lives, we need to monitor our responses to the moral prompts we read. When we do, we can find ourselves sharing God's love of what is good.

With the true and the good in literature, Christians need to read as partly resistant readers. We need to keep up our guard against possible error and immorality and, when we encounter them, resist them with truth and goodness. In the words of Milton, we should read "with wariness and good antidote."[10]

With beauty, the third in our triad of divine qualities, we can largely relax our vigilance. Beauty is beauty, and when we see and delight in it, we are seeing and delighting in a quality God has created. God is the source of beauty. He created a beautiful world and gave beauty as a gift to the human race. To delight in beauty is to delight in a quality of God himself. The classic comment on how we can make beauty a part of the spiritual life comes from Jonathan Edwards: "For as God is infinitely the greatest being, so he is allowed to be infinitely the most beautiful and excellent: and all the beauty to be found throughout the whole creation, is but the reflection of the diffused beams of that Being who hath an infinite fullness of brightness and glory."[11] When we revel in the artistry and beauty of literature, we can trace the diffused beams of that beauty to God.

Near the beginning of this chapter, we noted how the Christian faith enables readers to raise their literary experience "over and above" what non-Christians experience. Secular people can value the true, the good, and the beautiful in literature, though they usually seem less ardent about it than Christians. The "value added" component by which we pursue the true, the good, and the beautiful part of the spiritual life is twofold: we can actively look for these three pillars of life in our literary journeys, and we can consciously relate them to their divine Creator, being grateful to God for his gifts.

Notes

Chapter 1: Is Reading Lost?

1. Eric Partridge, *A Dictionary of Catch Phrases: American and British from the Sixteenth Century to the Present Day* (Lanham, MD: Scarborough House, 1992), 254.

2. Stephen Nichols, "Read Any Good Books Lately?" 5 Minutes in Church History, August 20, 2014, https://www.5minutesinchurchhistory.com /read-any-good-books-lately/; Sinclair Ferguson, *Read Any Good Books?* (Carlisle, PA: Banner of Truth, 2005).

3. Gene Edward Veith Jr., *Reading between the Lines: A Christian Guide to Literature* (Wheaton, IL: Crossway), 25.

4. National Endowment for the Arts, *Reading on the Rise: A New Chapter in American Literacy*, January 2009, https://www.arts.gov/sites/default /files/ReadingonRise.pdf. National Endowment for the Arts, *Reading at Risk: A Survey of Literary Reading in America*, June 2004, https://www .arts.gov/sites/default/files/ReadingAtRisk.pdf.

5. Andrew Perrin, "Who Doesn't Read Books in America?" Pew Research Center, September 26, 2019, https://www.pewresearch.org/fact-tank /2018/03/23/who-doesnt-read-books-in-america.

6. The Royal Society of Literature, "Literature in Britain Today: An IPSOS MORI poll of Public Opinion Commissioned by the Royal Society of Literature," March 1, 2017, https://225475-687350-raikfcquaxqncofqfm .stackpathdns.com/wp-content/uploads/2017/02/RSL-Literature-in -Britain-Today_01.03.17.pdf.

7. "Average Daily Time Spent Reading per Capita in the United States in 2018, by Age Group," June 2019, https://www.statista.com/statistics /412454/average-daily-time-reading-us-by-age.

8. Rob Marvin, "Tech Addiction by the Numbers: How Much Time We Spend Online," PCmag.com, June 11, 2018, https://www.pcmag.com

/article/361587/tech-addiction-by-the-numbers-how-much-time-we
-spend-online.

9. Andrew Perrin and Madhu Kumar, "About Three-in-Ten U.S. Adults
Say They Are 'Almost Constantly' Online," Pew Research Center, July
25, 2019, https://www.pewresearch.org/fact-tank/2018/03/14/about-a
-quarter-of-americans-report-going-online-almost-constantly.

10. *Encyclopaedia Britannica Online*, s.v., "War and Peace: Novel by Tolstoy,"
by Margaret Anne Doody, accessed June 1, 2018, https://www.britannica
.com/topic/War-and-Peace.

11. Nicholas Carr, "Is Google Making Us Stupid? What the Internet Is Doing
to Our Brains," *The Atlantic*, July/August 2008, https://theatlantic.com
/magazine/archive/2008/07/is-google-making-us-stupid/306868.

12. Clay Shirky, "Why Abundance Is Good: A Reply to Nick Carr," *Encyclopaedia Britannica* (blog), July 17, 2008, http://blogs.britannica.com
/2008/07/why-abundance-is-good-a-reply-to-nick-carr.

13. Alan Jacobs, *The Pleasures of Reading in an Age of Distraction* (New York:
Oxford, 2011), 105.

14. Stacy Conradt, "The Quick 10: The 10 Longest Novels Ever," Mental
Floss, May 16, 2008, http://mentalfloss.com/article/18661/quick-10
-10-longest-novels-ever.

15. James Wood, "Movable Types: How 'War and Peace' Works," *The New
Yorker*, November 19, 2007, https://www.newyorker.com/magazine/2007
/11/26/movable-types.

16. Philip Hensher, "War and Peace: The 10 Things You Need to Know
(If You Haven't Actually Read It)," *The Guardian*, January 22, 2016,
https://www.theguardian.com/books/2016/jan/22/war-and-peace-guide
-philip-hensher.

17. Michael Harris, *The End of Absence: Reclaiming What We've Lost in a World
of Constant Connection* (New York: Penguin, 2014).

18. Clive Thompson, "Reading War and Peace on my iPhone," accessed
February 16, 2019, https://br5.bookriot.com/quarterly/bkr07/amp. This
article is no longer available online.

19. Jacobs, *The Pleasures of Reading in an Age of Distraction*, 81.

20. Nicholas Carr, *The Shallows: What the Internet Is Doing to Our Brains*
(New York: Norton, 2010), 115–16. Interestingly, Carr reprised the
subtitle of his 2008 article as the subtitle of this 2010 book.

21. Richard Freed, "The Tech Industry's War on Kids," Medium, https://
medium.com/@richardnfreed/the-tech-industrys-psychological-war-on
-kids-c452870464ce.

22. Maryanne Wolf, *Proust and the Squid: The Story and Science of the Reading Brain* (New York: HarperCollins, 2007), 221, 225.

23. Sven Birkerts, *Changing the Subject: Art and Attention in the Internet Age* (Minneapolis: Graywolf, 2015), 146–47.

24. Annie Murphy Paul, "Reading Literature Makes Us Smarter and Nicer," *Time*, June 3, 2013, https://ideas.time.com/2013/06/03/why-we-should-read-literature.

25. Carr, "Is Google Making Us Stupid?"

26. Michael Harris, "I Have Forgotten How to Read," The Globe and Mail, February 9, 2018, https://www.theglobeandmail.com/opinion/i-have-forgotten-how-toread/article37921379.

27. Sven Birkerts, *The Gutenberg Elegies* (New York: Farrar, Straus & Giroux, 2006), 74.

28. Philip Yancey, "The Death of Reading Is Threatening the Soul," *The Washington Post*, July 21, 2017, https://washingtonpost.com/news/acts-of-faith/wp/2017/07/21/the-death-of-reading-is-threatening-the-soul/?utm_term=.922e7e252282.

Chapter 2: What Have We Lost?

1. C. S. Lewis, *An Experiment in Criticism* (Cambridge: Cambridge University Press, 1962), 140.

2. Francis Bacon, "Of Studies," from Essays of Francis Bacon, Authorama, accessed March 5, 2020, http://www.authorama.com/essays-of-francis-bacon-50.html.

3. T. S. Eliot, preface to *The Sacred Wood* (London: Methuen, 1920, 1960), viii.

4. Robert Lee, *Religion and Leisure in American Life* (Nashville: Abingdon, 1964), 35.

5. Richard Winter, *Still Bored in a Culture of Entertainment* (Downers Grove, IL: InterVarsity Press, 2002).

6. Helen Gardner, *In Defence of the Imagination* (Oxford: Oxford University Press, 1982), 29.

7. Abraham Kuyper, *Calvinism* (Grand Rapids, MI: Eerdmans, 1943), 142.

8. Matthew Arnold, "The Function of Criticism at the Present Time," in *Criticism: The Major Texts*, ed. Walter Jackson Bate (New York: Harcourt, Brace & World, 1952), 458.

9. C. S. Lewis, "Learning in War-Time," in *The Weight of Glory and Other Essays* (New York: Macmillan, 1949), 50–51.

10. Northrop Frye, *Spiritus Mundi: Essays on Literature, Myth, and Society* (Bloomington, IN: Indiana University Press, 1976), 43.

11. Wendell Berry, *Living by Words* (San Francisco: North Point Press, 1983), 14.

12. Felix Timmermans, as quoted in Bob Claessens, preface to *Brueghel* (New York: Alpine, n.d.).

13. Ralph Waldo Emerson, "The Poet," in *Major Writers of America*, ed. Perry Miller (New York: Harcourt, Brace & World, 1962), 1:530–31.

14. William Faulkner, Nobel Prize acceptance speech, (speech, Nobel Banquet, City Hall, Stockholm, December 10, 1950), accessed March 5, 2019, https://www.nobelprize.org/prizes/literature/1949/faulkner /speech/.

15. Carl Jung, *Psychological Reflections*, ed. Jolande Jacobi (Princeton, NJ: Princeton University Press, 1953), 47.

16. Malcolm Muggeridge, *Jesus Rediscovered* (Garden City, NY: Doubleday, 1969), 79.

17. Lewis, *An Experiment in Criticism*, 140; Bacon, "Of Studies."

18. Lewis, *An Experiment in Criticism*, 137.

Chapter 3: Why Consider Reading an Art?

1. Maryanne Wolf, *Proust and the Squid: The Story and Science of the Reading Brain* (New York: HarperCollins, 2007), 216.

2. Timothy Spurgin, *The Art of Reading*, Course No. 2198, The Great Courses audio CD. The Teaching Company, 2009.

3. Peter J. Leithart, "Author, Authority, and the Humble Reader," in *The Christian Imagination: The Practice of Faith in Literature and Writing*, ed. Leland Ryken (Colorado Springs, CO: Shaw, 2002), 209–10.

4. Damon Young, *The Art of Reading* (London: Scribe, 2018), 3, 6.

5. C. S. Lewis, *An Experiment in Criticism* (Cambridge: Cambridge University Press, 2013), 19.

6. Hans R. Rookmaaker, *Art Needs No Justification* (1978), accessed March 5, 2019, http://dickstaub.com/staublog/art-needs-no-justification-complete -hans-rookmaaker.

7. Young, *The Art of Reading*, 8, 14.

8. C. S. Lewis, "The Christian Reader," as reprinted in *The Christian Imagination: The Practice of Faith in Literature and Writing*, ed. Leland Ryken (Colorado Springs: Shaw, 2002), 226–27.

9. James Sire, *How to Read Slowly: Reading for Comprehension* (Wheaton, IL: Shaw, 2000), 15.

10. Lewis, *An Experiment in Criticism*, 137–38.

11. Dorothy Sayers, *The Mind of the Maker* (San Francisco: Harper, 1987), 113–15.

12. Sayers, *The Mind of the Maker*, 111.
13. *Merriam-Webster Dictionary*, s.v. "aesthetic," accessed March 5, 2020, https://www.merriam-webster.com/dictionary/aesthetic.
14. Clyde S. Kilby, *The Arts and the Christian Imagination* (Brewster, MA: Paraclete, 2016), 121.
15. Kilby, *The Arts and the Christian Imagination*, 42.
16. *The Belgic Confession* (sometimes called simply *Confession of Faith*), written primarily by Guido de Brès in 1561, Article II.
17. John Calvin, *Institutes of the Christian Religion*, I.l.i, iii (Grand Rapids, MI: Eerdmans, 1983).
18. Kilby, *The Arts and the Christian Imagination*, 107–8.
19. Kilby, *The Arts and the Christian Imagination*, 132.

Chapter 4: What Is Literature?
1. R. F. Daubemire, *Plants and Environment* (New York: Wiley, 1973), 434–35.
2. Mark Twain, *Life on the Mississippi* (New York: Penguin Books, 228–29). *Life on the Mississippi* exists in many editions and this quotation can be found in chapter 30, no matter what edition you happen to be holding.
3. Louise M. Rosenblatt, *Literature as Exploration*, 3rd edition (New York: Noble and Noble, 1976), 38.
4. C. S. Lewis, "The Language of Religion," in *Christian Reflections*, ed. Walter Hooper (Grand Rapids, MI: Eerdmans, 1967), 133.
5. Dorothy Sayers, "Toward a Christian Esthetic," in *Letters to a Diminished Church* (Nashville: W Publishing Group, Thomas Nelson, 2004), 160.
6. C. S. Lewis, *Reflections on the Psalms* (New York: Harcourt, Brace & World, 1958), 5.
7. C. S. Lewis, "On Stories," in *Essays Presented to Charles Williams*, ed. Lewis (Grand Rapids, MI: Eerdmans, 1966), 103.
8. Northrop Frye, *The Educated Imagination* (Bloomington, IN: Indiana University Press, 1964), 63.
9. Joyce Cary, *Art and Reality: Ways of the Creative Process* (Garden City, NY: Doubleday, 1961), 105, 174.
10. Gerard Manley Hopkins, "Poetry and Verse," in *Gerard Manley Hopkins: The Major Poems*, ed. Walford Davies (London: J. M. Dent and Sons, 1979), 38.
11. Dylan Thomas, "Poetic Manifesto," in *The Poet's Work*, ed. Reginald Gibbons (Boston: Houghton Mifflin, 1979), 185–86.

12. "New Edition Includes 39 Different Farewells to 'Arms,'" NPR, July 22, 2012, https://www.npr.org/2012/07/22/156991302/new-edition-includes-39-different-farewells-to-arms.

13. C. S. Lewis, *An Experiment in Criticism* (Cambridge: Cambridge University Press, 2013), 82–83.

14. C. S. Lewis, *A Preface to Paradise Lost* (1942; repr. New York: Oxford University Press, 1970), 1.

Chapter 5: Why Does Literature Matter?

1. J. B. Broadbent, *Paradise Lost: Introduction* (Cambridge: Cambridge University Press, 1972), 101.

2. Stephen Mallarmé, from a conversation with the French artist Degas, recorded in *The Collected Works of Paul Valéry* (New York: Pantheon Books, 1960), 12:62.

3. Joseph Conrad, preface to *The Nigger of the Narcissus* (New York: Collier Books, 1962), 19.

4. Flannery O'Connor, *Mystery and Manners*, ed. Sally and Robert Fitzgerald (New York: Farrar, Straus & Giroux, 1957, 1962), 96, 84.

5. Nathan A. Scott Jr., *Modern Literature and the Religious Frontier* (New York: Harper and Brothers, 1958), 52.

6. Robert Frost, "The Figure a Poem Makes," in *Writers on Writing*, ed. Walter Allen (Boston: The Writer, Inc., 1948), 22.

7. Matthew Arnold, "To a Friend," line 12, and "Maurice de Guérin," in *The Norton Anthology of English Literature*, ed. M H. Abrams (New York: W. W. Norton, 1962), 2:879, 927.

8. Denise Levertov, *The Poet in the World* (New York: New Directions, 1973), 116.

9. Ralph Waldo Emerson, "The Poet," in *Major Writers of America*, ed. Perry Miller (New York: Harcourt, Brace & World, 1962), 1:534.

10. R. A. Scott-James, *The Making of Literature* (London: Martin Secker, 1928), 343.

11. Matthew Arnold, "Wordsworth," in *The Norton Anthology of English Literature*, ed. M. H. Abrams (New York: W. W. Norton, 1962), 2:939.

12. Robert Frost, quoted in Elizabeth Drew, *Poetry: A Modern Guide to Its Understanding and Enjoyment* (New York: Dell, 1959), 84.

13. C. S. Lewis, *A Preface to Paradise Lost* (1942; repr., New York: Oxford University Press, 1970), 3.

14. Auriel Kolna, "Contrasting the Ethical with the Aesthetical," *British Journal of Aesthetics* 12 (1972): 340.

15. Thomas Aquinas's Latin statement *"id quod visum placet"* has been variously translated; the translation used here is from Jacques Maritain, *Creative Intuition in Art and Poetry* (Cleveland, OH: World Publishing Company, 1953), 122.

16. Samuel Taylor Coleridge, *Biographia Literaria*, ed. John Shawcross (Oxford: Oxford University Press, 1907), 2:221.

17. Matthew Arnold, "Literature and Science," in *Prose of the Victorian Period*, ed. William C. Buckley (Boston: Houghton Mifflin, 1958), 493–94.

18. Annie Dillard, *The Writing Life* (New York: Harper and Row, 1989), 72–73.

Chapter 6: What Does Literature Offer?

1. J. R. R Tolkien, *The Hobbit* (New York: Random House, 1978), 15.

2. Joseph Epstein, "The Bookish Life: How to Read and Why," First Things, November 2018, https://www.firstthings.com/article/2018/11/the-bookish-life.

3. Emily Dickinson, "There Is No Frigate Like a Book," Poetry Foundation, accessed October 8, 2020, https://www.poetryfoundation.org/poems/52199/there-is-no-frigate-like-a-book-1286.

4. Elizabeth Goudge, *A Book of Comfort* (Glasgow: William Collins Sons, 1964), 5.

5. C. S. Lewis, *An Experiment in Criticism* (Cambridge: Cambridge University Press, 2013), 138.

6. Sven Birkerts, "Reading as a State of Being," in *The Christian Imagination*, ed. Leland Ryken (Colorado Springs, CO: Shaw Books, 2002), 229–30.

7. Lewis, *An Experiment in Criticism*, 19, 21–22.

8. Lewis, *An Experiment in Criticism*, 138.

9. John Keats, "On First Looking into Chapman's Homer," in *The Complete Poems and Selected Letters of John Keats* (New York: Random House Modern Library, 2001), 43.

10. T. S. Eliot, *On Poetry and Poets* (London: Faber and Faber, 1957), 68.

11. Kenneth Burke, "Literature as Equipment for Living," in *The Philosophy of Literary Form* (Baton Rouge, LA: Louisiana State University Press, 1941), 293–304.

12. Dorothy Sayers, "Toward a Christian Aesthetic," in *Unpopular Opinions* (London: Victor Gollanz, 1946), 39–40.

13. Joseph Addison, "The Spectator, Nos. 411–421," Minnesota State (website), accessed March 14, 2020, http://web.mnstate.edu/gracyk/courses/web%20publishing/addisoncontents.htm.

Chapter 7: Reading Stories

1. Isak Dineson quoted in Dan B. Allender and Lisa K. Fann, *To Be Told Workbook* (Colorado Springs, CO: WaterBrook, 2005), 30.
2. John Shea, *Stories of God* (Chicago: Thomas More Press, 1978), 7–8.
3. Elizabeth Bowen, *Pictures and Conversations* (New York: Knopf, 1975), 34.
4. Kenneth Burke, *A Grammar of Motives and a Rhetoric of Motives* (Cleveland, OH: Meridian, 1962), 3, 6–9, 15.
5. Flannery O'Connor, *Mystery and Manners*, ed. Sally and Robert Fitzgerald (New York: Farrar, Strauss & Giroux, 1957), 75.
6. Shea, *Stories of God*, 8.
7. Simon O. Lesser, *Fiction and the Unconscious* (Chicago: University of Chicago Press, 1957). The title of this book conceals the wide-ranging nature of the book, which is an excellent overview of narrative in general.
8. Daniel Taylor quoted in *Tell Me a Story*, in Dan B. Allender and Lisa K. Fann, *To Be Told Workbook* (Colorado Springs, CO: WaterBrook, 2005), 34.
9. Homer, *The Odyssey*, trans. W. H. D. Rouse (New York: Signet Classics, 2007), 105.
10. Sir Philip Sidney, *Apology for Poesy*, in *Criticism: The Major Statements*, ed. Charles Kaplan (New York: St. Martin's Press, 1964), 124.
11. O'Connor, *Mystery and Manners*, 107.
12. Thomas Hardy quoted in Frank B. Pinion, *Thomas Hardy: Art and Thought* (London: Palgrave Macmillan, 1977), 8.
13. Shea, *Stories of God*, 9.

Chapter 8: Reading Poems

1. John Calvin, *Calvin's Commentaries*, Vol. IV (Grand Rapids, MI: Baker, 2003) Psalms, xxxvi–xxxvii.
2. Edward Hirsch, *A Poet's Glossary* (Boston: Houghton Mifflin, 2014), 473.
3. Northrop Frye, *The Well-Tempered Critic* (Bloomington, IN: Indiana University Press, 1963), 18.
4. Owen Barfield, *Poetic Diction: A Study in Meaning* (New York: McGraw-Hill, 1964), 63–64.
5. M. L. Rosenthal, *Poetry and the Common Life* (New York: Oxford University Press, 1974), 10.
6. Winifred Nowottny, *The Language Poets Use* (New York: Oxford University Press, 1962).
7. C. S. Lewis, *Christian Reflections* (Grand Rapids, MI: Eerdmans, 1967), 131.

8. Emily Dickinson, "After Great Pain, a Formal Feeling Comes," Poetry Foundation, accessed October 8, 2020, https://www.poetryfoundation .org/poems/47651/after-great-pain-a-formal-feeling-comes-372.

9. Robert Frost, "Education by Poetry," an essay originally delivered at Amherst College in 1931, accessed March 5, 2019, http://www.en.utexas .edu/amlit/amlitprivate/scans/edbypo.html.

10. John Keats, "On First Looking into Chapman's Homer," in *The Complete Poems and Selected Letters of John Keats* (New York: Random House, 2001), 43.

11. William Shakespeare, Sonnet 73 ("That Time of Year Thou Mayest in Me Behold"), Poetry Foundation, accessed October 8, 2020, https:// www.poetryfoundation.org/poems/45099/sonnet-73-that-time-of-year -thou-mayst-in-me-behold.

12. Edgar Allan Poe, "The Poetic Principle," in *Major Writers of America*, ed. Perry Miller (New York: Harcourt, Brace and World, 1962), 1:471.

13. Ben Jonson, *The Works of Ben Jonson* (London: Bickers and Son, 1875), 9:213.

14. See the George Herbert's "Easter Wings" poem at https://www.poetry foundation.org/poems/44361/easter-wings.

15. For examples, see Elizabeth Bishop's "Sestina" at http://staff.washington.edu /rmcnamar/383/bishop.html and Dylan Thomas's "Do Not Go Gentle into That Good Night" at https://poets.org/poem/do-not-go-gentle-good-night.

16. C. S. Lewis, "Edmund Spenser," in *Major British Writers*, ed. G. B. Harrison (New York: Harcourt, Brace & World, 1959), 1:102. Elsewhere Lewis wrote that in a great work of literature "we demand what I should call Deliciousness—what the older critics often called simply 'Beauty'" (Lewis, *Williams and the Arthuriad* [Grand Rapids, MI: Eerdmans, 1974], 374).

17. Samuel Taylor Coleridge, *Table Talk* in Hirsch, *A Poet's Glossary*, 474.

18. Flannery O'Connor, *Mystery and Manners*, ed. Sally and Robert Fitzgerald (New York: Farrar, Straus & Giroux, 1957, 1962), 84.

Chapter 9: Reading Novels

1. C. S. Lewis, *Christian Reflections* (Grand Rapids, MI: Eerdmans, 1995), 10. The latter part of the quotation is his translation of a Latin saying he attributes to Thomas Aquinas.

2. Os Guinness, *Invitation to the Classics* (Grand Rapids, MI: Baker, 1998), 16.

3. Bret Lott, *Letters and Life: On Being a Writer, on Being a Christian* (Wheaton, IL: Crossway, 2013), 14.

4. Bret Lott, *The Best Christian Short Stories* (Nashville, TN: Westbow, 2006), VIII.

5. Gene Edward Veith Jr., *Reading between the Lines: A Christian Guide to Literature* (Wheaton, IL: Crossway, 1990), 64.

6. Jane Austen, *Pride and Prejudice* (New York: Penguin, 1996), 7.

7. Thomas Brooks, *The Mute Christian under the Smarting Rod* (London: Nicholson, 1806), x.

8. Marilynne Robinson, *Gilead* (New York: Farrar, Strauss & Giroux, 2004), 3.

9. Justin Taylor, "R. C. Sproul: A Novel Every Christian Should Consider Reading," TGC (blog), September 12, 2014, https://thegospelcoalition.org/blogs/Justin-taylor/r-c-sproul-a-novel-every-christian-should-consider-reading.

10. R. C. Sproul, "The Unholy Pursuit of God in Moby Dick," *Tabletalk*, August 1, 2011, ligonier.org/learn/articles/unholy-pursuit-god-moby-dick.

11. Marilynne Robinson, *Gilead* (New York: Farrar, Strauss & Giroux, 2004), 9.

12. Michael D. O'Brien, *Island of the World* (San Francisco: Ignatius Press, 2007), 11.

13. Related by Brian Clark, "Ernest Hemingway's Top 5 Tips for Writing Well," Copyblogger (blog), November 11, 2019, https://www.copyblogger.com/ernest-hemingway-top-5-tips-for-writing-well.

Chapter 10: Reading Fantasy

1. C. S. Lewis, *English Literature in the Sixteenth Century Excluding Drama* (Oxford: Oxford University Press, 1954), 170.

2. J. R. R. Tolkien, "On Fairy-Stories," in *Essays Presented to Charles Williams*, ed. C. S. Lewis (Grand Rapids, MI: Eerdmans, 1966), 67.

3. Tolkien, "On Fairy-Stories," 63.

4. Tolkien, "On Fairy-Stories," 74.

5. J. R. R. Tolkien, *The Two Towers* (Boston: Houghton Mifflin, 1982), 41.

6. G. K. Chesterton, "The Ethics of Elfland," in *Orthodoxy*, in *The Collected Works of G. K. Chesterton*, ed. David Dooley (San Francisco: Ignatius Press, 1986), 1:252.

7. Tolkien, "On Fairy-Stories," 74.

8. Franz Kafka, *Metamorphosis* (New York: W. W. Norton, 1996), 21. Again all you need to know is that you can find this opening sentence in any edition.

9. Tolkien, "On Fairy-Stories," 74.

10. Samuel Hynes, "Guardian of the Old Ways," *The New York Times Book Review* (July 8, 1979), 3, 26.

11. Madeleine L'Engle, *Walking on Water* (Wheaton, IL: Harold Shaw, 1998), 154.

12. L'Engle, *Walking on Water*, 65, 68.

13. C. S. Lewis, *An Experiment in Criticism* (Cambridge: Cambridge University Press, 1961), 68–69.

14. Lewis, "On Stories," in *Essays Presented to Charles Williams*, ed. C. S. Lewis (Grand Rapids, MI: Eerdmans, 1966), 100.

15. Ursula LeGuin, *The Language of the Night* (New York: Putnam, 1979), 57–58.

16. Tolkien, "On Fairy-Stories," 75.

17. Pablo Picasso, *The Arts*, May 1923, 315, accessed July 27, 2020, https://babel.hathitrust.org/cgi/imgsrv/download/pdf?id=mdp.39015020076041;orient=0;size=100;seq=339;attachment=0.

18. C. S. Lewis, "On Three Ways of Writing for Children," in *Of Other Worlds* (New York: Harcourt Brace Jovanovich, 1966), 29–30.

Chapter 11: Reading Children's Books

1. "Newbery Terms, Criteria, Submission, and Committee Information" ALSC (website), accessed July 27, 2020, http://www.ala.org/alsc/awards grants/bookmedia/newberymedal/newberymedal/criteria-submissions -com-info#Terms%20and%20Criteria.

2. Daniel A Gross, "The Mystery of the Hardy Boys and the Invisible Authors," *The Atlantic*, May 27, 2015, https://www.theatlantic.com/entertainment /archive/2015/05/hardy-boys-nancy-drew-ghostwriters/394022.

3. Geoffrey Trease, *Tales Out of School* (London: Heinemann, 1964), 26.

4. Jill Carlson, *What Are Your Kids Reading?* (Brentwood, TN: Wolgemuth & Hyatt, 1991), 5–6.

5. David Mills, "Bad Books for Kids," *Touchstone*, July/August 2009, https://touchstonemag.com/archives/article.php?id=22-06-022-f.

6. In an act of shameless self-promotion, we'll mention the *Matthew in the Middle* series by Glenda Faye Mathes.

7. Gladys Hunt, *Honey for a Child's Heart: The Imaginative Use of Books in Family Life*, 4th edition (Grand Rapids, MI: Zondervan, 2002); and Gladys Hunt and Barbara Hampton, *Honey for a Teen's Heart: Using Books to Communicate with Teens* (Grand Rapids, MI: Zondervan, 2002).

8. Elizabeth Laraway Wilson, *Books Children Love: A Guide to the Best Children's Literature* (Wheaton, IL: Crossway, 2002).

9. Michael O'Brien, *A Landscape with Dragons: The Battle for Your Child's Mind* (San Francisco: Ignatius, 1998).

10. Kathryn Lindskoog and Ranelda Mack Hunsicker, *How to Grow a Young Reader* (Colorado Springs, CO: Shaw, 2002).

11. Sarah Clarkson, *Read for the Heart: Whole Books for WholeHearted Families* (Anderson, IN: ApologiaPress, 2009), 16.

12. The Read-Aloud Revival website is readaloudrevival.com. Also see Sarah Mackenzie, *The Read-Aloud Family* (Grand Rapids, MI: Zondervan, 2018).

13. Janie B. Cheaney's website is https://www.janiebcheaney.com, and the Redeemed Reader website (https://redeemedreader.com) is a leading children's book review website for Christian parents and teachers.

14. Madeleine L'Engle, "Is It Good Enough for Children?" *The Christian Imagination: The Practice of Faith in Literature and Writing*, ed. Leland Ryken (Colorado Springs, CO: Shaw, 2002), 431.

15. J. R. R. Tolkien, "On Fairy Stories," in *The Christian Imagination: The Practice of Faith in Literature and Writing*, ed. Leland Ryken (Colorado Springs, CO: Shaw, 2002), 461.

16. C. S. Lewis, "Three Ways of Writing for Children," quoted in *The Christian Imagination: The Practice of Faith in Literature and Writing*, ed. Leland Ryken (Colorado Springs, CO: Shaw, 2002), 461.

17. Deuteronomy 6:6–9 reads: "And these words that I command you today shall be on your heart. You shall teach them diligently to your children, and shall talk of them when you sit in your house, and when you walk by the way, and when you lie down, and when you rise. You shall bind them as a sign on your hand, and they shall be as frontlets between your eyes. You shall write them on the doorposts of your house and on your gates."

18. Tom Jacobs, "Home Libraries Confer Long-Term Benefits," Pacific Standard (website), October 8, 2018, https://psmag.com/education/home-libraries-confer-long-term-benefits.

19. Harper Lee, *To Kill a Mockingbird* (Philadelphia: Lippincott, 1960), 22.

20. Jim Trelease, *The Read-Aloud Handbook: Seventh Edition* (New York: Penguin, 2013), 24.

21. Richard C. Anderson, et al., *Becoming a Nation of Readers: The Report of the Commission on Reading* (Urbana, IL: University of Illinois, 1985). A PDF is available online at https://files.eric.ed.gov/fulltext/ED253865.pdf.

22. Perri Klass, "Reading Aloud to Young Children Has Benefits for Behavior and Attention," *The New York Times*, April 16, 2018, https://www.nytimes.com/2018/04/16/well/family/reading-aloud-to-young-children-has-benefits-for-behavior-and-attention.html.

23. Trelease, *The Read-Aloud Handbook: Seventh Edition*, 6.

24. Sigmond Brouwer, foreword to *How to Grow a Young Reader* by Kathryn Lindskoog and Ranelda Mack Hunsicker (Colorado Springs, CO: Shaw, 2002), xi. Brouwer has a heart for encouraging kids, especially boys, to read. See his website: sigmundbrouwer.com.

25. At each reading, Glenda's children begged for more from *Story Bible for Older Children* in Old Testament and New Testament volumes by Anne DeVries (which is pronounced Anna and, who is, surprisingly, a man). His *The Children's Bible* may be better for younger children with its larger print, shorter stories, and color illustrations. The following accessible recommendations feature modern artwork: *The Jesus Storybook Bible: Every Story Whispers His Name* by Sally Lloyd-Jones (includes pictures of Jesus) and *The Biggest Story: How the Snake Crusher Brings Us Back to the Garden* by Kevin DeYoung (the face of Jesus is not shown).

26. Sarah Mackenzie, "RAR #24: From Picture Books to Chapter Books & Novels," Read-Aloud Revival (podcast), https://readaloudrevival .com/24.

27. Our highly-recommended reading order, according to dates of publication: *The Lion, the Witch, and the Wardrobe* (1950), *Prince Caspian* (1951), *The Voyage of the Dawn Treader* (1952), *The Silver Chair* (1953), *The Horse and His Boy* (1954), *The Magician's Nephew* (1955), *The Last Battle* (1956).

28. For an exploration of Christian themes in the series, see John Granger, *How Harry Cast His Spell: The Meaning behind the Mania for J. K. Rowling's Bestselling Books* (Carol Stream, IL: Tyndale, 2008). To read thoughtful cautions, see Michael O'Brien, *Harry Potter and the Paganization of Culture* (Czech Republic: Fides et Traditio Press Vero, 2010).

29. Richard Freed, "The Tech Industry's War on Kids: How Psychology Is Being Used as a Weapon against Children," Medium (website), March 12, 2018, https://medium.com/@richardnfreed/the-tech-industrys -psychological-war-on-kids-c452870464ce.

30. For more of Freed's perspective and advice, see his *Wired Child: Reclaiming Childhood in a Digital Age* (North Charleston, SC: Create Space, 2015).

31. Some people advocate waiting until eighth grade to introduce smartphones; www.waituntil8th.org. S. J. Dahlstrom, author of the Wilder Good young adult series, offers ten reasons why he will not buy smartphones for his children, "Dare to Be Different," *World*, December 8, 2018, https://world.wng.org/content/dare_to_be_different.

32. Andy Crouch, *The Tech-Wise Family* (Grand Rapids, MI: Baker, 2017), 40.

Chapter 12: Reading Creative Nonfiction

1. Quoting James Frey, "Oprah's Questions for James," interview by Oprah Winfrey, *The Oprah Winfrey Show*, January 26, 2006, https://www.oprah.com/oprahshow/oprahs-questions-for-james.

2. Laura Barton, "The Man Who Rewrote His Life," *The Guardian*, September 15, 2006, https://www.theguardian.com/books/2006/sep/15/usa.world.

3. Quoting James Frey and Oprah Winfrey, interview by Larry King, *Larry King Live*, CNN, January 11, 2006, http://transcripts.cnn.com/TRANSCRIPTS/0601/11/lkl.01.html.

4. Edward Wyatt, "Author Is Kicked Out of Oprah Winfrey's Book Club," *The New York Times*, January 27, 2006, https://www.nytimes.com/2006/01/27/books/27oprah.html.

5. See https://www.creativenonfiction.org. Gutkind uses the definition repeatedly in his speaking and writing and has adopted it as the tagline on his website.

6. Phillip Lopate, "Curiouser and Curiouser: The Practice of Nonfiction Today," *The Iowa Review* 36.1 (2006): 3–15, also available at https://doi.org/10.17077/0021-065X.6151.

7. Based on the James Frey author page on HarperCollins Publishers website, https://www.harpercollins.com/author/cr-103938/james-frey.

8. Sylvester Clark Long had a difficult youth and achieved success with *Long Lance* in 1928 but was exposed for ethnic pretensions; see Jamie Frater, "Top 10 Infamous Fake Memoirs," Listverse (website), updated June 16, 2014, http://listverse.com/2010/03/06/top-10-infamous-fake-memoirs. For a sympathetic biography of Clark, see *Dictionary of Canadian Biography*, s.v. "Long, Sylvester Clark," https://www.biographi.ca/en/bio/long_sylvester_clark_16E.html.

9. Clifford Irving spent seventeen months in prison for his completely unauthorized *The Autobiography of Howard Hughes* (although he went on to write *The Hoax* about his experience, which was made into a 2007 movie starring Richard Gere). A magazine editor and a forger each spent four and a half years in prison for their roles in convincing the magazine to buy faked *Hitler Diaries*. For more on these and other examples, see Lyn Garrity, "Five Fake Memoirs That Fooled the Literary World," *Smithsonian*, December 20, 2010, https://www.smithsonianmag.com/arts-culture/five-fake-memoirs-that-fooled-the-literary-word-77092955.

10. For examples of inauthentic authors see the sections on *Misha: A Mémoire of the Holocaust Years* (1997) and *Love and Consequences* (2008) in Frater, "Top 10 Infamous Fake Memoirs," http://listverse.com/2010/03/06/top-10-infamous-fake-memoirs.

11. See *Forbidden Love* (2003) or *The Education of Little Tree: A True Story* (1976) in Frater, "Top 10 Infamous Fake Memoirs," http://listverse.com /2010/03/06/top-10-infamous-fake-memoirs. Oprah Winfrey promoted the latter in 1994 as a "very spiritual" book but withdrew her recommendation in 2007, after the author was revealed as a former Ku Klux Klan member.

12. John D'Agata and Jim Fingal, "Doubling Down: An Interview with John D'Agata and Jim Fingal," interview by Weston Cutter, *Kenyon Review*, February 23, 2012, https://www.kenyonreview.org/2012/02/doubling -down-an-interview-with-john-dagata-and-jim-fingal.

13. Dinty W. Moore, "In Fairness to John D'Agata," Brevity (blog), February 12, 2012, https://brevity.wordpress.com/2012/02/12/in-fairness-to -john-dagata.

14. Gideon Lewis-Kraus, "The Fact Checker Versus the Fabulist," *The New York Times*, February 26, 2012, https://www.nytimes.com/2012/02/26 /magazine/the-fact-checker-versus-the-fabulist.html?ref=books.

15. Hannah Goldfield, "The Art of Fact-Checking," *The New Yorker*, February 9, 2012, https://www.newyorker.com/books/page-turner/the-art -of-fact-checking.

16. William Giraldi, "The Unforgivable Half Truths of Memoir," *The New Republic*, January 15, 2016, https://newrepublic.com/article/127747 /unforgivable-half-truths-memoir.

17. Lopate, "Curiouser and Curiouser," https://doi.org/10.17077/0021 -065X.6151.

18. Lee Gutkind, *You Can't Make This Stuff Up* (Boston: De Capo, 2012), 22.

19. Uriah Courtney with Glenda Faye Mathes, *Exoneree* (Eugene, OR: Wipf and Stock, 2017).

20. Robert Root, *The Nonfictionist's Guide: On Reading and Writing Creative Nonfiction* (Lanham, MD: Rowman & Littlefied, 2008), 6–9.

21. Lopate, "Curiouser and Curiouser."

22. Lopate, "Curiouser and Curiouser."

23. Giraldi, "The Unforgivable Half Truths of Memoir," https://newrepublic .com/article/127747/unforgivable-half-truths-memoir.

Chapter 13: Reading the Bible as Literature

1. C. S. Lewis, *Reflections on the Psalms* (New York: Harcourt, Brace & World, 1958), 3.

2. Samuel Taylor Coleridge, *Confessions of an Inquiring Spirit* (Stanford: Stanford University Press, 1967), 43.

3. For a comprehensive overview of the literary forms and techniques found in the Bible, see Leland Ryken, *A Complete Handbook of Literary Forms in the Bible* (Wheaton, IL: Crossway, 2014). Among my (Leland's) numerous books on the Bible as literature, the following two provide the best amplification of the material covered in this chapter on the Bible as literature: Ryken, *How to Read the Bible as Literature* (Grand Rapids, MI: Zondervan, 1984); and Ryken, *Words of Delight: A Literary Introduction to the Bible* (Grand Rapids, MI: Baker, 1992).

4. Flannery O'Connor, *Mystery and Manners* (New York: Farrar, Straus & Giroux, 1957), 73. Italics added.

5. For helpful guidance in recognizing literary aspects in all Scripture, see *The Literary Study Bible, English Standard Version* edited by Leland Ryken and Philip Graham Ryken (Wheaton, IL: Crossway, 2020).

6. Martin Luther, "Letter to Eoban Hess," in *Luther's Correspondence and Other Contemporary Letters*, trans. Preserved Smith and Charles M. Jacobs (Philadelphia, PA: Lutheran Publication Society, 1918), 2:177.

7. See Ryken, *How to Read the Bible as Literature* and *Words of Delight: A Literary Introduction to the Bible.*

Chapter 14: Recovery through Discovery

1. Annie Murphy Paul, "Reading Literature Makes Us Smarter and Nicer," *Time*, June 3, 2013, http://ideas.time.com/2013/06/03/why-we-should-read-literature.

2. J. R. R. Tolkien, *The Two Towers* (Boston: Houghton Mifflin, 1993) 320–21.

3. Gene Edward Veith Jr., *Reading between the Lines: A Christian Guide to Literature* (Wheaton, IL: Crossway, 1990) 19.

4. Frequently attributed to Harper Lee (Goodreads, Brainyquote, and other online sites), but it seems at least the first part of this quote comes from Scottish philosopher James McCosh, http://interestingliterature.com/2017/04/who-said-the-book-to-read-is-not-the-one-that-thinks-for-you-but-the-one-which-makes-you-think.

5. C. S. Lewis, *Of Other Worlds* (New York: HarperCollins, 1966, 1994) 25.

6. Daniel 7 uses this term for God.

7. Clyde S. Kilby, *The Arts and the Christian Imagination* (Brewster, MA: Paraclete, 2016), 120.

8. John Calvin, *Calvin's Commentaries*, Vol. XXI (Grand Rapids, MI: Baker, 2003); Titus 1, 300.

9. Kilby, *The Arts and the Christian Imagination*, 117.

10. *The Belgic Confession*, Article II.

11. Vishal Mangalwadi, *The Book That Made Your World: How the Bible Created the Soul of Western Civilization* (Nashville: Thomas Nelson, 2011) 52–53.

Chapter 15: Truth In Literature

1. Douglas Bush, "Tradition and Experience," in *Literature and Belief*, ed. M. H. Abrams (New York: Columbia University Press, 1958), 52.
2. William Wordsworth, preface to *Lyrical Ballads*, in *Criticism: The Major Statements*, ed. Charles Kaplan (New York: St. Martin's Press, 1964), 311.
3. Joyce Cary, *Art and Reality: Ways of the Creative Process* (New York: Harper and Brothers, 1958), 158.
4. Flannery O'Connor, *Mystery and Manners*, ed. Sally and Robert Fitzgerald (New York: Farrar, Straus & Giroux, 1957), 65.
5. Jonathan Culler, *Structuralist Poetics: Structuralism, Linguistics, and the Study of Literature* (Ithaca: Cornell University Press, 1975), 115.
6. Gerald Graff, "Literature as Assertions," in *American Criticism in the Poststructuralist Age*, ed. Ira Konigsberg (Ann Arbor, MI: University of Michigan Press, 1981), 161.
7. T. S. Eliot, "Religion and Literature," in *The Christian Imagination: The Practice of Faith in Literature and Writing*, ed. Leland Ryken (Colorado Springs, CO: WaterBrook Press, 2002), 207.
8. Francis A. Schaeffer, *Art and the Bible* (Downers Grove, IL: InterVarsity Press, 1973), 41.
9. Sir Philip Sidney, *Apology for Poetry*, in *Criticism: The Major Statements*, ed. Charles Kaplan (New York: St. Martin's Press, 1964), 120.
10. Walker Percy, "Walker Percy, the Man and the Novelist: An Interview," *The Southern Review*, n.s., 4 (1968): 279.

Chapter 16: The Moral Vision in Literature

1. Oscar Wilde, preface to *The Picture of Dorian Gray* (1891), in *The Norton Anthology of English Literature*, ed. M. H. Abrams, 4th ed. (New York: W. W. Norton, 1979), 2:1682. Ironically, *The Picture of Dorian Gray* is a moral story.
2. C. S. Lewis, *English Literature in the Sixteenth Century, Excluding Drama* (Oxford: Oxford University Press, 1954), 346.
3. Plato, *The Republic*, Book 10, in *Criticism: The Major Statements*, ed. Charles Kaplan (New York: St. Martin's Press, 1975), 14. Italics added.
4. Sir Philip Sidney, "Apology for Poetry," in *Criticism: The Major Statements*, ed. Kaplan, 123.
5. Sidney, "Apology for Poetry," 134.

6. T. S. Eliot, "Religion and Literature," as reprinted in *The Christian Imagination: The Practice of Faith in Literature and Writing*, ed. Leland Ryken (Colorado Springs, CO: WaterBrook Press, 2002), 201.

7. Sheldon Sacks, *Fiction and the Shape of Belief* (Berkeley: University of California Press, 1964), 250.

8. Harry Blamires, *The Christian Mind* (London: S.P.C.K., 1966), 98.

9. Samuel Taylor Coleridge, *Shakespearean Criticism*, ed. Thomas Middleton Raysor (London: J. M. Dent and Sons, 1960), 2:30

10. Boccaccio, *Boccaccio on Poetry*, trans. and ed. Charles G. Osgood (New York: Liberal Arts Press, 1956), 74.

11. Keith F. McKean, *The Moral Measure of Literature* (Westport, CT: Greenwood Press, 1961), 11.

12. Frank Chapman Sharp, *Shakespeare's Portrayal of the Moral Life* (New York: Haskell House, 1971), ix.

13. Plato, *The Republic*, 16.

14. Karen Swallow Prior, *On Reading Well: Finding the Good Life through Great Books* (Grand Rapids, MI: Brazos Press, 2018), 15.

Chapter 17: Beauty in Literature

1. Clyde S. Kilby, *The Arts and the Christian Imagination: Essays on Art, Literature, and Aesthetics* (Brewster, MA: Paraclete, 2016), 14.

2. Kilby, *The Arts and the Christian Imagination*, 13–14.

3. *Merriam-Webster Dictionary*, s.v. "concinnity," accessed April 1, 2020, https://www.merriam-webster.com/dictionary/concinnity.

4. Kilby, *The Arts and the Christian Imagination*, 14.

5. John Keats, *Endymion*, Book 1, Poetry Foundation, accessed March 6, 2020, https://www.poetryfoundation.org/poems/44469/endymion -56d2239287ca5.

6. Kilby, *The Arts and the Christian Imagination*,131.

7. William Wordsworth, preface to *Lyrical Ballads*, in *Criticism: The Major Statements*, ed. Charles Kaplan (New York: St. Martin's Press, 1964), 311.

8. Brother Azarias, "The Beautiful in Literature," in *Philosophy of Literature* (1890), Jacques Maritain Center, University of Notre Dame, accessed March 6, 2020, https://maritain.nd.edu/jmc/etext/pl28.htm.

9. Kilby, *The Arts and the Christian Imagination*, 121.

10. Roger Scruton, *Beauty* (New York: Oxford, 2009), 16.

11. Leo Tolstoy, *What Is Art?*, trans. Aylmer Maude (Indianapolis: Hackett, 1996), 131.

12. Azarias, "The Beautiful in Literature."

13. Scruton, *Beauty*, 72, 196.
14. Makoto Fujimura quoted in Glenda Mathes, "Makoto Fujimura: Refracting Light and Reflecting Grace," *Christian Renewal*, July 12, 2006.
15. Fujimura quoted in Mathes, "Makoto Fujimura." For more of his perspective, see https://www.makotofujimura.com or his books: *Refractions: A Journey of Faith, Art, and Culture* (Carol Stream, IL: NavPress, 2009); *Silence and Beauty: Hidden Faith Born of Suffering* (Downers Grove, IL: IVP Books, 2016); and *Culture Care: Reconnection with Beauty for Our Common Life* (Downers Grove, IL: InterVarsity Press, 2017).

Chapter 18: Discovering Literary Excellence

1. Jane Austen, *Pride and Prejudice* (New York: Oxford University Press, 1988), 3.
2. Jack London, *White Fang* (New York: Puffin Books, 1994), 3.
3. "Examples of Assonance Poems," YourDictionary, accessed March 6, 2020, https://examples.yourdictionary.com/examples-of-assonance-poems.html.
4. Natalia Sanmartin Fenollera, *The Awakening of Miss Prim* (New York: Simon & Schuster, 2013), 4.
5. Alan Bradley, *The Sweetness at the Bottom of the Pie* (New York: Bantam, 2010), 1.
6. Bradley, *The Sweetness at the Bottom of the Pie*, 3.
7. Alan Bradley, *The Golden Tresses of the Dead* (New York: Delacorte, 2019), 16.
8. Leo Tolstoy, *Anna Karenina* (New York: Signet, 2002), 176.
9. The technique is variously identified as free indirect speech, free indirect style, or free indirect discourse.
10. Jane Austen, *Emma* (Peterborough, ON: Broadview, 2004), 69.
11. Charlotte Brontë, *Jane Eyre* (Ware, UK: Cumberland House, 1992), 3, 401, 397.
12. Brontë, *Jane Eyre*, 153.
13. Brontë, *Jane Eyre*, 166.
14. Brontë, *Jane Eyre*, 166.
15. Brontë, *Jane Eyre*, 443.
16. Brontë, *Jane Eyre*, 500–1.
17. Tolstoy, *Anna Karenina*, 37.
18. Roger Scruton, *Beauty* (New York: Oxford, 2009), 123–24.
19. Anthony Trollope, *Barchester Towers* (New York: Penguin, 1994), 242.
20. T. S. Eliot, *Selected Poems* (New York: Harcourt Brace, 1958), 14.

21. Charles Dickens, *Great Expectations* (New York: Penguin, 1996), 354.

22. Katherine Mansfield, "Bliss" (1918), Katherine Mansfield Society, accessed March 6, 2020, http://www.katherinemansfieldsociety.org/assets/KM-Stories/BLISS1918.pdf.

23. Quoting from Woiwode's remarks during his fiction class, attended by Glenda Faye Mathes from July 28–August 4, 2013, at the Glen West Workshop, hosted by *Image Journal* in Sante Fe, NM.

24. Charles Johnson, *Middle Passage* (New York: Scribner, 1990), 1.

Chapter 19: Freedom to Read

1. Kevin DeYoung, *Crazy Busy: A (Mercifully) Short Book about a (Really) Big Problem* (Wheaton, IL: Crossway, 2013), 11.

2. Augustine, *Confessions: Modern English Translation* (Grand Rapids, MI: Spire, 2008), Book 1, chapter 1.

3. Mark Buchanan, *The Rest of God: Restoring Your Soul by Restoring Sabbath* (Nashville: Thomas Nelson, 2006), 4. Buchanan's writing is lyrical and thoughtful. The latter part of this quotation refers to Psalm 46.

4. *Trinity Psalter Hymnal* (Willow Grove, PA: Trinity Psalter Hymnal Joint Venture, 2018), 891.

5. See for instance Leland Ryken, *Redeeming the Time: A Christian Approach to Work and Leisure* (Grand Rapids, MI: Baker, 1995) or Glenda Mathes, *A Month of Sundays: 31 Meditations on Resting in God* (Grand Rapids, MI: Reformation Heritage, 2012).

6. Mary Oliver, "The Summer Day," *New and Selected Poems* (Boston: Beacon Press, 1992), 94. We consider this one of her best poems.

7. Twyla Tharp, *The Creative Habit: Learn It and Use It for Life* (New York: Simon & Schuster, 2003), 6.

8. Search for their current reading challenges on their websites: challies.com or redeemedreader.com.

9. Visit Goodreads at www.goodreads.com or Pinterest at www.pinterest.com.

10. Tim Challies, *Do More Better: A Practical Guide to Productivity* (Minneapolis: Cruciform Press, 2015).

11. DeYoung, *Crazy Busy*, 118.

Chapter 20: Reading Good Books

1. The Great American Read home page, *PBS*, accessed August 6, 2018, https://www.pbs.org/the-great-american-read/home/.

2. Adam Kirsch, "The Way We Read Now," *The Wall Street Journal*, August 3, 2018, https://www.wsj.com/articles/the-way-we-read-now-153330 7226.

3. Clive Thompson, "Reading War and Peace on my iPhone" by Clive Thompson, accessed February 16, 2019, https://br5.bookriot.com /quarterly/bkr07/amp. This article is no longer available online. Although Thompson read Tolstoy's masterpiece on a small screen, he still loves reading physical books.

4. C. S. Lewis, *An Experiment in Criticism* (Cambridge: Cambridge University Press, 2013), 85, 11, 18.

5. Lewis, *An Experiment in Criticism*, 132.

6. Quote Investigator traces the sources of the joke here: https://quote investigator.com/2015/12/08/speed-reading (December 8, 2015).

7. Charlotte Mason, *Parents and Children* (Radford, VA: Wilder, 2008), 178.

8. Susan Hill, *Howard's End Is on the Landing: A Year of Reading from Home* (London: Profile, 2010), 171–72.

9. Annie Murphy Paul, "Reading Literature Makes Us Smarter and Nicer," *Time*, June 3, 2013, https://ideas.time.com/2013/06/03/why-we-should -read-literature.

10. Lewis, *An Experiment in Criticism*, 93.

11. Lewis, *An Experiment in Criticism*, 113–14.

12. Walker Percy, "Another Message in the Bottle," *Signposts in a Strange Land* (New York: Picador, 1991), 364.

13. Percy, "Another Message in the Bottle," 363.

14. Clyde S. Kilby, *The Arts and the Christian Imagination: Essays on Art, Literature, and Aesthetics* (Brewster, MA: Paraclete, 2016), 14.

15. Lewis, *An Experiment in Criticism*, 94.

16. Lewis, *An Experiment in Criticism*, 114.

17. Lewis, *An Experiment in Criticism*, 84.

18. Percy, "Another Message in the Bottle," 364.

19. Lewis, *An Experiment in Criticism*, 2.

20. Roger Scruton, *Beauty* (New York: Oxford, 2009), 24–25.

21. Lewis, *An Experiment in Criticism*, 32.

22. Scruton, *Beauty*, 25.

23. Percy, "Another Message in the Bottle," 364.

24. Lewis, *An Experiment in Criticism*, 141.

Chapter 21: Calling and Creativity

1. For example, read Jeremiah's call in Jeremiah 1:5, Isaiah's call in Isaiah 49:5, John the Baptist's call in Luke 1:15, and Paul's call in Galatians 1:15.
2. Dorothy Sayers, *The Mind of the Maker* (San Francisco: Harper, 1987), 22.
3. Larry Woiwode, *Words for Readers and Writers: Spirit-Pooled Dialogues* (Wheaton, IL: Crossway, 2013), 67.
4. Madeleine L'Engle, *Walking on Water: Reflections on Faith & Art* (New York: Crosswicks, 2001), 66.
5. Bret Lott, *Before We Get Started: A Practical Memoir of the Writer's Life* (New York: Ballantine, 2005), 13.
6. Nicholas Carr, *The Shallows: What the Internet Is Doing to Our Brains* (New York: Norton, 2010), 74.

Chapter 22: Literature and the Spiritual Life

1. T. S. Eliot, "Religion and Literature," in *The Christian Imagination: The Practice of Faith in Literature and Writing*, ed. Leland Ryken (Colorado Springs, CO: WaterBrook Press, 2002), 207.
2. All testimonials shared in this chapter not attributed to a source are to be understood as having been given to Leland Ryken over the course of his teaching career by students at the time, former students, or professional colleagues, in the form of emails, notes, paragraphs in class assignments, or oral communications.
3. Content of the testimonial was shared with us by this person's pastor, Dr. Philip Ryken.
4. Simone Weil, *Waiting for God* (London: Routledge and Kegan Paul, 1952), 27. The reference is to George Herbert's poem "Love (III)."
5. "The Real Cry of China," *Trinity Magazine*, Summer 2001, 15.
6. John Milton's "Sonnet 19" can be found here: https://www.poetry foundation.org/poems/44750/sonnet-19-when-i-consider-how-my-light -is-spent.
7. Matthew Arnold, "Wordsworth," in *Criticism: The Major Texts*, ed. Walter Jackson Bate (New York: Harcourt, Brace & World, 1952), 478.
8. The biblical data on which this summary is based can be found in Leland Ryken, "Man's Search for Truth," *Christianity Today* 22, November 1968: 8–9.
9. William Shakespeare, *Hamlet*, ed. A. R. Braunmuller (New York: Penguin, 1970), 70 (3.2.22).

10. John Milton, "Of Education," in *John Milton: Complete Poems and Major Prose*, ed. Merritt Y. Hughes (New York: Odyssey Press, 1957), 635.

11. Jonathan Edwards, *The Nature of True Virtue*, in *The Works of Jonathan Edwards* (New Haven, CT: Yale University Press, 1989), 8:550–51.

General Index

Brother Azarias. *See* Mullany, Patrick
Francis (Brother Azarias)
Brouwer, Sigmond, 275n24
Brueghel, Pieter, 33
Buchanan, Mark, 215
Burke, Kenneth, 76

Calvin, John, 89–90, 148, 164
Carlson, Jill, 124
Carr, Nicholas, 19, 23, 248
Cary, Joyce, 59, 171
Challies, Tim, 219, 222
characterization, 67
Chaucer, Geoffrey, 118
Cheaney, Janie B., 127
Chekov, Anton, 235
Chesterton, G. K., 114
children's literature, 121–22; and the
control of technology, 134–35;
current concerns of, 123–25; and
an integrated lifestyle, 128–29;
tips for choosing good, 125–28;
tips for reading aloud, 129–33;
uniqueness of, 122–23
Christianity, 64, 192, 241
Christian books/bookstores, 163
Christians, 24, 30, 32, 35, 44, 60, 99,
100–1; as artists, 198; awareness
of the Creator in, 47–48; and the
commitment to excellence, 201–
2; and the defense of literature,
64; and the experience of beauty,
194–96; and faith, 261; faith and
belief of, 175–77; and fantasy
literature, 114, 116–17; and the
moral authority of the Bible, 180;
negative portrayal of, 125; the
obligation of as readers, 77; and
the promotion of gritty realism,
163; and a Sabbath perspective,
215–26; and self-imposed moral
censorship, 186; and the writing
of fiction, 103

Chronicles of Narnia series (Lewis),
131–32
Clarkson, Susan, 127
Coleridge, Samuel Taylor, 149; on
moral tone, 183–84
Confessions (Augustine), 139, 145–46
Constable, John, 172
Crazy Busy (DeYoung), 222
creative nonfiction, 135–36; and curiosity, 143–45; reading recommendations for, 145–46; and scene
recreation, 143; traits and forms
of, 137–39; truth or consequences
of, 139–43; what is creative nonfiction?, 136–37
creativity: and a person's calling,
237–38; process/progression steps
of, 243–46; the role of inspiration
on, 242–43; what is creativity?,
240–242; why write creatively?,
238–40
Crouch, Andy, 133

D'Agata, John, 140, 141
Dahlstrom, S. J., 275n31
David, 191
"Death of Reading is Threatening the
Soul, The" (Yancey), 24
deconstructionism, 42
DeVries, Anne, 275n25
DeYoung, Kevin, 213
Dickens, Charles, 27, 195, 210
Dickinson, Emily, 72–73, 93
Dillard, Annie, 69
Dinesen, Isak, 79, 139
Do More Better (Challies), 222
Don Quixote (Cervantes), 101
Doody, Anne, 19

"Easter Wings" (Herbert), 95
edification, loss of, 35–36
Eliot, T. S., 28, 76, 175, 182, 251
Emerson, Ralph Waldo, 34

stories: reading of, 79–80; interchangeable with narrative, 80; tips for
reading stories, 87–88
Stratemeyer, Edward, 123

Taylor, Daniel, 84
"Tech Industry's War on Kids, The"
(Freed), 22, 133
Tech-Wise Family, The (Crouch), 133
Thomas, Dylan, 60
Thompson, Clive, 21, 227
Thoreau, Henry David, 139
Timmermans, Felix, 33
To Kill a Mockingbird (Lee), 235
Tolkien, J. R. R., 71, 112, 114, 128,
162; on fairy stories, 118–19
Tolstoy, Leo, 206, 209
Trease, Geoffrey, 124
Trollope, Anthony, 209–10
truth in literature, 169, 177; assessing
truth claims, 174–77; fallacies
concerning, 169–71; ideational,
173–74; representational, 172–73
Twain, Mark, 55–56
Two Towers, The (Tolkien), 114, 162

Veith, Gene Edward, Jr., 17, 104
vision, loss of, 36–37

Walden (Thoreau), 139
War and Peace (Tolstoy), 18–21, 220,
251
Weil, Simone, 253
What Is Literature?, 53
White Fang (London), 202–3
Wilde, Oscar, 179, 187
Wilder, Laura Ingalls, 131
Wilson, Elizabeth, 127
Wind in the Willows, The (Grahame),
118
Winfrey, Oprah, 135, 136, 277n11
wisdom, biblical, 30
Wodehouse, P. G., 221
Woiwode, Larry, 241–42
Wolf, Maryanne, 22, 41
Wood, James, 20
Wordsworth, William, 74, 171

Yancey, Philip, 24
Young, Damon, 43

Scripture Index